CW00549021

Roll Out the Beryl!

Roll Out
the
Beryl!

The authorised biography of Beryl Reid
by Kaye Crawford

Foreword by Dame Siân Phillips DBE

fantom
publishing

First published in 2016 by Fantom Films
fantomfilms.co.uk

A catalogue record for this book is available from the British Library.

Hardback edition ISBN: 978-1-78196-265-7

Material appears courtesy of © BBC Archives, Strithon Ltd and the Estate of Beryl Reid.

Quotes have also been sourced from *So Much Love*, © Strithon Ltd, 1983 with kind permission of Sue Reid-Povall. Quotations from Beryl Reid's personal archives appear with kind permission of Paul Strike.

All photographs not specifically credited are copyright © the Estate of Beryl Reid.

Typeset by Phil Reynolds Media Services, Leamington Spa
Printed and bound by CPI Group (UK) Ltd, Croydon, CR0 4YY

Jacket design by Will Brooks
Jacket photo © Rex Features

For Charlotte, with so much love

Contents

Acknowledgements

THERE IS SOMETHING SO COMFORTING ABOUT NOSTALGIA that, every so often, the British audience rediscovers its most beloved and iconic performers all over again. With each generation, a new legion of loyal fans is won and the demand to know more about these unique figures from our recent past increases. Performers such as Joan Sims, Yootha Joyce, Hattie Jacques, Tony Hancock and Joyce Grenfell are reminders of happier times when we sat curled up in front of the television on Sunday evenings with our grandparents who roared with laughter at the comedians they grew up hearing on the wireless, now made available to a brand new generation by the wonder of television.

Beryl Reid had a nagging fear, ever present in her later years, that she would be forgotten, allowed to slip out of our collective memory as just another comedienne of yesteryear. When I first discovered Beryl's 1984 memoirs *So Much Love*, I knew there was so much more to her than the book suggested; and, as the pieces began to fall into place, I came to adore Beryl in the way so many others have over the years. She inspired joy, she brought fun and perhaps even a little anarchy in a career that spanned over five decades and won her the praise of her peers, the press and a devoted fan base that still exists to this day.

With every handwritten note, in every interview and in every photograph, I began to see that Beryl was so much more than just that eccentric old lady caricature she is now remembered as. Despite her flaws and foibles which all human beings possess, she inspired so much loyalty, respect and gratitude among her family, friends and colleagues that she quickly became much more to me than some remote celebrity from the past; and it is a testament to how universally treasured she was that every contributor to this book began with 'Oh, I loved Beryl Reid!' It is my sincere hope that what you're about to read will not only rekindle memories of Beryl's most popular roles but that it will encourage those who are able to show more of her work to do so, ensuring that her place can be well and truly secured in the great Hall of Fame to which so many of our performers now departed belong.

I could not dream of thanking anyone who took part in the book before first sending my thanks to the great lady herself, who I am certain is sitting in that big green room in the sky, brandy in hand, surrounded by cats and probably swapping dirty stories with Sir Noël Coward. To be allowed to wander through her life, to be able to spend so much time watching, listening and learning about her has been a delight – and, on more than one occasion, heartbreaking. So my initial thanks go to the wonderful, the glorious, the irreplaceable and the unforgettable Beryl Reid.

It would have been impossible to launch the project in any real sense without the help of Beryl's niece, Susan Reid-Povall, who kindly allowed me to quote Beryl's own words from her 1984 autobiography *So Much Love* and who has been a constant source, not only of information, but of support. I am indebted to Sue and her husband Michael who have become dear friends, always happy to respond to my endless questions – or just to chat about our cats! It is not hard to see why Beryl adored Sue so much. Her kindness, generosity and warmth have made the process of getting to know Beryl not only easier but also a joy.

Thanks must also go to Paul Strike and Will Small, Beryl's close friends who now reside at Honeypot Cottage and who have a treasure trove of Beryl-abilia to which they very kindly gave me access as well as sharing their own memories of times shared. I'd also like to thank Elaine Pantling who allowed me to use the title of this book which first appeared as the title of her one-woman show dedicated to Beryl's life and who does such a superb job of bringing Monica and Marlene to the masses in Beryl's absence!

There have been so many contributors who took time out of their busy schedules to share their memories of working with Beryl, some of whom have sadly left us during the writing of this book. Thanks go to the late George Cole who offered reminiscences about his time working with Beryl in the 1950s and again in the mid-1980s, and also to the late Sir Terry Wogan whom Beryl completely adored in every sense and who could not have been more generous or thoughtful in the help he gave. Beryl was fiercely loyal to Sir Terry and it was not hard to see why.

Sincere and heartfelt thanks must go to Dame Siân Phillips who provided the foreword for this book – a true 'is this really happening?' moment in life! So many of Beryl's friends and colleagues have taken part and my eternal gratitude goes out to: Dame Eileen Atkins, Michael Pennington, Stephen Boxer, Steve Nallon, Dame Barbara Windsor, Jan Linden, Ruby Wax, Eleanor Fazan, Peter Bowles, Rosemary Anne Sissons, Susan Penhaligon, Maureen Lipman, Amanda Waring, Barry Cryer, Peter Nichols, Rula Lenska, Barbara Flynn and Nicky Henson.

Thanks are also extended to Trish Hayes at the BBC Written Archives and to Glen King who allowed me to quote an interview with the late Bill Pertwee she conducted shortly before his death in 2013. I'd also like to thank Jane Ireland, Mary Hunwicks, Charlotte Woollett, Roshni Radia, Meg Poole, Michelle Burke, Laura MacNeill, Lisa Foster, Marcus Prince and Daniel Albert who arranged many of the interviews which made this book possible; and Phil Reynolds for his conscientious proofreading and copy-editing. A special thank you must go to the artist June Mendoza who kindly allowed her stunning portrait of Beryl to be reproduced for this work.

Over the past year, many people have offered press cuttings, reviews and copies of Beryl's appearances in magazines, newspapers, on television, radio and even stage. It would have been impossible to piece together Beryl's career without these precious documents and so huge thanks must go to Ian Lifsey – The Oracle! – who turned out to have an exhaustive Beryl library which he was only too happy to make available to me. Thanks also to Penny Cooke, who kindly allowed me to quote letters sent to her mother Sheila from Beryl in the 1970s.

Of course, I owe a huge debt of gratitude to my beloved grandmother Jenny who is now familiar with every TV, radio and film appearance Beryl Reid ever made! Her unconditional support and encouragement can never be measured nor repaid, and I'm sure she'll be relieved to be able to answer the telephone again without fear of being confronted with a theatre legend at the other end. To my darling Dylan who has listened to my whinging and supplied endless bottles of gin when things seemed as if they would never happen, thank you, the drinks are now on me. And in true Beryl fashion, I have to thank my cats: Endora, Daisy, Maggie and little Beryl who didn't quite make it to the end but who was a source of joy and constant companionship throughout the project.

To my supportive parents, to my grandmother Betty, and to my much missed grandfathers Bill and Colin who inspired me so much – thank you.

Kaye Crawford
2016

Foreword

I KNEW BERYL REID SO WELL THE FIRST TIME I EVER MET HER. In an unlikely piece of casting I was to play her sister in a revival of Alan J. Lerner's musical *Gigi*. On the morning of the first day of rehearsals, I looked down from my five feet and seven and a half inches at the petite, rounded form of the most interesting person in the room. Not for her the working actor's uniform of unobtrusive, appropriate trousers and sweater with maybe a hint of something a trifle more interesting in the scarf department. Everything about Miss Reid was a statement: the witty little hat artfully angled above thoroughly coiffed hair, the silk, pussy-cat bow softening the immaculately tailored suit. The bag and shoes looked royal (she who wears such will still be standing erect here for as long as required). Clearer and brighter than any silk or ornament was the face. Shrewd, improbably large eyes and a smiling mouth with just a hint of trouble at the corners dominated the space around her.

She was exactly as I'd remembered her from hours of looking at photographs of her as I listened to recordings of her music-hall acts and, peering at her figure on an early, tiny television screen, laboriously transcribed Monica and Marlene's monologues. Dr Johnson rightly remarked on the absurdity of imitating those we couldn't possibly resemble; and even as I stood there in front of the long mirror in a chilly hall in a house in west Wales, struggling to capture Monica's diction ('did you notice when I said that all thspit came out?'), I knew perfectly well that I could never be like her, nor did my inclinations or ambitions lie in the direction of music hall; but above everyone else she fascinated me and I really wanted a tiny understanding of what she did, how it came about. So I learned her material. And it did help me understand more about her extraordinary talent.

Although I never told Beryl about the huge effect she'd had on me when I was a student, she must have sensed that I knew what cloth she was cut from because, even before we became enduring friends, she treated me with exquisite professional generosity – not always the case on the part of people who, starting young in the business, have had to rise the hard way. This was the sixteen-year-old girl left stranded at Crewe as the rest of the performers departed on the train to the next music hall. She had over-packed, there was no free porter, she couldn't move her trunk and she learned 'never pack what you can't carry.' She learned at an early age to keep up. And, soon after, to stay ahead.

No one could have imagined early in her career that she possessed major acting talent. No one who saw her play Restoration comedy or Joe Orton's plays or, most famously, Sister George or Connie in John Le Carré's *Smiley's People*, could prevent themselves from vainly wishing that she'd played *The Merry Wives* on stage or given her Lady Bracknell. I have a long list of parts that I can 'hear' Beryl playing.

The musical we appeared in was not particularly successful, but I treasure it. Going to work every day was a joy. I loved working with Beryl but equally I loved the nuggets of observation she accumulated each day (she followed people and eavesdropped!). There was the interesting-looking small boy she followed in the shop in Wraysbury who rewarded her by crying out as his mother put a box of white loo-paper in the trolley: 'Oh, not white again! My arse just cries out for a bit of colour.'

People who get laughs because they are funny are rare and precious. I had been lucky enough to have been through a painful mill as a fill-in comedy 'feed' in radio, and consequently appreciated what funny people need in the way of support, so there was no power on earth that could keep me chained to the page on the nights when some mishap led Beryl to depart from the script or just abandon it momentarily. The brief moments when the three of us – Beryl, the audience and I – spun together in a bubble of wordless nonsense are among my treasured delights.

On such nights I felt we shared a secret, but I have no idea what the secret was. In her own way Beryl was evasive. She talked about her life, but I think she had an edited version that she was prepared to share. And, eloquent though she was in speech, in a way I don't think she did herself justice in her own written account of herself; so I welcome a biography. Talent is unknowable, they say, but I want to know more about Beryl.

Dame Siân Phillips DBE
February 2016

Chapter One

'If I'm any good as a person at all, I owe that entirely to the way that I was brought up.'

WHEN THE PETITE BERYL REID, resplendent in a vivacious pink suit and hat with dainty netting covering her elf-like features, stood before the Queen to collect her OBE, there was no doubt in anybody's mind that she had earned those precious three letters. Indeed, Beryl could get quite sniffy if a presenter or journalist forgot to make mention of her coveted honour; and, that afternoon as she dined at the Garrick Club quaffing champagne and Courvoisier brandy, waited on by handsome waiters and feted by her dearest friend and loyal agent Robert Luff, she couldn't help but be struck by just how far she had come. Fearless in her fight against a male-dominated industry and committed to her craft, Beryl Elizabeth Reid was now a national treasure, long before the moniker was applied to anyone who can last a year in the very unstable world of showbusiness. Tony award-winning, honoured by her Queen, beloved by audiences and very much a gay icon, it all began for Beryl in Hereford, a leafy cathedral town in the West Midlands noted for being the birthplace of Nell Gwynn.

Her parents, Leonard and Anne, were chalk and cheese, neither having much in common with the other. Beryl's father was an auctioneer and came from a humble background, his father John being a brush salesman who was forever on the move. Day after day, Beryl's grandfather would pound the streets of whichever town or city looked to be the most promising, selling all kinds of things door to door in the hope of supporting his family. More often than not, the door would be slammed in his face by furious butlers; and, in the homes without domestic staff, money was extremely tight and the goods John was trying to sell would have been regarded as luxuries.

Leonard was born in Streatham in East London, but given the nature of John's profession the Reids were forever on the move. This didn't suit the rather dour and eminently sensible young Leonard, who wanted a solid career that not only paid well but came with a bit of a reputation. The thought of spending his time being rejected at the doorstep pushed Leonard into a stable profession and he trained as an auctioneer. As his granddaughter Sue recalls, 'He was a showman and that's where the performing gene came from. Nana was shy, but Grandams was totally the opposite.'

Nana was Elizabeth Anne Reid (known as Annie), a refined and gentle girl from Edinburgh. Unlike Leonard who had seen first-hand the slums of East London, Annie was from proud middle-class stock, the daughter of a cabinet maker with the unmistakably Scottish name of Alexander MacDonald. Annie was refined, genteel and sweet, not to mention extremely pretty. She came from a happy family full of laughter and the finer things in life. Though the MacDonalds were by no means wealthy, they enjoyed holidays in the Highlands and there was always jam for the bread. It's hard to know what she saw in the very strict and slightly temperamental Leonard, but nonetheless the pair were married at St Mary's Cathedral in Glasgow on 19th May 1913. Like any young bride leaving home, Annie must have wondered what on earth she'd agreed to when the hustle and bustle of family life with her eccentric siblings was suddenly replaced by a strict husband and a rather tiny house in Grenfell Road, Hereford. Two years later, however, Annie found her consolation: she gave birth to a son, Roy. Roy would always be studious and serious, intelligent and a deep thinker, and this was something of a relief to Leonard who was determined that his children should find respectable professions that would offer security and a level of comfort that was decent without being excessive. Roy was a skilled musician yet academia came first. It was a typical Presbyterian morality which was about to get a sharp shake to the roots.

On 17th June 1919, Beryl Elizabeth Reid was born in Hereford, in a house called 'Marlas' in Grenfell Road. Beryl always felt that houses should have a name and over the years she'd enjoy stays at 'Noroc', 'Willow Way' and eventually 'Honeypot'. She was by no means a bonny bouncing baby, being completely bald with tiny deep-set eyes and a sallow complexion. She was prone to coughs and colds, which ultimately led to pneumonia leaving her fragile and pencil-thin. This wasn't helped by her finicky attitude to food. Annie took to making two different choices of pudding in the hope that the young Beryl would at least nibble one and this might help to fill her out a little; and, eventually, she grew out of her fussy eating and in later years became something of a self-proclaimed gastronome, even publishing a cookery book.

Despite her physical weakness, emotionally the young Beryl was a little ray of sunshine in a gloomy postwar household. All over Britain, people were coming to terms with the loss of their sons, fathers and brothers killed in the Great War and still being found all over Belgium and France. There was a huge national debt to pay off; unemployment was rife and the country had failed to build homes fit for heroes to live in, which meant that uniformed beggars bedecked in medals, often with limbs missing, were a regular sight on street corners.

For Leonard, who had known the topsy-turvy life of unemployment, providing a comfortable and secure home for his family was a priority. So when a position at Kendal Milne, the 'Harrods of the North', was offered to him in 1922, he moved his family from Grenfell Road to Manchester. Kendal's promised to give its customers anything they could ask for. Known locally as 'the Bazaar' because of its seemingly endless array of goods, it had been bought by Harrods at the end of the First World War; and, though the company had disposed with an experimental 'Harrods of the North' campaign, Kendal Milne was still regarded as an exclusive and slightly better class of store.

With Roy now at school and showing great promise, Annie naturally spent more time with her daughter: and what a daughter she was. From the outset, Beryl was mischievous and self-assured. Annie was a quiet wife but an exceptionally strong mother, prepared to support her children in whatever they decided to do, whilst Leonard hoped Beryl might grow out of her theatrical temperament. Annie encouraged Beryl's creativity al-though she was a little taken aback by the bundle of talent that was baby

Beryl. 'I don't know who you belong to,' she once said, 'but you're nothing to do with us!'

To the delight of her mother, Beryl would lurch from room to room in her father's top hat giving her best Uriah Heep impression; and then came a new best friend. 'Envigamees' was born, not a little boy, but a fully grown man, and any misdemeanour was immediately laid firmly in his lap. One day Beryl slipped out of the house alone and wandered the streets for a while. When she returned, a frantic Annie scolded her daughter only to be told, 'It's all right Mummy! Envigamees was there and guess what? He saved me from being eaten by a lion!' This proved to be a little too much for her paternal aunts who saw the young Beryl as precocious. In an age where children were to be seen but not heard, one couldn't ignore Beryl and her impish behaviour. When an aunt told Annie to tell Beryl off for telling tall tales, Annie defended her proudly: 'She isn't lying!' she said. 'She just has a very vivid imagination!'

The house was often filled with laughter and if it wasn't provided by Beryl, it was provided by her mother. One day a visitor came to call. Annie said, 'Say hello to Mr Peabody everyone,' to which the assembled company fell about with a bad case of the giggles. It wasn't an unhappy home but Leonard could be extremely difficult; and, when Beryl later spoke of her childhood, her mother was the jewel in the crown. Annie could do no wrong: she had always supported Beryl and this led to a rift with her father that would only get worse as she remained dedicated to her dream of becoming an actress. Indeed, when Beryl finally wrote her memoirs in the mid 1980s, she didn't even mention her father's name but dedicated the book to her mother, a clear indication of where Beryl's loyalties had been placed.

The summer months brought the excitement of a holiday in Scotland, specifically to a little fishing cottage in Dunure in South Ayrshire. Her uncles and aunts joined the Reids; and, together, the children ran around the harbour watching the herring boats come in or played in the ruins of Dunure Castle. These were carefree days and when her grandfather John came to stay at the cottage, there was the reward of half a crown which they could spend on sweets in the village.

Like many children with a creative flair, Beryl had an inexhaustible supply of energy, her sickly days now over. She was enrolled in a dancing school where she had her first opportunity to shine – as a firefly. Wrapped in a cyclamen tutu on a tiny platform raised above the other children, she suddenly realised the joy of performing. As Annie walked her home, she looked up full of certainty declaring, 'This is what I'm going to do Mummy! I'm going to go on the stage!' Annie wasn't at all pushy but she did encourage her daughter. As Beryl later recalled, 'She absolutely supported me at home but she was realistic. Much later she got me used to the sound of my photographs hitting the doormat when nobody wanted me.'

In later life, Annie would always try to keep Beryl's feet firmly on the ground. When Beryl told her that she was to entertain the Queen at Windsor Castle, Annie wasn't at all impressed, simply saying, 'Well, you make sure you've got a clean hankie and no wiping your nose on your sleeve!' Beryl was 34 at the time.

One thing, however, did concern Annie and it only came to light on Beryl's first day at the Withington Girls' School in Manchester. In later life, she'd become much loved as Monica, the naughty schoolgirl; and, whilst Beryl didn't have the toothy plum voice that made Monica so funny, she was a handful. Withington Girls' had been established by Manchester's social elite in the late 19th century to provide a rounded education as well as offering the usual deportment and elocution lessons which, in theory, would turn out a generation of perfect young ladies. Girls were educated to a high standard in the early 1920s but their job prospects were few. Marriage was a priority, morality was just as key as mathematics or English literature; but in scenes reminiscent of St Trinian's, Beryl broke the rules as often as she could. On one occasion she kicked a fellow pupil, Brenda Johnson, and was summoned to the headmistress's office. With no trace of contrition, the young Beryl bounded into the room to find the assaulted Brenda standing there with a dangerous glint in her eye. 'Now Beryl, I understand you have kicked Brenda?' said the headmistress. Beryl nodded. 'Well, just you stand over there then,' said Miss Jenkins-Jones, 'because now she's going to kick you.'

She was certainly popular at school, making close friends with a girl called Pat Kirkwood. Pat would later become a huge success as an actress and would just beat Beryl by a few years in becoming the first woman to have her own show on the BBC; but as children, Pat hadn't quite decided what she wanted to do whereas Beryl insisted, 'I'm going to be an actress, Pat, and my father knows the fella who runs the Floral Hall where they put on shows.' As Pat later explained, 'I was harbouring stage hopes myself and

I remember being consumed with envy at someone with such powerful theatrical connections!' It was bluff of course: Leonard never took his daughter to the local theatre, let alone promised an introduction via a thespian friend. Yet as children, Pat believed her of course and, in awe, sighed, 'You're so lucky, Beryl!' But she wasn't lucky in all things.

Something Annie had suspected was now being confirmed through Beryl's school reports. She couldn't read terribly well. 'I was bright at a lot of things,' Beryl later remembered, 'but when it came to reading round the class, I had my first real bout of fear. I used to count the girls and put my fingers in my ears and try to read the paragraph that was going to be mine so that I wouldn't look silly.' For a self-proclaimed fearless child who thought nothing of climbing trees and cliffs during her Scottish summers, this was a setback that could ruin everything. If she couldn't read, she couldn't learn scripts – and what was an actress without her script?

In later years, Beryl would always speak of her dyslexia and said that much of her struggle came directly from it; but, according to niece Sue and close friend Will Small, this seems to have been a self-diagnosis that maybe didn't always ring true. As Sue recalls, 'She always said she was dyslexic but I think she'd heard it as a buzzword and she just put two and two together. I never noticed that she had trouble reading, or if she did, it wasn't dyslexia.' When Will was going through Beryl's bookcase many years later, he was surprised to find not only heavy classics but books such as the collected poems of Robert Burns, well read and annotated in Beryl's own hand. Reading was a struggle for Beryl, but whether she actually did have dyslexia as we now understand it is questionable.

In her other subjects at school, however, early signs of her detailed observational skills helped her flourish. She was a whizz at languages, and Latin and German came easily to her as she could listen to the sounds the teachers made and then repeat them. Maths proved to be another challenge, but luckily she had Roy to help her with her homework. 'As a mathematician, she was a brilliant comedienne!' he said of her. 'Her adding up was an absolute scream!'

Her relationship with Roy would always be a close one and, as she grew older, she loved spending time with him, putting him on a pedestal as many little sisters do with their older brothers. They quickly found a brand new hobby: cars. Whilst most fourteen-year-old girls were playing with dollies and having teddy bears' picnics, Beryl was speeding along the roads of Manchester in a clapped-out Austin Swallow, a 1930s classic that resembled a large butter bean on wheels. Roy would buy the cars for a few guineas and then fix them up for resale to provide a little pocket money, but in reality, the only success he had was to provide wonderful childhood memories for Beryl. With the top down and her foot to the metal, Beryl drove Roy around the city and always remembered those days with great affection; her driving never really improved. As Will Small says, 'Beryl had two speeds: fast and stop. There were times when we narrowly missed pedestrians and it was all a bit hair-raising!' Roy was perhaps the only male role model she had during her childhood, never able to forge a close bond with her father but always able to turn to her brother for support and a kind word.

There were of course other relations, some disapproving but others sharing that same self-determination which helped Beryl carve out her own niche in the world. Her Aunt Belle had set herself up in the photography business which was quite something for a woman to attempt in the early days of the 1930s. Belle's photography shop would later come in handy for those early publicity shots that Beryl needed to send out to try and find theatrical work.

By the time she went to secondary school, her finicky eating had subsided, though she objected to many of the school canteen offerings with a particular nemesis being 'Smelly Lena'. The offending pudding was put into her handkerchief, then into her knickers and then into the first lavatory she could find! Whilst academia was beyond her reach, she was a likeable girl and the teaching staff at Withington Girls' had always made allowances for her, finding her eccentricities funny and sweet. This all changed when she moved on to Levenshulme Girls' School. Levenshulme was a fairly new school, founded by the Duchess of Atholl with a progressive education in mind, but the teaching staff were woefully old-fashioned and they took a dim view of Beryl's precocious personality. She took solace in friends Pat Kirkwood (who had also moved on to Levenshulme) and in Nancy Wrigley. Wrigley was the daughter of the Scottish soprano Dame Isobel Baillie, and Beryl would later delight in telling Roy Plomley that she cherished the memory of Dame Isobel frying baskets of chips in hot dripping for her and Nancy after school.

The one saving grace Levenshulme did have was that it encouraged the regular performing of school plays, and this allowed Beryl to focus on what she liked best. However, this was all becoming a bit too much for Leonard. His daughter was now reaching the age when she'd have to move on in life, to leave school and to find a well-paid job with a pension before her eventual marriage. Annie knew that Beryl had to at least try her hand at performing, but Leonard refused to accept it.

At weekends and during school holidays, Beryl would take herself off to old people's homes and hospitals to sing songs, tell jokes or perform monologues she'd written herself. She was courageous and refused to be told no; she was going to do the thing she loved best. She took the *Stage* newspaper and Annie kept a close eye on opportunities in the Manchester area whilst Beryl began to improve her skills at the Alice Dodds Dancing Academy. Perhaps aware of Leonard's objections, Alice urged Beryl: 'I don't care if you're standing on a dustbin doing it, you *must* perform!'

As the time neared for her to leave school, Beryl didn't care about her lack of qualifications. What she had couldn't be taught and she took confidence in her skills as a singer, dancer and actress. Annie and Roy felt she was funny (if not a little outrageous) but, unbeknown to anyone in the family, Leonard had already made Beryl's next step for her.

One afternoon, he told Beryl to be at Kendal's the following morning to start work. He had managed to secure her a place as a sales girl; but it wasn't exactly a big success. 'I was in six different departments in six weeks because nobody would have me!' she recalled. In the fur department, she brushed the expensive minks and sables incorrectly and ruined several. Then they tried her in the china department where she broke things and couldn't add up the bills. As a last resort, they sent her to the toy department where her natural flair for performing saved her neck. She demonstrated the toys and played with the children; she was a natural saleswoman in fact, but her honesty let her down. One day, she was doing a fantastic job of selling a new set of Bakelite bricks, fashioning them into houses and castles. As the crowd grew, the floor manager must have been thrilled that finally they'd found something Beryl could do. It didn't last. At the end of her demonstration, she declared in a loud voice, 'Don't have it because it's awful! It all falls to bits!'

Her wages from Kendal Milne were spent on publicity photographs provided by Aunt Belle and dancing lessons with a new teacher, Sally Lobel. Lobel had her own dancing school and, in exchange for help with the tots and toddlers class, Sally gave Beryl elocution lessons which were important in an era when regional accents had to be ironed out for performers to stand a chance. Ironically, it was a thick Brummie accent that Beryl would later be associated with when she found great success with her Marlene character.

Her lunch break at Kendal Milne began at 11.30 each day and, with a full hour to spare, Beryl began to hang around the local theatres in the hope of finding some kind of paid theatrical employment that would allow her to leave Kendal Milne. One night, a knock came at the door and in bounded Bernard Habgood who was a member of the South Manchester Operatic and Dramatic Society. He had noticed Beryl a day earlier when she had auditioned at the Leslie Pavilion, a music hall in Manchester which played host to all kinds of variety performers and 'spesh acts' such as fire eaters, female impersonators, jugglers and the obligatory Northern comic.

'Can your Beryl come and join our show?' he asked Mr Reid, who was none too impressed at the suggestion. But Annie insisted and Beryl took the part of Pauline in the SMODS production of *No, No, Nanette*, her very first stage role. She wasn't paid, of course, but as well as the larger productions she also performed each Sunday with the society's variety shows in which she excelled. Gawky and angular in stature, she was not a particularly pretty young ingénue; but she didn't want to be the girl the audience swooned over. She wanted the laughs.

Annie heard that a man called Fred Rayne was coming to the Leslie Pavilion to find players for his troupe, the North Regional Follies. Rayne had been in the business for some time and had taken his *A Breath From the Sea* show to Morecambe, Southport and Blackpool throughout the early thirties. He offered a complete package of singers, dancers, comedians and impressionists which toured seaside towns performing end-of-the-pier shows for summer seasons. With each new tour, Rayne liked to include some fresh faces for returning audience members; and so when Annie heard that he was holding open auditions at the Leslie, Beryl gave lunch a miss and rushed to the theatre to show Fred what she could do.

Not having any props or costumes, she decided to create a character called Ethel, dressed in the maid's outfit she wore for the Sunday SMODS shows, and came on stage carrying a pile of shoes. She'd drop them onto the floor and then try each pair on, portraying the character they might belong to, which allowed her to show off her range of accents, ages and gags which she had written herself. Rayne was so impressed that he agreed to put her into the 1936 summer season in Bridlington; but when she returned home, all hell broke loose. Taking the season meant leaving Kendal's and that all-important pension. Leonard was absolutely furious, and so it was left to the ever loyal Annie to help her daughter find digs and to see her settled in. It must have been a very daunting prospect for a sixteen-year-old girl. Away from home, alone in a strange town with people she didn't know, she was well aware that her father was livid with her decision; and he refused to speak to her for a year, finding it impossible to comprehend that she would throw away a steady position to risk everything at the end of the pier.

The Bridlington show gave Beryl £2 a week, but the majority of it went on her bed and board at a guest house. She was billed as 'the Blonde Comedienne', her hair then almost white and pin-curled, but Rayne didn't provide her with a script. She was very much thrown in at the deep end, performing alongside seasoned talent including a baritone called Wilson Harvey, a comedienne called Marjorie Marsh, a comedy duo called Horace and Edna and a man called Wally Ackworth who specialised in Al Jolson impressions. Another performer was a comedian called Horace Mashford: 'We were rehearsing a sketch in which she was behind a saloon bar. I was front of stage doing some comedy business that was supposed to be the high spot of the show. When she asked if she could have a word with me, I thought she wanted a bit of advice, because she was only sixteen after all.' But Beryl didn't want advice. 'Excuse me, Horace,' she said, 'I wonder if you'd mind moving to one side, because if you stay where you are, the audience won't be able to see me!'

Bridlington was also home that summer to Jimmy Jewel and Ben Warriss, a comedy double act formed in 1934 and now enjoying great success. Jimmy Jewel would later become best known for his role as Hylda Baker's rakish brother in the sitcom *Nearest and Dearest* whilst Ben Warriss would become a pantomime staple, performing well into his seventies. As a comedy duo, they were extraordinarily popular in the north and, in a local pub one night, Beryl was introduced to them. They immediately noticed something special about her, and Ben decided to take her under his wing.

Her lack of experience showed: she was even removing her make-up with large amounts of Trex, a lard substitute! Before every show, she'd apply her greasepaint, run to Jewel and Warriss's dressing room so they could give her the nod, and then run back to dash on stage and do her turn. She later remembered drinking pints of beer with Jewel and Warriss, which she hated but thought was terribly grown up.

As wonderful as the North Regional Follies had been, the summer season was now over and the cast had begun to look for alternative employment over the Christmas period. Wary of returning to Manchester and having to face her father, Beryl began to look for employment. There was a fabulous opportunity to audition for Jack Gillam, a producer who specialised in pantomime, forming his own production company in the 1950s that gave juveniles and veterans of the stage alike a chance to perform all over the country in popular pantomimes such as *Aladdin* and *Cinderella*. Gillam ran six pantomimes simultaneously bringing in around £600 a week. When this was broken down, it left theatres around £15 a week with which to pay the cast; so Gillam must have been delighted when Beryl walked into his office to audition. Unsure of what to say, she'd asked Annie for some advice. 'There is nothing you can't do Beryl, nothing,' she said. After doing her little sketch as Ethel the maid, Gillam said:

'What else can you do?'

Remembering her mother's wise words, Beryl enthused, 'Everything!'

'And how much do you want?' said Gillam.

'Three pounds a week,' Beryl pleaded.

'All my life,' said Gillam, 'I've been looking for someone who can do everything for £3 a week.'

She was cast as the Genie of the Ring in *Aladdin* at the Hippodrome in Salford; but, before the run even began, she entered a talent competition and won, the prize being a week's worth of appearances at the Paramount Astoria in the Old Kent Road with an additional cash prize of £20. The thrill of appearing on the London stage would never leave Beryl and, as a young girl travelling down to the capital for the first time with her mother, Beryl spent much of the train journey jotting down ideas for jokes. The whole enterprise had been a success but the money didn't last long. When Beryl disappeared and returned with a mink coat from Frith Street in Soho, Annie was horrified. 'But Mummy, I'm an actress and an actress has to have a fur coat!' Beryl protested.

Seeing her enormous potential, Jack Gillam then asked Beryl if she would join the *Arcadian Follies*, another revue which opened in late 1936 at the Empire Theatre in Morecambe. Her very first review boasted that 'Beryl Reid with her impressions has to be the best turn on the programme' and, buoyed by this success, she took a one-night theatre booking in Birkenhead. As she approached the theatre, her jaw dropped open as she noticed that the name 'Reid' was up in lights. Swelling with pride, she quickly discovered that the lights were for the singer-songwriter Billy Reid who was far too busy arguing with the Welsh torch song singer Dorothy Squires to even notice Beryl.

For Annie, Beryl's continued success meant that it was time to step things up a little. Even before the Second World War when radio took on a brand new role of national importance, the wireless was a sought-after addition to the home and the BBC had studios in Manchester which produced programmes under the name 'BBC North Regional'. With two summer seasons and a couple of pantomimes under her belt, Beryl now managed to secure an audition with David Porter who was the man to please at North Regional Programming. As a producer and presenter, he was always on the lookout for fresh talent and so, in February 1938, the young Beryl Reid faced her first audition for the British Broadcasting Corporation. She was extremely nervous and decided to show her range of impressions which at that time included the unlikely combination of Margaret Rutherford and Donald Duck. She was the twenty-ninth performer to audition on a Sunday night and a beleaguered Porter had sat through everything from ventriloquists to budding sopranos; but, when Beryl asked if she'd get a broadcast, Porter was certain she would.

Beryl always insisted that her first broadcast had been with Wilfred Pickles on *Children's Hour* but in fact it was as an impressionist during Porter's radio revue, *Between the Houses*. Her co-stars on that first broadcast didn't reach the successful heights Beryl did and, perhaps because she stood out so much from the other performers, Porter began to use her as much as he possibly could in the North Regional Schedule.

For Beryl, this was not only a wonderful opportunity and a great leap forward but it went some way to improving things with her father. A daughter on the stage was a very different thing to a daughter on the radio. His work colleagues would no doubt have been slightly in awe of him and, as a natural showman, the notoriety of Beryl's growing public fame was something of a compensation. It healed the rift slightly but the relationship would always remain a little tense on both sides.

North Regional was all very well and good, but London was the place to be. Not only were theatre opportunities more abundant, the BBC was based there and she'd have a chance to be heard nationally. Beryl was still busy with Gillam's *Arcadian Follies* and so Annie took matters into her own hands, writing to the BBC on her daughter's behalf: 'After my broadcast on 29th September I will be free for a week or two when I could come to London to audition for you if you so wish. I am 19 years of age.'

Annie was certainly taking on the role of an unofficial agent even though Beryl now had limited representation by the theatrical agent Ernest Binns. Binns perhaps never appreciated the talent he had on his books and the relationship quickly ended. During an appearance in *Mother Goose* in Scarborough, Binns went to see his client who tottered onto the stage in high heels and a little tutu. When she kicked her legs, she flashed her knickers to the fury of her agent who rushed round to her dressing room ranting, 'You're not paid to show your arse, Beryl!'

It didn't matter: she had been offered an appearance on the 'New Voices' segment of the radio show *Band Waggon*, to be recorded at Broadcasting House in London. The excitement was almost too much to bear and Beryl sent letters asking if she should prepare her own material or whether it would be provided. Certainly the BBC were intrigued and David Porter wrote a supporting letter in which he said, 'I consider Beryl Reid one of the cleverest impersonators up here. Some of her impersonations are extremely good and she has an enormous repertoire. It is perfectly easy to pick four or five to make a first class act.' A date was set for 2nd December and Beryl managed to get out of the matinee of *Mother Goose* to make the trip to London for her audition. But it was not to be.

Frank Risk was the head of the Programme Contracts Executive at the BBC and was slightly taken aback by Porter's recommendation. Whilst he was in no doubt that Beryl was good enough, he pointed out that the *Band Waggon* slot was a vehicle for new talent. In red pencil, Risk scrawled across Porter's memo: 'This correspondence shows that the lady is not qualified for "New Voices" having broadcast from everywhere except the Director General's bathroom!' Beryl was disappointed and she did suggest that she could still be considered for other programmes, but *Band Waggon* was definitely out. Her big break in London would have to wait.

On the bright side, she still had the loyalty of David Porter who then made sure that Risk knew exactly what he'd missed out on. She was used in everything and anything Porter could find for her and he included her in the 1938 Christmas broadcast, *A Right Good Do!*, hosted by 'the king of the ukelele', George Formby. Beryl would work with George several times in her radio years but, like many pretty young things with talent, she found that George's wife (also called Beryl) made for an unpleasant working atmosphere, often consumed by jealousy. Musical accompaniment for *A Right Good Do!* was provided by a pianist from Blackpool called Violet Carson. She would later become an icon in television history when she joined the cast of an experimental soap opera called *Coronation Street* as the matriarch of the cobbles, Ena Sharples.

Though *Mother Goose* had cost her her agent, it didn't take long before Beryl was able to get representation with the Hyman Zahl Vaudeville Agency thanks to the impressive reviews that appeared in *The Stage*: 'A popular artiste in this show is Beryl Reid who without the aid of anything but her own face impersonates all the well-known movie, stage and radio stars, not only obtaining their vocal characteristics but also their facial impressions.' It closed with the ringing endorsement, 'She is well deserving of the applause she receives.' Zahl offered her £8 a week, a fair amount of money in the late 1930s, and he secured her a few tours.

There was another, more long-lasting gift that came from *Mother Goose* that year: she formed a friendship with the actor Reg Vincent. Vincent never quite got the big break Beryl would later enjoy but they remained dear friends for decades. Reg would often claim that he was broke and that a Christmas Day usually involved peering through other people's windows as they sat down to a huge turkey and all the trimmings. Beryl never failed to invite him to Honeypot and Reg died a wealthy man.

It was during this pantomime that he played a classic prank Beryl always told with great relish. Reg explained that the ingénue always provided the snacks for opening night; and, spending her entire week's wages on potted meat and fish, she duly stayed up all night making endless rounds of sandwiches. Reg then said that she shouldn't forget the tradition of sharing Christmas presents and so, the next day, she ran to the nearest department store to buy a jolly tie for the men and a silk scarf for the ladies. Of course, it was all fabricated by a mischievous Reg and when the joke was revealed, Beryl thought it hilarious and said, 'I wanted you to have that tie anyway!' In a typically loving gesture, Reg wore it for his Christmas dinners at Honeypot.

Mother Goose had been a joyous experience, and another would come the following year when she got the chance to appear with Douglas Byng, a gay comedian and drag performer who titillated audiences with his risqué monologues and songs such as 'I'm a Mummy, an Old Egyptian Queen' and 'Oriental Emma of the 'Arem'. The material Beryl was performing during this period wasn't wonderful, but the chance to mix with some of the most famous names in the business gave her the contacts and the experience she needed. Max Wall, Dorothy Ward, Nellie Wallace, Harry Champion: these were the performers Beryl had listened to on the wireless at her mother's knee; now she was one of them and loving every bit of it.

When a dressing room wasn't quite up to scratch, a concerned Annie took one look at the cracked basin and dirty walls and said, 'Well, if this is what it's going to be, Beryl, I should give it up now!' She was joking of course. Annie was now acting as Beryl's companion, going with her to all her bookings and ensuring her digs were the best they could be given the money she was earning. Leonard stayed at home.

In Scarborough, Beryl met Arnold Crowther, a master puppeteer who excelled at Punch and Judy shows as well as creating various magic tricks that he performed with flair. He became a firm favourite with the young Princesses Margaret and Elizabeth, performing for them at Windsor Castle in 1935 and giving him the chance to use 'By Royal Appointment' (albeit unofficially) on his playbills. Crowther suggested that, whilst impersonations were all very well and good and Beryl was clearly very talented, Donald Duck could only take her so far. He suggested a schoolgirl persona which she could perform alongside his dummy, 'Horace the Sailor'. It was here that an embryonic version of Monica was born, a toothy schoolgirl with little material but with an awful lot of potential.

Hyman Zahl gave the BBC a gentle push. The *Band Waggon* fiasco had now been forgotten and as he explained, 'She is an excellent girl and she has done quite a lot of broadcasting from your Manchester studio but nothing from the South.' Frank Risk relented. He simply initialled a big red tick on the page, leaving his assistant Miss Lipscombe to ask in pencil: 'When do you want her then?'

Beryl's big break came with a radio series called *What's Yours?* to be broadcast from the grandest of venues, the London Palladium. Produced, written and devised by Ernest Longstaffe, *What's Yours?* was billed as 'a lightning programme of contrasts' but, in reality, was simply a revue for the wireless with a live audience at the Palladium. It was a very traditional set-up with 'Our Canadian Pals' Al and Bob Harvey providing a Flanagan and Allen style music act, and a comedian called Bruce Green who specialised in female impersonation in the 'Over the Garden Wall' style first made famous by Norman Evans before becoming the basis for endless Cissie and Ada sketches written by Terry Ravenscroft for Les Dawson and Roy Barraclough.

Performers were required to wear evening dress, but Beryl was having none of that. If she was to perform 'the schoolgirl' (Monica went without a name for quite some time), she would appear as the schoolgirl. As Susan Penhaligon who starred alongside Beryl in *No Sex Please, We're British* remembers, 'She gave me a piece of advice I've used ever since: "Get the character's shoes right and you'll crack how to play the role." I have a feeling Laurence Olivier used to say it but, for me, it came from Beryl.' And for Beryl, costume was just as important as the material she was performing. Whilst her fellow performers appeared smartly dressed before a rather fancy audience, Beryl leapt onto the stage with her hair in pigtails, freckles dotted across her nose with an eyebrow pencil and her original gymslip from her days at Withington Girls'.

'You just can't do it if you're not exactly like the character,' she told *The Stage*. 'You should look and feel like them as much as possible and then you'll sound like them, walk like them, you'll find all their mannerisms. It makes the thing so much more truthful.'

Although *What's Yours?* was only one broadcast, Beryl now had no choice but to relocate permanently to London. When war was declared in September 1939, Britain carried on as usual and it seemed that the entire thing had been blown out of all proportion. People called it 'the phoney war' and very little changed. Air raid shelters and gas masks became a common sight, but that Christmas was very much like any other and the British wondered if the whole thing hadn't been a big misunderstanding. That idea was quickly put to bed in early 1940 when the Germans began to carry out Blitzkrieg operations all over Europe, taking one city after another. The government experimented with theatre closures but this proved unpopular and, leading the example set by London's famous Windmill theatre, many fought to stay open.

Following the success of *What's Yours?*, Beryl had been booked for a Tom Moss pantomime in Sheffield, *Cinderella*, to star the matinee idol, Jack Buchanan. Buchanan was something of a national treasure, debonair and extremely handsome. Beryl would later say that she almost always fell in love with her leading men 'at least for a week!' but any chance at a romance with Jack was cut short when, tragically, an air raid brought devastation to Sheffield. Beryl's rented accommodation was bombed so badly that it burned through the night. Determined not to lose a thing, Beryl kept walking into the smouldering wreck to retrieve precious items such as her wireless which she'd called 'Wilhelmina', the first broadcast she'd heard on the set being made by the exiled Queen of the Netherlands on the run from Holland following the Nazi invasion. Beryl was badly burned and her hair and eyelashes were singed as she used an old pram to take anything she could salvage to Buchanan's hotel. The next morning, the theatre announced that his understudy had been killed in the raid and the production was scrapped as the local authority questioned the sense of keeping the theatre open.

The only suitable venue for the show was now the Hippodrome in Ilford, East London and this gave Beryl the final push to make the move she'd been pondering for some time. She found a room in a small three-up-two-down in Brixton with an Italian family called the Pellegras. For ten shillings a week, she had a room of her own and was invited to take her evening meal with the family: quite a treat considering that, whilst most of the country were existing on boiled beef and carrots, Beryl was being introduced to pasta dishes and ciabatta which she loved.

Despite theatres closing down or being temporarily vacant, the government still saw the benefits of keeping people entertained, and now a new force came to the fore to take that responsibility on. It was called the Entertainments National Service Association (or ENSA) and was formed by Basil Dean to offer free shows to troops fighting abroad and war workers on the Home Front. Dean, a film director and actor, held open auditions at London's Drury Lane Theatre; and, over the duration of the Second World War, around eighty per cent of those involved with the entertainment industry would contribute something whether it be performing, making props, creating costumes or providing lights. But whilst Basil Dean referred to his force as 'the Entertainment Army', the audiences had their own idea of what ENSA stood for: 'Every Night Something Awful!' Beryl joined ENSA but, unlike performers such as Joyce Grenfell who toured remote parts of the British Empire, Beryl Reid stayed firmly in the capital and this meant that she could take other work: most notably, the pure slog that was 'cine-variety'.

Cine-variety was a cheap and therefore extremely popular form of entertainment during the war where patrons could watch two films, a Pathé newsreel, a cartoon and a full stage show for around two shillings (10p). Unlike theatre which generally provided two performances, one in the afternoon and one in the evening, cine-variety programmes ran throughout the day. Beryl managed to secure a contract for two bookings at once, zipping from the Astoria in the Old Kent Road (where she had previously won £20) to Brixton where her last performance was given at 11 p.m. Exhausted, she would return to the Pellegras' to be fed before starting the whole thing over again the following morning.

It was by no means an easy life but it did provide a decent wage, and gentle reminders from her agent to the BBC that she was now London-based did wonders for her diary. Throughout 1940, she would make sporadic appearances on more episodes of *What's Yours* and variety shows including *Any Minute Now* and *Not So Brief Variety*. Neither were particularly well received by the public but, for £5/5s an appearance in addition to regular cine-variety bookings, Beryl was able to make quite a pleasant life for herself down in Brixton. She never failed to pay tribute to the Pellegras who she said had made the whole thing possible.

Unlike her contemporaries who may have gone a little dizzy at the idea of being modestly well off in a city that had so much vice to offer, Beryl wasn't one for going to nightclubs or parties. She loved to meet with her fellow cast members in the dressing room after a show but the idea of spending a night on the town didn't appeal to her at all. More often than not, she turned down invitations so that she could tuck herself up in her room at the Pellegras' and create material for 'the schoolgirl', a character that was now so popular with the public that she was asked to make an appearance in *Workers' Playtime*.

Although she couldn't have known it at the time, this made Beryl one of Britain's very first female stand-up comedians. There had always been a natural rivalry between the classically trained actresses who appeared in Shakespeare and those who made their way to the top by way of the music halls. But as Maureen Lipman told this author, 'Get rid of this word *comedienne*; she was an actress. A wonderfully talented actress who could do anything.' Beryl didn't simply learn lines and deliver them through a mouthpiece: she *was* that naughty schoolgirl who was always 'absolutely fed up' and had a best friend called Stephanie ('and I hate her!').

This made her an absolute must-have for *Workers' Playtime*, a government-sponsored radio variety show which began in 1941 as a way to boost the morale of factory workers in their lunch hour. The Home Front was as big a part of the conflict as the battlefields across Europe, and the government wanted to make sure that those confined to dreary manufacturing jobs (especially women taking the place of men who had gone off to fight) were kept bright and cheerful. Performers such as Terry-Thomas, Betty Driver, Eve Boswell, Dorothy Squires, Arthur English and Elsie and Doris Waters (in their guise as Gert and Daisy) would perform skits, songs and sketches with occasional appearances from the Minister of Labour and National Service, Ernest Bevin, to offer a sober but encouraging word of congratulation to the workers of Britain for soldiering on in the country's darkest hour. Beryl appeared on the programme in 1942 for which she received £5 and a subsistence allowance of a shilling to cover her bus fare.

With her list of credits growing, it would be easy to assume that Beryl was much in demand; but one London agent in particular put up a fight when she first expressed an interest in working for him in 1942. His name was Tom Arnold.

If it was a pantomime you wanted, Arnold was your man. With a fat cigar and a large brandy in hand, he was known as 'the king of panto' and his shows always included something out of the ordinary. Horses, ice shows, circus clowns, flying trapeze artists: you name it and Tom Arnold could put it into *Dick Whittington* and wow the audiences. Beryl knew that she could fit into Arnold's productions but to get the booking, she'd have to get five minutes with His Majesty.

Determined as ever, she found out Arnold's address and made her way to his office in a neat suit, her hair waved and her make-up just so. An old boy guarding the inner sanctum of the pantomime king told her that she'd need an appointment or else Mr Arnold wouldn't see her. The next day, she walked from Brixton to Shaftesbury Avenue with an armful of funny props, whistles, slapsticks and strange hats. She sat on a chair outside the office, hoping Arnold would notice her through the glass. He didn't. This was war.

Every afternoon, Arnold left the office for lunch and ignored her as he sailed past. But now Beryl would ensure he couldn't ignore her. When Arnold went for lunch, she quickly put on her Monica costume and began lurching round the room. Arnold returned to find this St Trinian's horror giving a one-woman show outside his quiet little office and boomed, 'For Christ's sake! Let's have her in!' Beryl would appear in Tom Arnold's pantomimes for the next nine years.

Arnold also put her in touch with a Scottish comedian called Dave Willis who was thrilling audiences with a show called *Half Past Eight*. Willis was a great comedian and beloved by his audiences, but he was also a master of improvisation and hated rehearsing. More often than not he was to be found in the nearest pub drinking whisky, only to totter round to the theatre at the last minute to give his all. Beryl would perform over two hundred sketches with Willis in the season of 1944 and not one of them was planned. When she asked him for advice, he replied in his thick Scottish brogue: 'Well, you come on and say so and so, and then I'll come on and say so and so. And then we'll do some domestic patter and we'll end on this…' Beryl later recalled that this was very much a baptism of fire but one for which she was forever grateful: 'Not being comfortable with reading scripts, it was a lovely way to get direction; I just wished there'd been more of it!'

Night after night, Beryl had to prove her worth and be prepared for anything Willis may throw her way. The *Glasgow Herald* said of *Half Past Eight*: 'The company maintains a high standard of entertainment in the fourth show of the series which opened last night. The pawky brand of humour which Willis provides is given full scope in half a dozen scenes which show him in such diversified characters as the henpecked husband over the washtub, a slapstick salesman and a vicar. Able support is given by all members of the company, especially Miss Beryl Reid who is an impressionist.'

The run also brought her into contact with Wilfred Pickles, a Yorkshire comedian who had just been selected by the BBC Home Service as an announcer for its North Regional Radio Service, despite his strong accent which caused a fuss at a time when people objected to any form of news not being delivered in the ever treasured RP (Received Pronunciation). It later transpired that the BBC were deliberately selecting people with regional accents to make it harder for the Nazis to imitate British broadcasters after the Lord Haw-Haw debacle in which William Joyce, an Irish fascist, broadcast regular anti-British news bulletins from Germany with his famous signature: 'Jairmany calling, Jairmany calling.'

*

The war was slowly drawing to a close and Beryl had by no means been short of opportunities, but times were changing and now there was a new medium to be considered. It was, of course, television.

In an age where a television show about people watching a television show is considered unmissable viewing, it is perhaps unthinkable that we Brits ever managed without our beloved gogglebox. But during the war, radio was king; and not only did people feel televisions were hideously expensive (given the fact that they were always presented in beautiful cabinets) but many felt them to be dangerous. Not until the Coronation of 1953 would television suddenly catch on, and even then most sets were rented and not owned. However, Beryl had been encouraged by the idea that Wilfred Pickles had made a broadcast on the box; and if the BBC at Alexandra Palace were on the lookout for comediennes, surely she should be first in line?

In 1947, Beryl approached the Head of Light Programming at the BBC, D. H. Munro, and said, 'I hear that television is short of photogenic comediennes. I am both and enclosed are two very small pictures. I finish in this pantomime on January 25th and I'll be in town for a couple of weeks after this; if you should be interested in seeing me, perhaps you could make an appointment with me. I have done lots of radio work but *no* television!'

Munro was initially reluctant but he must have known who Beryl was: after all, her fame was snowballing and she was becoming a permanent fixture on popular BBC radio shows such as *Workers' Playtime*. Her name was added to a list of potential candidates and, eventually, she got a chance to make a screen test.

The problem was that Beryl had never even seen a television pro-gramme, let alone had the chance to actually appear on one. She arrived with a suitcase full of props but instead of a friendly, cosy theatre full of an adoring public willing her to make them laugh (which she could do with ease), she was suddenly in a draughty studio full of bright lights, wires and no audience. Joyce Grenfell believed that comedy was like a tennis match and that performers needed an audience to keep the movement going. With the lack of an audience, Beryl struggled. 'I was very nervous and pretty bad to start with,' she said, 'but I got a bit better as I went on! I realise the technique is quite different from anything I've ever done before but with practice and direction I think I'd be all right. I do hope anyway that you'll try me in a programme of yours.'

However badly she thought it had gone, and even though she always found television a little terrifying, Eric Fawcett who auditioned her way back in 1947 was full of praise. 'She's obviously a very experienced performer doing good comedy, sophisticated or broad,' he wrote. 'She also did a very good character study of a drab. Would say she's definitely well worth including.'

With the war over and most of her radio work still coming from North Regional, it seemed as good a time as any to return home to Manchester. She was doing better than some of her contemporaries; regular theatre work and consistent casting on the wireless meant that she had a steady income in a profession which her father had refused to believe could ever offer stability. Tom Arnold wanted her for every pantomime he produced, David Porter consistently booked her for anything he produced at the Manchester studios; but somehow, she was in a rut. What she needed was a hit, something the nation took to in their droves and in which she played a central part. In London, BBC bosses were discussing something that could easily offer just that. It was a new radio sitcom that would feature a dummy called Archie.

Chapter Two

'I owe so much to radio; it cast its spell on my life because of course, it is a magic medium.'

BERYL'S DETERMINATION WAS A FORCE TO BE RECKONED WITH. The decision she had made to go against her father's wishes and go on the stage coupled with her early successes gave her confidence and sometimes this meant that she could be self-sabotaging in other areas of her life.

Indeed, it's easy to think of Beryl as the nation's favourite granny, a *grande dame* of the theatre with her tremulous voice and matronly warmth; but as a young woman, Beryl was blonde, vivacious and desirable. She didn't shy away from talking about sex and could be extremely risqué (yet never vulgar). As her niece Sue recalls, 'Beryl once said she needed to have sex every day to keep her spirits up but really, she just loved to flirt; she was a naturally loving person but she was also very outrageous which made her very attractive to men.' It may have been said in jest but she was always the first to admit that she had been a bit of a girl. She would later tell Peter Stuart in the *Woman's Weekly*: 'I've certainly played the field; mind you dear I'd be a bit of a poor show of an actress if I hadn't!'

Barbara Cartland always insisted that every woman has a dream lover, a perfect man whom she searches for until she finds him and secures her happiness, and Beryl perhaps fit that theory. 'I like men with a sense of humour,' she said. 'They mustn't be conceited and they must be the sort of men who can laugh at themselves. I like the sort of man who grows on you rather than coming on very strong.'

By the late 1940s, she'd had brief romances of course and mostly with members of the theatre companies she toured with, but the men in Beryl's life would have to accept one thing: her career came first. As Dame Eileen Atkins told this author: 'She had a typical actor's attitude to her relationships which a lot of people in this profession do. There's something in your head telling you that the most important thing in life is your career and so you don't accept any threat to that even if means not being there for a lover or a friend.'

The ideal relationships for Beryl at that time seemed to be with the young gay members of the company who could offer the affection she craved but expected nothing in return. 'I'm very fond of the poofs,' she said in 1987 with no trace of political correctness. 'They've always been devoted to me and they've got me through some pretty dark hours I can tell you.' Close friends Paul Strike and Will Small confirm that Beryl always felt more relaxed in the company of homosexual men, even though she did have quite a voracious appetite for the male sex. 'Gay men were safer, they didn't really want anything in return,' says Paul. 'She could simply be herself and have a few drinks and hold court without worrying if she looked right or if the man had other intentions.' Will agrees: 'She needn't be scared or prove anything and that's when you got the best of her.'

There's no doubt that from an early age, Beryl could turn heads. She was extremely proud of her femininity and didn't care for the frumpy frocks she often donned for her characters. Marlene was 'down with the kids', squeezed into the latest fashions of the day and always in two sizes too small. Beryl loved clothes, she was besotted by hats and whereas she always made sure that her hair was perfectly coiffed and her clothes were modern without being 'mutton', Marlene allowed her to be larger than life; most of Marlene's clothes in fact came from what Beryl called 'the tart shops' on Shaftesbury Avenue.

When she came to playing Kath, the hypersexual adult baby she portrayed in Joe Orton's *Entertaining Mr Sloane*, she found a pair of stilettos which she reasoned someone might have told Kath her legs looked nice in and so, whatever the weather, Kath wore them. Beryl put a lot of faith in shoes, keeping every pair she ever wore for a character, just in case she was called back to play the part.

But however grotesque she was willing to be and however eccentric, she did feel that women should remain feminine and that men only really cared for funny women who were not a threat to their masculinity. By way of return, Beryl didn't really care about the physical traits of men. 'Looks don't matter that much to me,' she said. 'They can be ugly or good looking – I like them with lived-in faces.' Whilst Marlene and Kath longed for the young, the hip and the trendy, Beryl preferred a father figure – one doesn't have to be Mr Freud to see why.

In the summer of 1949 whilst appearing in a summer season at the New Theatre in Newquay, Beryl began her first big love affair which would result in a whirlwind engagement. Taking everyone by surprise (including Beryl herself), she announced her engagement to Bill Worsley, a BBC producer whom she'd met during a recording of *Workers' Playtime*. Worsley was a well-liked face in the Variety department and had a hand in the early careers of many of Britain's best-loved comedy performers such as Bob Monkhouse and Eric Sykes. He had been married before and had a fifteen-year-old daughter, Priscilla, but that didn't worry Beryl at all. He was tall, slender and rather handsome in a bookish sort of way. And he was incredibly kind to her which helped the thing along.

Fate seemed to bring them together as the directors of *Workers' Playtime*, Jack Inglis and Brian Sears, offered Beryl another thirty episodes at £7/7s a pop, and so as well as appearing twice a day in Newquay, she also had to make the weekly dash to London each Saturday to record various skits and sketches which were almost always produced by Bill Worsley. Beryl didn't take to him at first. 'Our relationship was, in a way, very slow to develop,' she said, 'but I did fall in love with him and realised he was a person I could marry.'

In the time it took for her relationship with Bill to become serious, Beryl was also stepping out with a handsome lifeguard called Peter whilst at the New Theatre. Needing a little extra money, Peter the lifeguard had taken a job for the entire summer which happily coincided with Beryl's run; and so for one blissfully hot summer in Cornwall, Beryl had picnics with Peter on the cliffs and even introduced him to her mother whilst also spending the weekends with Bill Worsley up in London. Her mother was by now a travelling companion and acted as Beryl's secretary and so when

Annie was introduced to Peter and not to Bill, it seemed that Bill's ambition to marry Beryl was a little misplaced. 'I had a firm talk to myself,' Beryl remembered, 'and I accepted Bill's proposal.' In truth, Annie had stepped in and told her to make a decision one way or the other.

Bill and Beryl were engaged in August 1949 and the banns were read at the Quantock Church in Newquay with the big day scheduled to take place on 1st October. She made a beautiful bride and even though she had just turned thirty, she looked to be a young girl of eighteen. She wore a large bow in her hair with a huge cultured pearl at the centre to fix her veil, and her white wedding gown was fitted to show off her slender frame with white lace covering her shoulders. As she walked down the aisle in front of friends and family, Beryl was truly happy and the reception was small but recorded on camera for posterity by Pathé, a gentle reminder to all present that here was Miss Beryl Reid, a rising star at the BBC.

Looking back on her marriage in her later years, Beryl could never quite accept that she'd married in haste. 'I was engaged to Bill, an engagement that lasted two years which I suppose was pretty old fashioned,' she'd say, 'but that was the way you did things back then.' In reality, she had met and married Bill all within six months; but it appears there were two key reasons why she later tried hard to extend their courtship. The first of course was good old-fashioned 'keeping up with the Joneses'. By suggesting a two-year engagement, it made the thing more respectable.

The second was more serious. In the crazy, hazy days of that summer in Cornwall, Beryl clearly overlooked something in Bill that would later cause tremendous unhappiness between them. They were different people, out for different ends and each with their own emotional baggage. And then there was the professional stumbling block which was totally unavoidable and, for Beryl, potentially an axe to her early career. As with today's performers, the BBC was forever being accused of nepotism, of overpaying its stars and of failing to produce shows that were universally popular. Whilst that side of things maybe hasn't changed all that much, in the late 1940s the bigwigs at Broadcasting House went one step further in trying to keep such claims to a minimum. Anyone who was married to a BBC producer was limited to just six broadcasts a year and so by marrying Bill, Beryl had to cut short her contract. She was faced with a choice between the BBC or Bill. Bill won.

*

Bill had lived in Amersham in Buckinghamshire but now the newly-weds needed somewhere to call their own. They rented a little cottage called 'Noroc' in Sunbury-on-Thames where Bill could pursue his interests in sailing and where the couple could spend relaxing weekends together after his many hours in the smoky dark backrooms of Broadcasting House.

And then the reality hit her. Beryl realised she'd made a terrible mistake. Her regular jaunts to London hadn't just brought the chance to perform for the BBC; she'd also been able to see friends and paint the town red... or at least a charming shade of pink. Now, she was stuck alone at Noroc waiting for Bill to come home, and she was acutely aware that if she couldn't work in radio as much as she was accustomed to, she'd have to take more theatre work to keep her career alive. This got her out of the house but it also took her away from Bill. And yet suddenly, that didn't seem to be such a bad thing.

'When you start getting involved with someone then you lose the thrill of the unexpected,' she said in 1976. 'The man stops being a lover and starts being your husband and that's boring. It's not on.' Tension also came when Beryl didn't exactly see eye to eye with her new stepdaughter, Priscilla. Their relationship was strained and didn't make for a pleasant family atmosphere at home.

Travelling around the country constantly, trying to grasp scripts despite her difficulty with words, and now facing suggestions that her material was becoming predictable, it didn't take long before the strain started to show. Beryl was enduring a rather miserable run in Great Yarmouth at the Wellington Pier Pavilion, a far cry from the Palladium where she could have been recording *Workers' Playtime*; and when she did manage to grab a few weeks at Noroc, her efforts to improve the marital home went unappreciated. She redecorated it and made it her own, the entire house was repainted and Beryl put her own modern twist on things but when Bill returned home he was horrified and demanded they move.

'He sometimes behaved a bit like a U-boat commander,' Beryl said. 'He took me for granted and I wasn't terribly happy.'

Sue believes that the initial decision to marry Bill had been well meant: 'She married him because she loved him. I don't doubt that. But she was a very passionate person and she fell in love at the drop of a hat. The stress that came with it all meant that it just didn't work out and she was sad about that, she really was.'

From Noroc, the couple moved to Ripple Cottage and there was a chance for a fresh start. She used her allowance of six episodes at the BBC wisely and was booked to do a handful of episodes for *Henry Hall's Guest Night*, yet another variety showcase of the kind so beloved by the BBC. But her stint at Yarmouth had seen a few bad reviews with one critic writing, 'Beryl Reid's act is the same word for word as it was five years ago.' To which Beryl retorted, 'If he can remember it word for word after five years, it must be a bloody good script!'

With radio work a rarity, Beryl joined the company of *After the Show*, a revue to be played at the Watergate Theatre in which she would present a series of songs and sketches. One of Bill Worsley's fellow producers was a man named Ronnie Waldman and he had it in mind to use Beryl in a television series called *Vic's Grill*. Aware of the criticism she'd received that her material was starting to become a little stale, she was on the lookout for writers when she was introduced to Bill and Jon Pertwee, two cousins who would both play important roles in two of the greatest British television shows of all time: Jon as the third Doctor in *Doctor Who*, and Bill as the frustrated ARP Warden Hodges in the eternally successful Home Guard comedy, *Dad's Army*. 'Jon invited me to a party and Beryl Reid was there,' Bill recalled. 'She said to Jon, "I'm doing this revue at the Watergate Theatre to try out some material for a television programme." I interrupted and said, "Excuse me but I could write you some very funny material." So she gave me the number of the producer and I sent him one or two pieces. He rang me and said, "We're definitely very keen on one bit you've written for Beryl. You'll get £2 a week," and I thought, "Good Lord, that's marvellous just for writing a few lines!" '

The series in question was *Vic's Grill* and would mark Beryl's very first TV appearance. Written by Sid Colin and produced by Bill Lyon-Shaw, it was set in an East London café with a young Norman Wisdom tumbling around and John Hanson warbling 'The Desert Song' as was his wont. When Waldman saw Beryl at the Watergate performing Pertwee's material, he was immediately impressed and wrote a hasty note to Lyon-Shaw: 'She has tremendous verve and an uncanny gift for mimicry,' he said. 'Extremely amusing ideas, well carried out with great attention to detail. She should prove very suitable for television, variety or revue type programmes.'

After her disastrous audition in 1947 for an experimental medium called television, she was now in demand and it was around this time that a marvellous opportunity presented itself to Beryl. But before she could even think about taking any kind of television work, there was another big decision to make. She'd learned the hard way that if she wanted a successful and busy career in showbusiness, that must come first and that meant separating from Bill. She would never again put a relationship with a man before her craft and this would cost her dear at times.

It was 1951 and whilst the couple had been married for two years, Bill and Beryl had spent very little time together. 'It's terribly difficult to have a successful marriage if you are a success in the theatre because absence doesn't make the heart grow fonder and you're always on the go,' she remembered wistfully. She'd tried her best but, by her own admission, she longed for affection and she'd chosen badly in marriage: 'My husbands did tend to have a bit of the gypsy in their soul but that was just my hard luck. I did my best for them. They always had perfect food and a nice home.' And yet what they didn't have was Beryl.

One day, she asked Bill to join her in the garden at Ripple Cottage and told him that she thought things had reached their conclusion. She was going to London for her revue show and explained that she didn't want to come back. Bill was shocked but he must have been aware how difficult things had become. Beryl later explained that they would argue and then not speak for days on end, after which time he would invent some other problem because he'd forgotten what he was originally upset about.

She was realistic and practical about the failure of the marriage. 'It's nobody's fault really,' she explained. 'You just can't get home. You can do the shopping, cook the meal and have it on the table but if you're not there, it doesn't matter. And men are the kings you know. Men are men in their own right but women should have their own place. It's hard for a man to be married to a woman who is a success.' And naturally, with her marriage now ending in divorce, it was Beryl who was left without a home.

She left Bill in February 1951 and began to look for a home of her own. As a temporary measure, she moved into a caravan park called the Willows in Windsor so that she could be close to friend Sue Stauffer who no doubt provided a shoulder to cry on. The 'temporary' move would last for three years and when one caravan was not enough, she took another which was filled with props, costumes, fur coats, pretty hats and – of course – endless pairs of shoes.

With the loss of Bill came the freedom to work in radio again; also, Ronnie Waldman was now able to give her two months' worth of bookings with *Vic's Grill* which aired from 18ᵗʰ April 1951 until 27ᵗʰ June that same year. But if Beryl thought her success was now going to be limited to television, she was very much mistaken. Indeed, her television appearance only served to showcase her talent for creating funny characters and that was something that the critics welcomed. 'Miss Reid's delightfully naughty piece of the lady of the streets who meets a business recession with a cut price sale is a joy that lives beyond the moment's passing pleasure,' said one impressed viewer.

Yet for all her outrageousness, and whilst the material she penned herself verged on the bold, she insisted that it should always be enjoyable for a family audience. When her close friend Terry Wogan interviewed her alongside the late Joan Rivers in 1989, Beryl offered a rather curt judgement of blue humour: 'There is a difference between suggestiveness and dirt, dear!' she lectured Miss Rivers. Beryl respected the boundaries and, whilst she was the queen of the outrageous quip in private, in her early appearances she never crossed the line. She didn't want to be controversial, she didn't want to be noticed for the wrong reasons.

Barry Cryer says, 'It was stunning really because in those early days, we didn't have many female comics getting up and doing their own thing. She was like our Lucille Ball: it was entertainment for everyone, the whole family and so she didn't alienate any particular audience.' Much like Lucille Ball, she made every effort to get to know every single member of the crew on whatever it was she was working on. In this way, she managed to get the lighting she wanted or to get another take at the end of a long day. Whilst Miss Ball was sometimes feared by those around her, Beryl was adored and one more take for Miss Reid was given gladly rather than suffered in frustration.

*

When a comedian called Peter Brough began to look for new talent for his radio sitcom that year, Beryl Reid seemed a natural addition to the cast being equally popular with adults and children. Spanning generations is never easy but Beryl had potential in that department and Brough too had mastered this, enjoying huge success with his radio sitcom in which he rather bizarrely performed a ventriloquism act with his dummy, Archie Andrews. Supported by some of the finest names on the comedy roll of honour, Brough (as Archie always called him) was aided and Archie abetted by Tony Hancock, Hattie Jacques, Benny Hill and a young singer who played Archie's girlfriend. Her name was Julie Andrews. No doubt Dame Julie was in high demand even then but, if she was leaving, Archie would need a new squeeze and Ronnie Waldman knew the perfect comedienne – that funny schoolgirl he'd used for *Vic's Grill.*

A telegram was dispatched to the Willows and Beryl travelled up to London assuming that they wanted to review her contract or offer her another episode or two of *Vic's Grill.* Brough was absolutely certain that she was right for the show but the BBC insisted Beryl audition. She trudged up to London under the shadow of her impending divorce, which everyone at the BBC knew about. She had no real home of her own other than two draughty caravans and, slightly dejected and a little depressed, she did her audition and waited for the news. As soon as she'd read the last line on the script, Brough turned to the panel and said, 'Now what did I tell you? Now are we having her or not?' The answer was yes. With no idea how to celebrate, Beryl ran outside and headed to a greasy spoon where she ordered two banana splits.

Educating Archie was a strange premise and indeed it has become the stuff of legend. A ventriloquist on the radio sounds utterly ludicrous today; but Brough had honed his act for years, it was seasoned and polished – even if he didn't always take care of his little friend in the striped blazer. Archie was often 'misplaced' and even stolen, usually from Brough's car. When Brough left Archie in the luggage rack of his train carriage, the porter was promised a small fortune if he'd send Archie back in a taxi to make the Sunday recording. The problem was that there was only one Archie. The factory that made him was destroyed during the Blitz and the mould for his head had been lost. If Archie went missing, Brough would need an entirely new sidekick and the act would be lost. Archie was insured for a small fortune as a result, and a clever toy company managed to replicate miniature versions to be sold exclusively at Hamley's toy shop in London. These were among a wave of Archie memorabilia to be snapped up by children including annuals, yo-yos, replica blazers and there was even a *Sound Like Archie* booklet which offered young ventriloquists advice on how to perfect the art of throwing one's voice.

Much of the early material she was given was written by Eric Sykes but the two quickly fell out, Beryl believing that he kept most of his best lines for co-star Hattie Jacques. Beryl's friendship with Hattie was genuine and she considered her to be a true ally and someone she could talk to about anything – usually men! But Eric loved writing for Hattie and so it was to her that Beryl thought the best gags were being given. She took matters into her own hands, finding a writer who could give her material which was equal to Hattie's, and bypassed Eric Sykes entirely.

A brief stint on *Starlight Hour* helped her discover Ronnie Wolfe. Wolfe was a young writer who was contributing small scenes here and there; but, to Beryl, he was ideal. As Wolfe remembered: 'She was living in a caravan park in a field and I remember arriving with my first script. She carefully selected the gags she liked, working them to me in her Monica voice. She said she didn't like one of the gags, one I really fancied. "Ronnie," she said, "just all right isn't good enough! We can do better!" And of course she was right.'

Ronnie knew that Beryl was a scriptwriter's dream and though she often dabbled in writing the odd script here and there, as she prepared to join the cast of *Educating Archie* full time, only the best would do. 'You tried never to let her down because she would never let you down,' Ronnie remembered. 'I never knew her to ruin a line or miss a gag; she got every laugh in the script and usually a few extras along the way.' Because Ronnie wasn't actually employed by the BBC at the time, Beryl had to submit a pay request for him and this meant naming the sketch. The schoolgirl was now officially 'Monica'.

Monica was a bundle of energy, a St Trinian's prototype with buck teeth and a frightfully posh voice. She was inspired in part by the girl next door who was forbidden to come through the fence. One day, Annie caught her and the little girl lisped through her braces, 'Oh Mrs Reid, aren't I squeezy?' Once again, it was Beryl's attention to detail that wowed audiences. 'Beryl just slipped straight into the shoes of her character and then she simply was,' recalls Maureen Lipman who was a childhood fan of Monica. 'She was the first radio voice I responded to as a child and I used to do impersonations of her when I was a little girl – we all knew Monica and we all loved her.'

And for children and adults alike, Monica had an irresistible impish charm. She encouraged Archie to be naughty and break the rules with absolute glee in her voice. A typical exchange went as follows:

MONICA: Don't let's be too awful, let's do something to really please old Brough.
ARCHIE: Should I give him back my pocket money?
MONICA: No! I mean like, cleaning the windows or washing the ceiling or getting that ink stain out of the carpet.
ARCHIE: Ink stain?! Where?
MONICA: Well give me a chance to knock the bottle over!

Monica had delightful little catchphrases such as 'Jolly gymslips!' and 'I'm absolutely fed up!' A memorable gag was a large gobstopper she'd find tucked in her knickers; Monica would describe her discovery with glee, licking the fuzz from it and then popping it back, covered in spit, into her pocket. Beryl was thrilled when, during her *This is Your Life* appearance, Peter Brough brought Archie along to pay tribute to her career… and a pair of knickers complete with gobstobber which Beryl dutifully popped into her mouth!

When not working with Archie, Monica told stories about her best friend Stephanie whom she absolutely hated (a line gleaned from her soon to be ex-stepdaughter) and it was this material which she chose to take to a revue at St Martin's Theatre in September of 1951. The idea that she might do a revue with herself as the lead was practically unheard of. It had been done, of course, but it was rare that a woman was able to lead such a revue, usually depending on men to both lead the scene and bring in the audience. And yet for Beryl, her new-found fame packed the house and the material was so solid that she didn't need anyone else to push things along.

The reviews were staggering. The *Evening News* said, 'She is a superb comedienne. That was established last night at St Martin's when she treated us to cruelly scintillating character studies.' There were comparisons drawn between Beryl and the 'Two Hermiones', Gingold and Baddeley. This was perhaps a little unfair as the three women had their unique and individual styles, Miss Gingold specialising in the obscure and slightly dark delivered in a husky smoker's drawl whilst Miss Baddeley could turn her hand to cockney sparrows or dowagers in their dotage. Still, the *News Chronicle* insisted, 'Notable new talent in the matter of comedy is led by Beryl Reid who is sometimes wickedly like Miss Gingold, sometimes grotesquely like Miss Baddeley, sometimes distractingly like both of those revue queens rolled into one.' This review found its way into Beryl's file at the BBC, furiously underlined with a pencil inscription 'NOW'.

At Christmas 1951, Beryl finally joined the cast of *Educating Archie* as a permanent fixture. In typical Beryl fashion, she dismissed entirely the suggestion that she should wear evening dress for the recordings. Whilst her co-stars wore black bow ties or pretty evening gowns, Beryl appeared in her own school uniform with 'B. Reid' sewn in the back and a straw boater with '*Temperet Omnia Veritas*' (truth governs all things) printed across it. Monica was given an uncle played by Brian Reece, and her debut was the ideal opportunity to put her ill-fated marriage to Bill behind her. Now she could concentrate on forming friendships with some of her co-stars, and also on making a name for herself in the BBC as a whole.

She would count Tony Hancock among her admirers, and he often tried to push for Beryl's inclusion in programmes he was making. It wasn't always feasible, but the two had a very good working relationship. Suddenly, the word on everyone's lips at the BBC was 'Beryl'. She became so inundated with requests that she needed a new agent, someone who could represent her but also someone who could understand her mentality and her approach to her work.

In 1951, Beryl put her career firmly in the hands of theatrical agent Robert Luff. Luff was not the sort of agent who was content to simply sit in his office and wait for the telephone to ring, neither was he simply a go-between. Shortly after being demobbed from the Gordon Highlanders at the end of the war, Luff had begun his theatrical life arranging bookings for swing bands, when he came across a chartered accountant called George Mitchell. Mitchell had a choir like no other: a sixteen-piece all-male revue chorus who specialised in minstrel numbers. It was Robert Luff who encouraged George Mitchell to take them on the road, establishing one of Britain's best-loved musical entertainment troupes (though frowned upon today of course), the Black and White Minstrels. But Luff didn't simply represent the Minstrels: he helped to stage their early shows before the transition to television which saw them pull in millions of viewers between 1958 and 1976. Once he was done with the Minstrels, he turned his attention to promoting the Tiller Girls. Through the 1950s and 1960s, Robert Luff was running endless variety shows up and down the country;

and this made him an ideal agent for Beryl, with many of her early appearances being made in shows which Luff had produced personally.

His reputation made him a force to be reckoned with, and his first task when it came to handling the career of Beryl Reid was to insist that the BBC increase her wages, considering how well she had been received by an audience of fifteen million listeners. The fact that the Archie Andrews Fan Club was selling Monica badges meant that Beryl could safely be regarded as a household name; and, despite the misgivings of the variety bookings department, Luff managed to secure her £26 a week which was enough to allow Beryl to live comfortably and to seriously consider buying a house. Her first appearance as Monica was broadcast on 18th September 1952 and the audience adored her from the start, so it wasn't out of the realms of possibility that she was in it for the long haul, offering her a very real chance of financial security. She might not have the pension her father had hoped for but she was becoming quite a wealthy woman and her wages were consistently increased.

Requests for autographs flooded in and, with Beryl totally overwhelmed, these letters were sent to Manchester where the ever loyal Annie diligently acted as a secretary for her daughter. Beryl was so much in demand that whenever she was asked to give an interview, the accompanying photograph had to be of her in full schoolgirl regalia; whilst Beryl never objected to this, it did mean that she was totally invested in one series and one character. Monica was written into pantomimes, she was given sketches in revues and summer seasons, but offers for other stage roles were conspicuous by their absence. She'd learned that the performer with the tag line got the biggest laugh but she was now struggling with writers once again. Whilst Wolfe had provided some excellent material for her, the BBC were not keen on importing scripts from an outside source; and what was acceptable for appearances in other shows could never have been tolerable to someone like Eric Sykes who came down hard on the arrangement, saying that it was his job to write the sketches for Brough and Beryl and that the only person he'd consider working with was Brough himself.

Beryl felt this was unreasonable; she believed that Sykes didn't find her very funny at all and that, in his devotion to Hattie, she was being overlooked. It was the first sign of a side of Beryl's character that could make friendships difficult. Whilst she never 'played up' to the star image, she did relish the attention she was given, and the idea that she wasn't the star of the show could rankle with her so much that she could be deliberately difficult or even openly hostile. There were occasions when she'd simply say, 'I don't like you dear, go and sit somewhere else,' or 'I should really have that line you know, I'd say it better,' and these didn't come from cruelty but from a sense of inferiority. It was rare that she was gripped by such crises of confidence but, when they came, a slightly cutting side to Beryl could show itself and those who were treated to the cold shoulder never forgot it.

In reality, of course, Eric Sykes did find her funny, and he later protested that while he had absolutely no doubt that he had favoured Hattie, he admired Beryl enormously. When the row was hinted at in the press, Eric took great pains to write to Beryl and ask if she'd like to appear in the remake of his 1969 film, *Rhubarb, Rhubarb*. All was forgiven and forgotten.

Monica was a blessing but also a curse. As Eileen Atkins says, 'When you do a television piece, you're stuck with that character and people only want to see that. It lasts.' Brough felt that Monica risked getting a little stale and, whilst audiences longed to hear her, he suggested Beryl find another character she could play in a new series of *Archie* which was to broadcast in 1953. The death of Queen Mary that year meant that all comedy shows were put on hiatus for a brief period of court mourning, and this gave Beryl the time to try out a few new ideas with Brough before broadcasting resumed.

Her first creation was a cockney charwoman called Fuchsia, and Ronnie Wolfe was happy to help in the form of a script. She was entirely wrong for *Archie* but made one appearance in a Christmas special of *Henry Hall's Guest Night* at the Playhouse Theatre in London for which she was paid £30. Most of it went to Ronnie for the script. Fuchsia was funny but not quite distinctive enough. 'I tried a few like that,' Beryl explained, 'but when I performed as Fuchsia, everyone said, "Oh wonderful! Just like Joyce Grenfell." I thought Joyce was the most talented person in the world but it's no good being like anybody, you've got to be original.'

Her admiration of Joyce was returned. After seeing a revue Beryl did in 1953, Joyce wrote a personal note which said: 'You are a joy. Reticent, brushed in ever so lightly and so deftly with so much affection and understanding in your performances. Oh! I had such a fine time in your company and I feel I want to say thank you.' Beryl kept the letter for the rest of her life, clearly moved by such a glowing tribute from one of her personal heroines.

Understanding of a character was important to Beryl, though as Monica she wasn't really getting the chance to show her range as much as she would like; and, in trying out different successors for Monica, she knew she could only find the right one if she really had a firm grasp on it. Beryl was an avid people-watcher and she collected little anecdotes as if they were china ornaments, always aware that a mannerism or joke would come in handy. Tucked away in her memory was a meeting with one of those repertory theatre legends, the great British landlady. As a travelling player, Beryl was forever staying in guest houses run by eccentric landladies. More often than not they were spinsters or widows who opened their doors to theatricals, only to provide endless inspiration for the performers who stayed with them. One such landlady hosted Beryl during a pantomime run in Birmingham and would give her the basis for a brand new character: Marlene.

'She pretended she didn't eat anything, but she was at it all the time!' Beryl recalled, adopting Marlene's thick Brummie accent: 'I never have bacon and egg you know, well I can't eat breakfast so I force it down and then I won't eat till ten o'clock when I have a cup of tea and a few biscuits and then not a bite passes my lips till eleven. But I don't have nothin' then till twelve, just a bit of bread and dripping or something you know.' Beryl thought this hilarious enough, but the landlady also provided the perfect catchphrase for Marlene: 'Goodnight each.'

She performed a little skit for Peter Brough who thought it may just have possibilities but he advised her to write a script and submit it to the BBC. Not that she had much time to do so; a pantomime with Ken Dodd had secured the popularity of Marlene when she was written into a version of *Snow White and the Seven Dwarves* as 'the Grand Duchess of Dresden'.

Marlene had yet to make it onto the wireless, but when Leslie MacDonnell was putting together a spring revue in Coventry, he decided to team Beryl (based on the Marlene performance) with Jimmy Edwards, the moustached tubby comedian who was best known for his role as Pa Glum in the radio sitcom *Take it From Here*. Whilst they worked together wonderfully, Jimmy helped Beryl on something quite different and much unexpected.

As well as being well liked as a comic, Jimmy Edwards was a war hero serving with the Royal Air Force. In 1944, his Dakota aircraft was shot down over Arnhem and he suffered injuries to his face. He was put in the care of Sir Archibald McIndoe, a prominent plastic surgeon from New Zealand who had gained a reputation as 'The Maestro' for his amazing work with injured servicemen during the Second World War. Indeed, 'Big Jim' grew his trademark moustache to hide the scars McIndoe couldn't avoid. Sir Archibald developed many new techniques for cosmetic surgery but the real appeal was that he could operate quickly and ensure that the patient didn't need much time to recover.

So, when Beryl confessed that spring that she didn't like the shape of her nose, Jimmy Edwards handed over McIndoe's card and told her to give him a call. She had her rhinoplasty after the run at Coventry ended and McIndoe promised her faithfully that she'd be back in time for the autumn reprise of the show as well as the recording of the new series of *Educating Archie*. The operation was a success but the results subtle. Her recovery would take place in Majorca and, as she baked in the Spanish sun in a privately rented villa, covered up in bandages and sipping sangria, she busied herself with writing Marlene sketches and sending them across the channel to the BBC.

She was no doubt cheered by the reviews for her first theatre appearance as Marlene, but nothing could have prepared her for the public's reaction when Marlene finally joined Archie. Letters poured in and the reviewers agreed that Beryl had created a character who would no doubt become part of the showcase of great British comedy icons. Writing in *The Stage* in 1953, one critic said, 'Beryl Reid, whose comedy work has been seen in intimate revue as well as in variety, here gives us a blending of two styles. Her familiar radio schoolgirl "Monica" is still as odiously amusing but her gallery is now expanded by the addition of "Marlene", a *femme fatale* from the Midlands, a caricature admittedly broad but alarmingly true to life.'

Another review proclaimed, 'Frankly we did not expect to find Miss Reid accorded the patience of the full development of her act but we were delighted to find her able to dictate her own terms to the audience and keep them quietly entranced while the full flavour of her clever artistry was being developed. Miss Reid can do it because she is an artist of considerable talent with something good to offer. Her methods are not recommended to the average budding aspirant to comic fame.'

The secret of Marlene's success was perhaps that she was an adult and, whereas Monica was restricted to childlike naughtiness and a schoolroom setting, Marlene could travel and be a little more risqué which suited Beryl's sense of humour. Whilst Monica became known for her boater hat and gobstobber, Marlene's fashion sense was a wonder to behold in itself, especially her fondness for large earrings. Just as Monica had become a national institution, the public took to Marlene so much that Beryl began to receive novelty earrings from devoted fans through the post in the hope that she might appear wearing them. When Beryl became the face of Mitchell and Butler pale ale in 1954, beer bottles were suspended from her ears and her collection would grow to include shoes, buckets and eggs. She drew the line, however, at a pair of toilets. The commercial deal with M&B beer paid handsomely and there was even talk of a film appearance.

It was just a year since she had divorced Bill and life at the Willows was becoming impractical. For one thing, the telephone was at the end of the road into the camp site and she couldn't talk to her agent or to any writers who may wish to throw something her way. She needed a home she could call her own; but it now appeared that she may well be ready to share it with someone else. Beryl was in love.

Chapter Three

'The theatre is mad, it's bizarre and frantic. What you need is a little getaway where you can hide from the world. If I didn't have that, I'd probably be an absolute basket case by now.'

THE BELLES OF ST TRINIAN'S WAS SET IN A FICTIONAL girls' school inspired by the cartoons of Ronald Searle. The cast list read as a who's who of British comedy history with Alastair Sim playing two roles: the criminal mastermind Clarence Fritton and his sister, the headmistress of the school, Millicent. Not a dainty actor, Sim was naturally hilarious as he towered over the girls clad in Edwardian style frocks.

In *The Belles*, Clarence tried to knobble a horse race, the horse's owner having just lodged his daughter at the den of inequity that was St Trinian's. The girls smoked, made their own bootleg gin and were aided and abetted by George Cole as a spiv called Flash Harry. There was an undercover policewoman played by Joyce Grenfell and the dysfunctional teaching staff were portrayed by Irene Handl, Joan Sims, Renee Houston and Hermione Baddeley, all wanted by the police for gambling debts or even murder.

The big draw for Beryl was that the film was to be made at Shepperton Studios with the Oakley Court hotel in Windsor providing all the exterior shots. This meant that she could work from the caravan, and a driver was sent to collect her for each day's filming. Oddly, however, for someone known to the public as the naughty schoolgirl, it was as a teacher that she was cast.

Miss Wilson was the chemistry teacher, decked out in plus fours and a monocle. She had an almost Clarissa Dickson-Wright quality to her as she swung a golf club in the teachers' lounge and looked on idly as the girls pounded at a pot of nitroglycerine. Beryl adored the part: 'Absolutely everybody was in that; it was wonderful and we had very little responsibility. We had a few lines to say each, we charged about a bit and then we had to throw flour and soot at each other. It was the most carefree film I think I've ever done!'

St Trinian's was a huge success and quickly became a cult classic with four further additions to the franchise being made between 1954 and 1980; but, for Beryl, her days as a teacher at the war-torn girls' school would be restricted to the first instalment. When her brief venture into film concluded, Beryl packed her trunk for Scarborough's Floral Hall for a variety show. Providing the music was a jazz trio first formed by the bandleader Hedley Ward in 1948. The trio comprised Derek Franklin, a bass player, Jack McKechnie on guitar and Bob Carter on the piano. They were no strangers to Beryl as they'd provided musical interludes for *Archie*, but one of the trio had an appeal that wasn't restricted to music. He was a man she'd met just a few weeks earlier in the BBC canteen. His name was Derek Franklin.

Derek joined the Hedley Ward trio shortly after returning from active service in North Africa during the Second World War with the 49th LAA Regiment. Like her first husband Bill, Derek was older than Beryl but, unlike Bill, Derek was a variety performer. He knew the ways of the stage; he understood the time constraints and the demands of touring. Their relationship blossomed and, whilst Beryl had not long been divorced, she now considered Derek something of a permanent presence in her life.

They became engaged, again remarkably quickly; but naturally the two of them couldn't remain living at the Willows in a caravan and Derek was constantly in digs. Beryl began to peruse magazines for a suitable home, but she was rather taken with caravan life and so, at first, she trawled the *Slough and Windsor Gazette* for a houseboat, desperately wanting to live by the river. A strange little property was on the market that could have been designed especially for Beryl Reid. Prone to flooding, almost inaccessible without a car and slap bang on the banks of the River Thames in the little village of Wraysbury, Honeypot Cottage was her ideal.

She loved it from the moment she saw it. The cottage was a bizarre property in that it was constructed of three perfect circles. Built by an Edwardian called Eric Munro, the house itself was whitewashed with a thatched roof. The largest 'pot' was the living room which featured an imposing circular fireplace with a copper panel set into it, with the inscription 'Our true intent is all for your delight' from Shakespeare's *A Midsummer Night's Dream.*

Beryl's first view of the kitchen was hardly impressive. The cooker was on bricks, as was the refrigerator; and the estate agent explained that, if the Thames flooded, so did Honeypot. A set of stone steps led down to the garden, and from there Beryl could sit on the riverside in the midst of the wild flowers, occasionally taking a dip in the hot summer months. It had two bedrooms, and hidden away on the river itself was a cement bench, carved into the side of the bank with a large cement column. In the concrete were the names of children from Eastern Europe, most likely to have been refugees who stayed with Munro at Honeypot. After the war, the place seemed incredibly small to him and so he left in 1947 after decades of making it the perfect dwelling. But luckily for Beryl, it was absolutely perfect.

She bought it without hesitation for £500, but she very quickly realised that the issue of flooding was not one she should take lightly. Though not yet married, Derek was a regular visitor to Honeypot and had helped her get settled in, finding contractors to sort out the kitchen and to repaint the house to make it habitable. But within two weeks of being there, the Thames flooded and Derek was away with the band in a show called *Music for the Millions.* Beryl had to fight the flood waters on her own as they poured over the brand new kitchen floor. She was devastated but quickly came to accept this may well become a regular feature of life.

Luckily, it only happened once more during her forty years of living at Honeypot and provided her with a favourite story she told often, here recounted by close friend Jan Linden: 'Two friends were due to visit when the river flooded and the garden was totally under water. Beryl explained that they'd have to arrive by fishing boat; and then she came up with a little joke. She went into her bedroom and put on a stripy bathing costume, flippers, a snorkel, a floral swimming cap and a pair of frog earrings sent to her no doubt by a Marlene fan. When she saw a boat nearing the cottage, she rushed out to greet them only to find the postman in a rowing boat delivering her fan mail!' When she tried to explain, the postman laughed and said, 'Oh, you theatricals!'

The postman and the window cleaner featured in many of Beryl's stories about life in Wraysbury, such as the time she'd had friends for lunch one very balmy summer's afternoon. Stripping off, she fell asleep on the bed only to find that someone had left a note on the side table when she woke up. 'Your windows have been cleaned,' it read. When she next saw the window cleaner, he said, 'Nice to see you with some clothes on this time, Beryl!'

Beryl's relationship with Derek was a happy one and, determined not to make the same mistake she had made with Bill, she made him wait for a marriage even if she had jumped into an early engagement. They married in April 1954 in Blackpool whilst on tour.

Music for the Millions had taken a small fortune at the box office and now it was a travelling production. Honeypot lay empty for the first year as the couple focused on theatrical engagements, and so the only chance they had to get married was during a break between appearances. The wedding was held at Blackpool Registry Office on a quiet Monday afternoon with the wartime singer Anne Shelton and the opera singer John Turner as witnesses. A small reception was held at the Grand Hotel in St Annes-on-Sea; Beryl's only bridesmaid was the vaudeville star Bunty Meadows who was in rehearsals with Derek for *On With the Show*, an end-of-the-pier piece which would see Derek stay in Blackpool whilst Beryl went on with *Music for the Millions* in Bournemouth, Llandudno, Cheltenham and Harrogate.

Noting her happiness, producer Bill Lyon-Shaw was aware of the problems Beryl had faced during her first marriage and how sad she had been to see it end so badly. He wrote her a letter offering his congratulations after her marriage to Derek, saying: 'I do wish you every happiness for your forthcoming marriage. Being a Scot you are obviously following the example set by Robert the Bruce. However, I believe he was successful at his second attempt so I am quite sure things will be hunky-dory this time!'

When an opportunity came to do an interview with the *TV Mirror* in February 1955, Beryl was only too happy to show off her marital bliss and, whilst the majority of the photographs were Monica larking about at

Honeypot, she gave some insight into how the couple lived. Beryl explained: 'Breakfast is a precious time as it's about the only opportunity we get to talk about events of the day. Derek being married to "Beryl Reid" means that I'll be out all day busy on a TV show and as I'm married to Derek Franklin of the Hedley Ward Trio, I won't see my husband until he comes back from Broadcasting House after late night variety. But that's us.'

The following year saw not only another film but a touch of royal recognition. She was cast in *The Extra Day* with Sid James, a film in which a disgruntled cast face the ire of the management when a movie reel is lost and they must reshoot the entire thing all over again. It wasn't a rip-roaring success but it clearly pleased someone in high places. The Queen and the Duke of Edinburgh had recently completed a Commonwealth tour taking in New Zealand, Australia, the Cocos Islands, Ceylon, Aden, Uganda, Malta and Gibraltar, and to celebrate its success a special revue called *The World's the Limit* was put together for a command performance at Windsor Castle. Each of the sketches was to reflect a part of the Commonwealth, and for Beryl that meant teaming up with Peter Brough to play the part of 'Tongan Wife' in front of twenty-eight members of the Royal Family including the Queen Mother, Princess Margaret and of course the Queen and Prince Philip.

Such an extravaganza may seem archaic to our less deferential society but, for Beryl, that appearance at Windsor Castle was perhaps the confirmation she needed that she'd made it. She was as much a part of the establishment as her male colleagues at the BBC; and, encouraged by her agent Robert Luff, she was well aware of her star quality. And now she took advantage of it.

She'd been asked to record a brief appearance in Leeds, but her schedule didn't allow for it unless she could be driven there and back from Lime Grove in London. Thinking she'd found the perfect solution, Beryl simply went to Lime Grove and recorded *Archie*, then hopped into a private taxi and went to Leeds. She made the driver wait for an hour whilst she recorded the show, and jumped back into the taxi to be taken back to Honeypot Cottage. When the BBC were given the receipt, they almost wept with shock and refused to pay up. But Beryl carefully worked out the cost of train tickets, waiting times and the loss to them if she'd had to cancel either BBC booking. 'Will Mr BBC Cock Esq pay up NOW?' she demanded. They did.

It was now Beryl's dressing room that co-stars came to, it was Beryl the press wanted to speak to before a show and as Eileen Atkins recalls, 'She was the star, she had to be the leading lady and she loved all that. It wasn't enough for her to be in the part, she had to do the publicity, she had to present the whole thing and that brought her a lot of joy.'

But her new-found fame threatened to jeopardise the very thing that had given her that much sought-after position. With *Archie* due to start recording again at the end of the summer, the BBC wanted to bring the series up to date a little and this meant not only a new name, *Archie's the Boy*, but some rather big cast changes. Beryl had no issue with that of course – she knew she'd be included – but now she felt (as did Robert Luff) that perhaps she wasn't being paid her dues. When the new scripts came, Beryl took herself off to Broadcasting House to record a pilot with Peter Brough, Graham Stark, Ken Platt, Shirley Eaton and James Robertson-Justice.

The show had a new producer, Roy Speer, the man responsible for discovering the genius of Peter Sellers – or rather, Sellers gave Speer no choice but to discover him. Shortly after his discharge from National Service in 1948, Sellers called Speer and impersonated the radio presenter Kenneth Horne so well that Speer arranged a meeting with him and was so amused by the whole thing that he gave Sellers an interview and thus began his career.

Speer had a very set idea of what kind of a show he wanted *Archie's the Boy* to be and he didn't want to compromise. He liked the idea of a pretty young voice being provided by Shirley Eaton, and he was also keen to include James Robertson-Justice, then an extremely well-respected name in the business. Robertson-Justice was one of Britain's most celebrated character actors having made a name for himself in films in the late 1940s. Extremely tall with a great round belly and a bushy beard, he was a great bear of a man and he'd form a key part of the *Doctor in the House* series of farces led by Leslie Phillips. Shirley Eaton was no stranger to Beryl having worked with her two years earlier in *The Belles of St Trinian's*, and she'd also appeared in the first *Doctor* movie with Robertson-Justice. With the cast assembled, a pilot was made; but when the BBC put in a secret reviewer (who remains anonymous in the BBC Archives), his impressions of the pilot were scathing.

He didn't care for Shirley Eaton at all, saying: 'What is her purpose in this? I cannot see her worth.' And he found the whole thing vulgar. 'There are too many crude gags,' he explained. 'And Graham Stark sounds nothing like a woman!' Quite what role Stark was playing has been lost to the imagination, but even those cast members reprising original roles came under fire. 'Monica no longer sounds like the Ronald Searle type schoolgirl that originally made the character,' he ranted. 'The slapping of plaster into Brough's face was an example of how *not* to write a script. And as for Marlene, she is too slow and some of her material is bad. Although she gets a lot of laughs, both of Beryl's characters are extremely hammy and Music Hall.'

The problem was that Beryl was an integral part of the cast and crucial to the show's success. Robert Luff had now represented Beryl for five years and, under his careful guidance, she'd made two feature films, had made her first appearances on television and the fact that theatres now battled to secure her talents each summer meant that the £31 she was paid per episode for *Educating Archie* needed to be increased to reflect that. Luff knew that the BBC needed Beryl more than she needed them; and furthermore, he also knew that Brough wouldn't contemplate replacing her. When the BBC ummed and aahed over the fee, Luff wrote: 'Beryl wishes to go ahead with trying to make a full engagement book and I have reason to believe she has offers coming along (could it be commercial TV?) I have warned her that it is probably a bit too soon to ask us all this but she has done the right thing and I know she wants to be in this new series.'

The BBC panicked. Commercial television meant the newly launched ITV, the up-and-coming rival to the corporation. It wasn't that losing Beryl to ITV would be so terrible in terms of any future television roles; rather, word had reached Peter Brough that Beryl wanted more money and the BBC were considering replacing her as a result. Brough absolutely refused to do another series unless Beryl was in the cast and she became personally involved in the row, assuring the corporation that £40 an episode would be more than acceptable even if it wasn't the full £50 that Robert Luff had been fighting for. Producer Roy Speer took this extremely personally, suggesting that Beryl owed her fame to the BBC and therefore should simply accept the £35 he had in mind. 'There is no greater admirer of Beryl Reid's work than myself,' he said, 'but if I don't think she should get more than 35 guineas then I don't mind saying that both she and her agent should pay some respect to that opinion.' Jim Davidson, the head of the accounts department, went on to suggest that £35 was fair considering that: 'Her importance is offset by the fact that it is a programme in which she doesn't have to provide us with any material.'

For a week or two, it seemed as if Beryl's time with Archie had come to an abrupt end. Various BBC names fought for her, including variety booking manager Patrick Newman. 'I saw her recent effort at Windsor,' he said, 'and if the show comes to town as intended, it puts her on the way to being in the star class. She has a mass of characters to do (seldom being off stage) and she really is the poor man's (and not as poor as all that) combination of the two Hermiones (Gingold and Baddeley)!'

Just when it seemed that things had been resolved, two new crises hit the production team. If Beryl's fee was a headache, James Robertson-Justice was about to bring on a full-blown migraine. Not only did he object to working on a Sunday, he also lived in Scotland and therefore wanted the BBC to increase his expenses to allow for an overnight sleeper train from Inverness each week. Whilst this may have been possible, his third demand was one the BBC simply couldn't swallow. 'You may know that Mr Justice, with ideas almost akin to the Lord Chief, is uninterested in this programme unless he can make £100 a time!' Newman reported. 'We could probably squeeze to the £40 but not £100!' Robertson-Justice was dropped. Brough was making £100 an episode but it was his show... and his dummy.

And if Newman thought it was all over, suddenly Robert Luff opened another can of worms by demanding £40 a week for Ken Platt. When he overstepped the mark by suggesting that the scripts were not terribly good, Roy Speer took action. At a lunch at the BBC, he laid the matter to rest once and for all. 'Before the discussion ended, I used my trump card which I had been keeping up my sleeve. I said I had had complaints from the studio audience about some lavatorial jokes Ken had used in his warm up, and neither he nor Luff could provide any excuses for this!' The opposition crumbled. 'They were so worried I agreed to make a gesture to spare them any further embarrassment; so if you would destroy this letter, we can consider the matter closed.' The letter wasn't destroyed and Platt settled for £35.

All Speer had to do now was agree to Beryl's £40 and all would be well. Speer had taken confidence from the Platt settlement: now he thought he could knock down Beryl's pay rise as well. 'You will recall my comment to you that although she has made considerable strides outside radio and there is no doubt that her work has improved,' he wrote to Robert Luff, 'her popularity outside has been enhanced very very considerably by her radio activities. The question therefore is this: is the Variety Department prepared to do without Beryl Reid? I hope this will be one of the occasions when we stand firm.'

Luff scrambled a response. He suggested that Beryl had been offered something else, this time on Radio Luxembourg with Peter Sellers, a kind of disc jockey affair which would undoubtedly be broadcast at the same time as *Archie…* or even the Goons. Newman had been asked to find a replacement for Beryl just in case and he settled on Dora Bryan who was sent scripts and contracts with a pay offer of £30. But was Luff telling the truth? If he was, there was no way the BBC could compete with Reid and Sellers as a comedy duo. The BBC gave in. Beryl got £45 and the promise of two more years with *Archie*.

A surprising part of the fallout of the whole debacle was that Beryl had been told that Dora Bryan was more than willing to replace Beryl and that she was cheaper. 'She's cheaper because Dora Bryan is cheap!' Beryl snapped. Whilst Beryl usually had a kind word for most people and never sulked, Will Small remembers that whenever Dora was mentioned, 'cheap' often came into Beryl's comments – and this was some thirty years later. Dora had been a threat, and even a nervous breakdown on Dora's part didn't heal the rift between them. Dora once included Beryl in a list of performers she most admired but, for Beryl, the damage had been done. She'd been part of a potential coup to get her out of *Archie* (in Beryl's mind at least) and that was unforgivable.

The entire episode could easily have soured her working relationship with the BBC but she retained a sense of humour and her notes to Patrick Newman following the pay dispute always contained a funny drawing or the odd swear word, clearly designed to amuse him. Her warmth, her generosity and her humour could always dispel tension, but she also had reason to be confident. She thought that *Archie's the Boy* was unlikely to run for more than one series and even though Peter Sellers didn't commit to the Radio Luxembourg proposal for every episode, Beryl managed to secure both with a delay of a year, meaning that even if the BBC axed her for wanting a pay rise, she'd still have an income and a regular radio presence.

Whether this was all of Beryl's making or whether Luff advised her, nobody at the BBC was aware of this and why should they be? She was becoming a shrewd businesswoman and, on many occasions, she would agree to take less money – for increased royalties. This meant that a fifteen-minute radio appearance for which she was seemingly getting very little would pay twice as much as what the headliners were getting, and so even if she wasn't working, something was always coming in.

*

If she'd ever had a trace of nervousness, it was now dissipating quickly – though Beryl would always claim that she was shaken to her core by anxiety before every stage performance. She was a household name, she'd secured the hottest radio ticket in town and film offers were starting to roll in.

In June 1955, Beryl was even talked into making a record as Marlene. Produced by Wally Ridley, 'The Tin Pan Alley Ball' was a dance record made with Ken Mackintosh in which Beryl didn't sing but had a 'dainty chatette' with bandleader Ken. It wasn't exactly a natural medium for Beryl and, though she could sing well enough for a pantomime or a musical, pop music wasn't really her forte. The redeeming feature was a Marlene monologue on the B side, but the record didn't shoot to the top of the charts.

What Beryl really wanted, of course, was a play. As she recalled in an interview with Russell Harty, she was being overlooked for serious parts in straight plays because of her fame as a comic. 'The writers would say, oh, here's Beryl Reid, that awful Scotch Presbyterian who won't say nasty things,' she said. 'When I came up for a part in revue, it was only ever as Monica or Marlene. It's very difficult to be known as a comedienne when you know you can be a dramatic actress. Someone had written that I was a comedy actress and I thought, yes, I've got the comedy but where's the actress?' It would take another two years before anyone would consider her for a dramatic role.

The Royal Command Performance of *The World's the Limit* had led to a summer season at the Theatre Royal in Windsor and this allowed Beryl to commute from Wraysbury each day. She loved Windsor, especially its closeness to the Royal Family; when they were in residence, the odd undercover trip to the theatre wasn't unusual, but Beryl was also a frequent guest at the castle itself for luncheon parties. She was almost invariably seated next to the Duke of Edinburgh and opposite the Queen, and in her diary (which was usually a simple schedule of appointments) Beryl noted after one dinner at the castle: 'Lovely evening with Queen. She chatted me up. Queen Mother too and Princess Margaret and Lord Snowdon... that is a thing I'll never remember...'

The appeal of working at Windsor was that Beryl could get back to Honeypot and hopefully catch a few hours with Derek; but now she was back to a full-time schedule in London their lives were beginning to separate. Beryl was seeing less and less of Derek, until their conversations were reduced to 'How's sound dear?' to which the reply was always 'Dreadful. How's TV?'

Pathé News took the opportunity to film Beryl at home, a three-minute reel shown in cinemas which painted her life as idyllic if not a little eccentric. The pair were seen loading rifles to take shots at wildlife which may find Honeypot's thatched roof an ideal nesting place. Indeed, Ronnie Wolfe remembered one dinner party where the meal was interrupted by a strange rustling from above. Quick as a flash, Beryl grabbed her gun and dashed outside shouting 'Bloody hell! There's a squirrel in my thatch again!' Ominously, Beryl described a typical evening with Derek as: 'He does a crossword, I read Daphne du Maurier. And that's it, time to turn in.'

In her later years, Beryl would suggest that Derek was jealous of her fame. 'Men should be so big they should be able to cope with my success but they can't, they just crumple,' she said. 'You're suddenly rivals and not lovers. I should have been supported but I was keeping my husbands and if I hadn't been working, the bills would never have been paid. But then they resented me for never being around. I could never win.' And it's certainly true that whilst Beryl was becoming a household name, the Hedley Ward Trio were still very much a support act. Beryl earned more than Derek and, whenever they appeared in the newspapers, Derek was always referred to as 'Beryl Reid's husband' and even 'Mr Reid' which must have wounded his pride in an age where the husband was always the breadwinner. As with her first marriage, her work was taking her away from Derek; but whereas at the start she'd made a conscious effort to take work in or around Windsor, now she was being offered work which required her to stay in the capital so that she could meet her BBC obligations and appear in variety shows in the evenings.

In 1956, she was asked to join the company of a new revue at the London Palladium, called *Rocking the Town*. It meant that, for the first time, her name would be up in lights – not just outside a provincial theatre, but in the West End. *Rocking the Town* was billed as 'The Biggest Show of the Year' and starred the singer and comedian Harry Secombe, the pianist Winifred Atwell, the 'girl with the laugh in her voice' Alma Cogan and Beryl Reid. The supporting players included comedy actress Toni Palmer and dancer Diane Holland who would later become known as Yvonne Stuart-Hargreaves, the snooty ballroom dancing partner of Barry Howard in the sitcom *Hi-de-Hi!* Beryl took bottom billing but the show, produced by Bernard Delfont and Val Parnell, was such a smash hit that the run was extended to eight months.

However thrilled she was by the show's success, *Rocking the Town* brought something more important to her life: her friendship with Harry Secombe. This was one of the most tender and most special relationships she had, though strictly platonic. The pair were incessant gigglers, sharing saucy jokes and enjoying large quantities of 'toffs' lemonade' – their pet name for champagne. There was no suggestion of a romance; Harry was devoted to his wife Myra whom he'd married in 1948, and Beryl's life with Derek may not have been harmonious but it was comfortable at least. Their letters to each other are touching, their relationship being that of an older brother looking after a naïve and innocent little sister – though their backstage banter was hardly the sort you'd expect to hear between siblings. When Harry Secombe noted that Winifred Atwell and Alma Cogan were selling their LPs in the foyer of the Palladium, he asked Beryl, 'Have you got anything to sell?' to which Beryl replied, 'Only myself, dear, and that's going cheap!' Harry Secombe always spoke of Beryl in glowing terms and when she named a cat after him, he said, 'What on earth will your neighbours think when you're at your door shouting out 'Sir Harry! Sir Harry!' Beryl retorted with a twinkle in her eye: 'They'll think I've got lucky!'

Beryl's exchanges with friends, especially male colleagues, seem totally different to the rather spartan life she had with Derek in which there doesn't seem to have been much fun at all. As soon as her stint at the Palladium was over, Beryl headed off to Coventry for pantomime rehearsals whilst Derek was in Southend-on-Sea supporting trumpeter Eddie Calvert at the Palace Theatre. It seemed that absence would not make the heart grow fonder. She began to notice that Derek's things were slowly disappearing from Honeypot

Cottage and they spoke mainly on the telephone. It was friendly, pleasant but by no means a marriage.

Whatever the pair expected, one thing was absolutely non-negotiable in Beryl's life: children. If Derek had hoped to have a little bundle of joy with Beryl at Honeypot, he was to be bitterly disappointed. For Beryl, it was hard enough visiting her own family, though she kept in touch with Roy by telephone every day, and when she was working in the Liverpool area she would always spend an afternoon with them. She saw her parents less and less but again, the telephone became the bond; and every now and then Beryl would arrange for Annie and Leonard to come to Honeypot for the day and then maybe take them to see a show and introduce them to the cast. By this time, Roy was married to his wife Pat and the couple had given Beryl a niece, Sue and a nephew, Peter.

In later life, Beryl almost specialised in playing grandmothers or aunties and the public have a perception of her in that mould. Paul Strike says, 'People talk about her and they smile because she came across always as so sympathetic and loving, she was the auntie everyone wanted and you wanted her to give you a great big cuddle. But that wasn't really how she saw herself, not as far as children or anything were concerned.'

For Sue, of course, Beryl Reid really was her auntie and she always adored being in her company. There were no presents for Christmas or for birthdays (though there were pretty cards) but, as Sue recalls, 'What she would do is give me things she thought a girl my age might like. Make-up or clothes. She gave me a fur coat once that was clearly very expensive; I'd never wear it now but I remember being really taken with it then.' As a special treat, Beryl would arrange for her niece and nephew to see her in pantomime; and once there was even a visit to see *Educating Archie* being recorded in London. 'I was far too young,' Sue says; 'I know I was definitely under the age limit printed on the ticket but I laughed so much and to see her there as Monica, in full flow, that's something I'll never forget. She introduced me to Brough and the other cast and yes, that day I was spoiled but it was never a regular thing with her. Beryl cared more about talking to you than she did about buying you things.'

And free time had become increasingly rare. Beryl had a manic desire to work and, aware that showbusiness is a fickle mistress, she took as much on as she possibly could which led to a bout of nervous exhaustion in between *Rocking the Town* and *Aladdin* in 1956. She was ordered to rest, yet BBC executives were stunned when a pale, drawn and slightly green Beryl Reid crashed into an audition at Earl's Court for a part in a thriller she desperately wanted.

It seems to be around this time that Derek moved out of Honeypot altogether and subsequent communication with him was restricted to letters: infrequent, businesslike. To all intents and purposes, she was now separated and her second marriage over. Neither wanted to call time on it officially yet; but just a decade after her career had hit the big time, Beryl was now the hottest ticket in town and she'd managed to find a careful balance, working incessantly before darting back to Honeypot where she could sit by the river and dip her toes into the water, where she could entertain friends or just have the peace that her hectic life so often lacked. The absence of Derek wasn't painful any longer, it was welcome. Beryl accepted that formality didn't suit her lifestyle. She had no time to mourn the death of her second marriage.

Many years later, Beryl confided that had she wanted to have a family of her own, her marriage to Derek had been her one chance. But the truth is, Beryl (whilst being quite fond of children in small doses) just didn't believe herself to be the ideal mother. A child would have meant sacrificing her career and, if she couldn't do that for Derek or Bill, she was unlikely to do it for a baby. In an age where choices were so restricted for women, even a husband was something of a novelty in her chosen profession let alone a son and heir.

As Dame Siân Phillips explains: 'I think it's still the case that you have to make choices like that and she'd had to learn the sense of being independent, the importance of succeeding as an independent woman. Variety isn't an easy life to live, the days of music hall were tough and to be a woman headliner must have been even more difficult. I can only imagine that she had to make herself as tough as she could be to protect her position and so maybe there wasn't any room for a husband; and she had no time to bring up children either, because she was just too busy.'

Certainly Beryl felt that way too. 'A mother needs to be there all the time for her children, just as my mother was there for me,' she said. 'But I couldn't offer that. So I didn't think it fair to have children of my own. You can't do two jobs at the same time.' Reflecting on her decision shortly before her death, she said, 'I'm totally unshockable you know. If someone told me they were having an affair with a goat I'd say, "Oh good! What colour is it?" The children wouldn't have got lectures about what they should or shouldn't do and I'd never have said, "That's the last time I warn you…" ' She certainly preferred young adults to whom she could be maternal and a little protective but she could, of course, make them laugh. When her niece complained about the changes puberty had brought, Beryl cried, 'Oh Sue! No! Don't complain. I love my chest! I just stuff it into absolutely anything!'

*

On one of Derek's last visits to Honeypot, the couple were having a rare afternoon together when they heard a squeaking noise coming from the roof. Upon closer inspection, it turned out that a large black cat had given birth to a litter of kittens behind the water tank. Not being *au fait* with cats at the time, Beryl cooed over the kittens but made the mistake of touching them so that when the mother returned, she killed them all except one. The chosen one was Footy and, eventually, his mother was christened Ella and accepted that Honeypot was now her home, no doubt encouraged by fresh fish and poached chicken which Beryl would lovingly prepare each day.

This began Beryl's lifetime love affair with cats; and indeed, it's become part of the legend, with some newspapers reporting that she lived with thirty and even fifty cats at any one time. Whilst those numbers are vastly exaggerated, Beryl absolutely adored cats and there's no doubt in anyone's mind that they became her substitute for children. Paul Strike says, 'We never really discussed anything like that but the way she was with the cats, the way she took care of them, especially the tiny ones, that was her being a mother. And she did mother people as well: she mothered me and I know she probably mothered Sue a lot as well after her parents died. She was a very maternal and loving person, but cats didn't interrupt her career as children would have done.'

Co-star Stephen Boxer was fascinated by what he found at Honeypot when he visited in the early 1980s. 'She lived a sort of fairytale existence and she struck me as the little girl who hadn't quite grown up, living in this beautiful cottage by the river with these cats, stepping through the bluebells as it were. She'd made her own little fairy kingdom and she was very happy there, but I think the cats were absolutely the only way she could get that need to mother across without actually having children.'

Two became three, three became four, until eventually cats were a permanent fixture at Honeypot and Beryl was absolutely devoted. In later years, Beryl would not only give large donations to the Cats Protection League, but she was always happy to offer a home to strays or kittens and more often than not they were named after friends and colleagues such as 'Eileen' (for Dame Eileen Atkins), 'Sir Harry' (for Sir Harry Secombe) or after the roles she'd played such as 'Kath' in *Entertaining Mr Sloane*. Friend Muriel Carey who worked for the Cats Protection League would often tell Beryl about an orphaned kitten or a stray that had been found in need and Beryl would immediately offer to pay for its medical bills and then give it a home. Will Small remembers that if the spare bedroom wasn't full of hats or clothes, it would be temporary accommodation for a new member of the cattery, separated from the others until Beryl was sure it would be able to become part of the brood.

But Beryl went one step further. To ensure that there was absolutely no chance of her falling pregnant, she turned once more to Dr McIndoe. Now all but retired, she asked him if she could have a hysterectomy. In 1954, such an operation was considered to be major surgery requiring many weeks of hospitalisation and also carried inherent risks that were only just beginning to be understood. Without the female reproductive system, the hormones were affected and so, to avoid complications, Beryl would have to be given an early form of hormone replacement therapy. She hadn't yet started menopause but, on the advice of McIndoe, she checked into the Chelsea Hospital for Women in the King's Road; whilst McIndoe couldn't perform the surgery himself, he recommended a good man who would make sure she was well taken care of. Her admission to the hospital was even reported in the *Daily Mail* and after three weeks of being hospitalised, she was considered fit enough to travel. She flew to Majorca once more, Derek accompanying her, to recuperate. Even though their marriage had clearly fallen apart, they remained friends and Derek was concerned for Beryl's health.

The step she had taken was drastic, incredibly severe and would have long-lasting repercussions. People have even suggested that Beryl changed after the operation, that her personality underwent a kind of transformation, perhaps due to the large amount of medication she was required to take following the surgery. In typical Beryl fashion, she couldn't put her career to the back of her mind. She sent letters, script ideas, long apologies for not being able to make BBC luncheons and dinners; nobody could tell Beryl to take a rest. Indeed, in a letter to Ned Sherrin who was trying to convince her to return early so that she could appear on a special tribute for Henry Hall who had been with the BBC for thirty-five years, Beryl wrote, 'I would have loved to come as Henry launched me as Monica and he has forwarded my career every time I've worked with him and I really am most grateful but you see dear… I am here in Majorca until May recovering from a large operation and as I just have to work as soon as I get back, it is necessary to stay as long as that. I am so sorry.'

Whether it was because of her insistence that children would never be a part of their marriage or whether it was because her workaholic tendencies now increased dramatically, Beryl last saw Derek at a New Year's Eve gathering in 1955. By that time, she had sufficiently recovered to begin working again; and whilst, for many women, a hysterectomy may have been a cause for sadness, for Beryl the whole thing was liberating. A husband couldn't interfere with her career any more, children wouldn't interfere either and so began a new way of life: Beryl had fun. She enjoyed herself at parties she would never have dreamed of attending before, she relaxed into life at Honeypot a little more and she took every role possible that allowed her to travel and meet new people, to form new friendships and of course, to have the odd fling here and there.

There would never be anything formal for Beryl; some men stayed longer than others and some brought with them baggage that she couldn't accept but, for the most part, Beryl (as she openly admitted without shame or regret) simply enjoyed the company of attractive men in the physical sense with no emotional ties. If she wanted emotional support, she had that in friends and family. Now Beryl was free to do what she wanted to do. And what she wanted to do was work.

Chapter Four

*'People kept calling me a comedy actress. And it was that word…
actress… that interested me.'*

THE ACTRESS ANGELA BADDELEY, best known for her role as Mrs
Bridges in the 1970s period drama *Upstairs, Downstairs*, once said
that television gave the public ownership over an actor. 'They see
us in that little box in their homes and they feel they know us because
we've been in their house,' she explained. By 1956, not only had Beryl been
into British living rooms through the medium of radio but she was also a
regular on television, and it was becoming harder for her to go about her
private life without being spotted by the public.

Unlike Kenneth Williams, however, who could be notoriously frosty
with autograph hunters, Beryl was always happy to talk. As her friend Jan
Linden recalls, 'There was no side to Beryl; her feet were very firmly
planted on the ground and she treated everyone the same whether they
were a superstar, a cleaner or a road sweeper. She was generous to people
and she never objected to someone wanting a bit of a chat on the street.'

She was loath to get caught up in a long-running series though they
were offered regularly. As Dame Eileen Atkins says, 'I share with Beryl that
view that to get caught in one role for too long can be death for an actor.
She really didn't like all that; she knew she had great versatility and so she'd

only stomach something for so long before she wanted to try her hand at something else.'

As would become the pattern for the rest of her life, Beryl was always in demand for stage roles: comedy roles, that is. But in 1957, the BBC audition she'd attended whilst under the weather finally secured her a dramatic role and she made no secret of the fact that it was something she'd wanted to try her hand at. She was offered the part of Alice the maid in a psychological thriller written by Donald Henderson called *Mr Bowling Buys a Newspaper*. Co-starring Hugh Sinclair, Everley Gregg and Kathleen Boutall, the play's title character commits murder only to find that it hasn't quite satisfied his thirst for homicide, and so he goes on to become a serial killer. The original radio adaptation had stunned post-war British audiences and the BBC hoped that a television adaptation would do the same.

Two weeks of rehearsals at St Mary Magdalene's Church just off Holloway Road in North London were followed by two four-hour rehearsals in Studio D at Lime Grove in the first weekend of June. The play was to be broadcast live on the Sunday evening. Today, it's almost unthinkable that a drama would be broadcast live, with or without rehearsals; but the cast were all trained in repertory theatre and, to them, a television film was no more than a stage play with cameras and lights.

Mr Bowling was produced by Stephen Harrison, and so thrilled was Beryl to be playing a dramatic role at last that she asked if she might be kept in mind for anything else he did. Harrison replied, 'I fear that my next production, *The Governess* by Patrick Hamilton, is completely grim with no hint of humour, let alone a Beryl Reid part!' A Beryl Reid part? In the late 1950s, there was a certain snobbery (which may still exist) that comics simply do not make good actors. 'In those days there was an enormous gulf between variety people and straight actors,' explains Dame Siân Phillips. 'Even straight actors going into musicals was quite rare and unusual. It was an enormous crime that Beryl wasn't offered more dramatic roles because, if you think of her performance in *Tinker, Tailor, Soldier, Spy*, it was truly magnificent. It's a crying shame she wasn't given more of a chance to show off that skill, but I know she always said her first love had been comedy.'

And the sort of people Beryl related to and got on best with were other comedians. Straight actors could be too dour and serious and, whilst many comedians had a hidden side of tragedy or prolonged bouts of depression, Beryl managed to carve out friendships with comedians who were on her level such as Ronnie Corbett or Harry Secombe. She was also extremely fond of the comedienne Peggy Mount who, like Beryl, had worked her way up from the amateur stage to BBC success and was now doing very well for herself. But Peggy never bemoaned her fate, she never regretted the choice she'd made to focus on her career and not a husband or children. This, along with a shared sense of humour, made Beryl and Peggy an unlikely but very affectionate duo.

The two had many friends in common and George Cole recalled one gathering at Russ Conway's house where Peggy and Beryl were the life and soul of the party: 'Russ was playing "Ragtime Cowboy Joe" which is quite a jolly tune and Peggy and Beryl did this kind of strange tap-dance to it; they can't have rehearsed but they were having a whale of a time and were holding up their long dresses and kicking their legs about. When Russ finished playing, they collapsed into each other's arms, all out of breath and laughing hysterically. It was one of the few times I saw Beryl really let her hair down.'

By 1957, the BBC confirmed that Beryl's time with *Educating Archie* had most certainly come to an end. They had honoured their side of the bargain for long enough and even turned a blind eye when she'd gone to Radio Luxembourg whilst still being on a BBC contract, an unthinkable slight to the corporation. Each year she had been given a small but welcome raise and these were gestures of respect which they hoped would be returned. But the truth was, audiences were getting tired of the same old thing and ventriloquism on the radio had had its day. The six- and seven-year-olds she'd entertained as Monica were now entering their teens in an era where teens could be teens; and whilst the BBC did offer her two more years at a reduced salary, they were already looking to other performers such as Hilda Braid – later known as Nana Moon in *EastEnders*, but then a comic actress who had hinted she could do what Beryl had done for just £10, one sixth of Beryl's new salary.

Producer Roy Speer explained to Robert Luff that Monica had gotten stale and that they no longer wanted her; she'd been all but written out. They were prepared to make an offer to keep Marlene as a semi-regular guest, but even Brough was accepting the inevitable now and he didn't put up a fight to keep her. Neither did Beryl expect him to. She accepted that her time with the series had come to an end and, in many ways, it allowed her to end her close association with the BBC. Her loyalty would always be there, but she didn't feel guilty in looking at offers from other employers such as ITV and she certainly didn't let the grass grow. Within two weeks of being told that the corporation thanked her but would not be renewing her contract, Beryl was to be found on ITV with Noele Gordon, a chat show host and interviewer way before she stepped into the role of Meg Mortimer in the kitschy soap extravaganza that was *Crossroads*.

ITV were offering Beryl better scripts and opportunities and in 1957 she appeared in her first ITV series, *The Most Likely Girl*. Again with Noele Gordon, it was a comedy in six parts in which Beryl played a kind of enchanted debutante called Arethusa Wilderspin. It sent out a powerful message to producers: Beryl was very much her own performer and she didn't need a sidekick to make her funny; neither did she need an army of suits at the BBC to help her get the roles she wanted. She could do it all on her own.

This made her a rare commodity. Other female comics had always been paired up with a better known, more established male comic to ease them in gently. Women like June Whitfield who were very funny in their own right had to take on the role of a 'comedian's labourer'; even Peggy Mount had to be teamed with Sid James, and the idea that a woman could have her own show was unheard of, in part due to the misogynistic view the BBC held at the time that women simply weren't funny enough. Beryl had made no secret of the fact that she'd like her own sketch show based on her favourite revue material, and she made enquiries both at the BBC and ITV.

Expecting nothing, she committed to her first Noël Coward revue at the Theatre Royal, Windsor alongside Graham Payn who also happened to be Noël's partner. Beryl's association with Coward would only strengthen as the years went on and she, like many who worked with 'the Master', fell hopelessly in love with him and clung to his every word. After one performance, Sir Noël found himself in Beryl's dressing room in a discussion about dying.

'Well you know, my dear, when you die, everything keeps on growing. Your teeth, your nails, the hair on your chest,' he said.

'Well, not on my chest, Noël,' Beryl said with a giggle.

'Oh!' he exclaimed, 'You give up hope so easily!'

The dressing room was very much Beryl's kingdom and the place to be. She was cared for devotedly by her dresser, Betty, who was meticulous and fiercely protective. Betty would turn Beryl's dressing room into a home away from home with pretty chintz curtains, cushions and endless photographs. The flowers that came flooding into the theatre were always arranged personally by Betty, though Beryl only ever kept the white ones, more colourful blooms being given away to other members of the cast who perhaps didn't get anything. Before the performance and during the interval, Betty would make sure that Beryl had her favourite tipple, a Courvoisier brandy, in her favourite cup: a tiny silver goblet which she took to every theatre she performed in as a good-luck charm. There was also another – a tiny golliwog called Basil who lived in Beryl's handbag and was carted around the country and popped onto her dressing table.

Betty quickly became the only person who could calm Beryl down. Although at home she was often very placid, at work she was now becoming prone to flashes of temper: again, this may be due to the hormonal problems she was facing after her hysterectomy. On one occasion, Beryl screamed at Betty in a fit of pique, 'Where are my fucking eyelash curlers?!' Betty calmly picked them up, put them in her hand and said, 'Where you left them, dear.' The relationship was a happy one, built on mutual respect and a silent promise to always support the other in a time of crisis.

After a performance, co-stars and crew alike were invited to the dressing room for impromptu parties where the booze was plentiful and Beryl provided little snacks she'd cooked herself or bought in from the nearest posh restaurant. But if Betty was her confidante and friend in the draughty corridors of theatreland, there was someone at home whom she relied on utterly, totally and whom she loved more than any husband who shared Honeypot Cottage with her.

Joan Bissett was one of Beryl's first housekeepers, coming to Beryl at a time when her marriage to Derek was privately deemed to be over but publicly still very much in existence. In the early days of their marriage, Derek and Beryl had decided the thing to do would be to take on a housekeeper who could look after the place when they were not around and ensure that it was warm and tidy when they got back home. Some were more successful than others. The first seemed to be perfect for the role: discreet and friendly, dutiful and happy to stay on and work long hours which others might have thought a little too much hard work for the money offered. Then, one night, the police came to the door. The housekeeper had been flogging things from the cottage and when they turned her bed over, they found all manner of things tucked under there awaiting sale. Another incumbent simply disappeared one day mid-dusting and never returned. But the third was Joan, someone Beryl took to immediately; and, with the absence of Derek, the two became firm friends.

Beryl had a small staff: her dresser, her agent, her housekeeper, a part-time driver for long journeys, someone to help with fan mail and, occasionally, someone to come and help her read through her lines when she found a script particularly difficult to learn; but nobody was invited to work for Beryl without first becoming a friend. Yet there were limits. Paul Strike was a young actor who was asked by a mutual friend to help Beryl learn her lines for Peter Nichols' play *Born in the Gardens* in 1979. The two became firm friends and Paul and his partner Will became an important part of Beryl's life. Paul explains: 'She was very sociable, very happy to see people and she loved entertaining. The staff she had were her friends, not just people who worked for her; but then you'd get too close and she'd shut down on you. It was like a candle flame, you could get only so close before you got burned.'

Beryl got bored very easily and she didn't suffer fools gladly. When she and the South African singer Eve Boswell worked together, the two clearly had nothing in common and didn't much care for each other. When Boswell said one morning, 'I suppose you're not talking to me today?' Beryl quipped back, 'Of course I'm talking to you dear! I just have absolutely nothing to say to you.' She had a name for it: 'people poisoning'.

One of Beryl's greatest passions in life was cooking for friends and family and she took to it with a staggeringly professional mindset. Every gadget, every herb and every spice, cookbooks and recipes galore were packed into the cupboards of her kitchen and she was always keen to impress. When people visited the cottage, they were given a stiff drink and then shown into the dining room which Beryl had had specially constructed onto the side of the building, the black structure a stark contrast to the white 'pots'. Fine china, crystal goblets and beautiful table linens were offset with her favourite white flower arrangements, and guests were regaled with her favourite stories in an atmosphere where Beryl was most certainly queen of her court.

Of course, it didn't always work. Sue recalls one Christmas at Honeypot where Beryl decided to try out a recipe called '*oeufs en gelée*', the sort of thing Fanny Cradock would create in her nightmares. A boiled egg set in a bowl of aspic, the brown mass quivered and wobbled leaving people to wonder how best to dispose of it politely. And the imperious Mrs Cradock was quite a fan of Beryl's, taking a recent impersonation of her in good spirits as opposed to her fury at Benny Hill's version of her and a battered and beleaguered Johnny.

Fanny dispatched a letter to the cottage in which she praised Beryl to the point of sycophancy and then casually remarked, 'My husband and I are giving a garden party here and we would be so delighted if you would come on after your show and join us. The *Daily Mirror* and *Evening News* will be here so quite apart from the pleasure of welcoming you to our home, we might dish up a little something for the press.' Such blatant publicity-seeking was not in Beryl's remit and there's no sign of the invitation being accepted – or even replied to.

Beryl much preferred to be the hostess, but only for a certain amount of time. She would suddenly announce to her guests that she was going to bed or she'd simply say, 'Well, I think that's enough now,' and shepherd people out of the house. She was never rude to friends, but people were left in no doubt as to when Beryl had a case of 'people poisoning'; and, after particularly busy periods in which she'd perhaps done a stint in the theatre followed by a few interviews and the odd cocktail party, the door of Honeypot was firmly closed to company and the telephone would go unanswered. Those closest to her respected it and understood it. It was never intended to be cruel but Beryl adored her own company and relished the chance to be alone.

There were inevitable periods of loneliness; sometimes she did feel that she'd like more than just her cats for company, but her inner circle insist that if Beryl was ever lonely, it was by her own design. She was never short of company if she wanted it and, whilst this applied to the odd casual relationship with a man, as Dame Siân explains: 'She was single minded and unless she married someone rich enough or wise enough to accommodate her success then there was very little chance of her making a happy marriage. She had decided not to bother with it; it hadn't worked before, it wouldn't really work again.'

Dame Eileen Atkins agrees but suggests that there was an element of self-sabotage involved too: 'Beryl had to be the star and she had to come first. She loved men, she loved the attention but in reality, she wanted to be at work and not at home so anything that did come her way was kept strictly informal.'

Joan Bissett perhaps became yet another substitute for a husband. She would work for Beryl for twenty years and the two had no secrets and no boundaries. It went beyond an employer and her housekeeper: this was a devoted friendship and Beryl took a keen interest in Joan's life, her family and friends. Her daughter Margaret was eventually asked to drive Beryl and to become a companion to her when she had to make long journeys for filming. Beryl and Joan took holidays together, though initially never abroad as Beryl had a crippling fear of flying.

One day, refusing to be beaten by any obstacle, Beryl announced that she'd like to go abroad and it was ridiculous that she couldn't because of her 'flight fright'. Whilst many might try the services of a hypnotherapist or ask a doctor for a few Valium to get over the worst of it, Beryl went one further. She took flying lessons and applied for a pilot's licence – which she got. Now, she could go anywhere she wanted to!

Whilst she may have thought the BBC would treat her a little coolly following her departure from *Archie's the Boy*, in fact there had been talks (at boardroom level) about offering Beryl her own series on the BBC. Whether it was the BBC trying to avoid losing her forever to commercial television or whether it was just good old-fashioned common sense, the BBC suggested that Beryl might like to do a six-part live revue series called (using Marlene's catchphrase) *Good Evening Each!* Ronnie Wolfe was brought in as a writer, and a script was pieced together from sketches Beryl had done in various revues or pantomimes. This would be the first time a woman had been given her own sketch show on the BBC, decades before Victoria Wood or French and Saunders could hope for the same. But in the planning stages, it was decided that it may not yet be suitable for television: the public were not quite ready for a female comic alone. It would be far better, it was suggested, to try the entire thing on the radio first and if it was a success, it could transfer to television.

Ken Platt, who had also been dropped from *Archie* for wanting too much money, was brought in to provide the voices for the male characters. It broadcast throughout August and September 1958 and it gave Beryl's agent Robert Luff an idea.

Teenagers across the country had fallen in love with rock and roll but they were also the first generation of teens to have a disposable income; well, enough to buy a few records with at least. Disc-jockey-led pro-grammes were all the rage and so Robert Luff put together a proposal for something called *The Dear Beryl Club*. She had appeared on Radio Luxembourg in a similar role and she was now keen to move away from the Monica and Marlene-based appearances so that she could introduce a little bit more of the uniqueness that was 'Beryl' to the audience; but the BBC got entirely the wrong end of the stick and asked Gene Crowley to put a Marlene script together. Beryl had taken off to Majorca for two weeks but, aware that the whole thing was under discussion, she asked to be kept in the loop and didn't want to miss out on any detail. The script by Crowley was sent to the villa, but by the time it reached Beryl lounging in the Spanish sunshine, the idea was considered dead in the water. 'I have read the script and I think it's quite good… sweet…' she mused. 'I have made several suggestions [quite proper you understand!] to Ronnie Wolfe because he has always written Marlene. So this is no reflection whatsoever on Gene Crowley!' To avoid any bad feeling, she excused herself by drawing a little picture of the sun with the explanation: 'My brain is quite rotten now! I'm having a wonderful holiday, glorious sun and heavenly food… and drink… and everything! Oh John dear, I do hope you approve of all this 'cos it's most difficult to be away from it all. But I'm sure everything will be wonderful! It's the sun you know. Wonderful!'

When Wolfe couldn't supply them with a script, another writer called Robert Bishop was brought in to try and patch things up and Gene Crowley was set to work on creating scripts for Ted Ray and June Whitfield instead. The BBC were still uncertain about the entire endeavour but Luff offered them exclusivity, always a popular proposal as it meant Beryl could only work for the corporation and not for anybody else. He suggested that if the BBC really didn't want it, Radio Luxembourg had already shown an interest and would 'happily secure Beryl's services with substantial remuneration'. In other words, pay up or lose Beryl Reid once again.

Producers Pat Osborne and Michael Bell were asked to review the Bishop script but their impression of it wasn't exactly positive. Indeed, it verged on the brutal. 'I have read the script,' wrote Osborne, 'and whilst it's basically not a bad idea for a peg to hang yet another request programme on to, using Beryl Reid as the compere (or should that be commere?), at the same time, it's all been done in the most nauseating way because bearing in mind that Beryl Reid is a comedienne, it is meant to be humorous from beginning to end and not just the odd humorous comment thrown in from time to time.' As far as Osborne was concerned, *The Dear Beryl Club* was to be avoided: 'The humour is terribly unfunny and the records are completely dragged in. To sum up, like you, I think it is dreadful but rather than condemn it out of hand, if planners like the basic idea of an excuse to use Miss Reid, to be any good it needs completely rewriting. In fact, I would suggest another script writer altogether judging by this poor effort.'

Douglas Lawrence, the Assistant Head of Gramophone Programmes, was tasked with telling the two Roberts (Bishop and Luff) that it was all over. But whilst Bishop lost out, Luff kept his promise and Beryl began a weekly show once more with Radio Luxembourg using the original Gene Crowley script but renamed *Beryl Reid's Monday Night Requests*, which did exactly what it said on the tin but failed to last beyond the October of 1958.

That Christmas, she whizzed down from Birmingham to make one last appearance with her old friends Peter Brough and Archie Andrews at Brough's insistence. In a Christmas special that would be the last ever *Educating Archie*, Monica and Marlene were brought back for one last shout; and though she couldn't know it at the time, the broadcast marked the end of Beryl's career in radio. Whilst she would occasionally appear on panel shows or grant an interview, she'd never take a regular role in a radio series again; and as the curtain came down that night, with Brough by her side and the applause of the audience ringing in her head, the reality hit her. Turning to Brough she said, 'It'll never be the same again, will it?'

Her diary for 1959 was all but empty. Actors live hand to mouth, they are only as successful as their next project and, for many, there can only be emotional security if there is also financial security, or a constant stream of applause and acclaim. Beryl had become used to recognition and she did like to be asked for an autograph whilst shopping, but there was an underlying fear that the work would never come in and that she'd be forgotten. It tormented her often during 'resting' periods, and it was at these times that she tended to take quite poor projects and throw herself into them, certain that it would be just enough or that it would lead to something more substantial. Beryl wasn't terribly religious, though she would often say that she felt there was no point in going to church as she had a direct line to 'The Management'. The Management stepped in.

Beryl was offered the chance to appear in a revue that would be the perfect Beryl Reid showcase with material from twenty writers including Dorothy Parker and Harold Pinter. Called *One to Another*, it didn't pay very much (Beryl could command £105 an appearance, the equivalent of around £1,600 today) but it would mean top billing in the West End and a chance to do something totally different, free of Monica and Marlene. Her male lead came in the form of Patrick Wymark, a Shakespearean actor trained at the Old Vic who, before going to the Lyric Hammersmith with Beryl's production, had only appeared in serious classical pieces such as *The Tempest, Danton's Death* and *The Cherry Orchard*. Directed by a young Eleanor Fazan ('who didn't look old enough to direct anything!' according to Beryl), the company included Patricia Bredin, Ray Barrett, Barbara Evans, Tony Tanner, Roddy Maude-Roxby, Joe Melia and a young actress called Sheila Hancock. Speaking to R. B. Marriott in *The Stage*, Beryl was under no illusion that the chance to star in a West End revue without the obligatory male comic lead was anything but daunting.

'The first thing that concerned me when I started to work on *One to Another* was my enthusiasm,' she said. 'I can never work without it; but I found I was fired with enthusiasm and ambition more than ever before so I got off on the right foot.' Her lack of enthusiasm was probably attributable to the fact that she was hung up on the idea that her next production should be a dramatic play. However, *One to Another* was a natural step on from her great success at the Watergate Theatre eight years earlier. Whilst the majority of the critics were kind about the Watergate revue and whilst it had secured her early television appearances, there had been that one negative review (which actors always remember above and beyond any praise) which had suggested her act was stale. 'I realise that this form of entertainment has changed a lot since 1951,' Beryl confessed, 'but I decided to keep my mouth shut and listen and learn.' This meant relying on the director, in this case Eleanor Fazan.

Beryl didn't always find directors easy to work with but if they understood her approach, the result could be magical. Dame Eileen Atkins recalls that Beryl generally needed an understanding director to get the best from her. 'She was totally technical and the director had to grasp that first,' she explains. 'She would stand on the stage and Val May (the director of *The Killing of Sister George*, 1966) would say, 'Now Beryl, I want you to tilt your head about thirty degrees stage left when you deliver that line.' And then she had it, she remembered it and that was her stage direction.'

But Beryl often remained suspicious of directors. During the promotion of *One to Another*, she told *The Stage* newspaper: 'I love a good director and I love direction. The artist who can't take direction is a dead duck as far as I'm concerned.' And yet in later life when she was a stalwart of the stage and the TV studio, she'd simply opt out of rehearsals or ignore a director entirely, citing her long experience as grounds for doing it her way.

There was no trace of that, however, when she began work on *One to Another*. Eleanor Fazan recalls that Beryl, whilst nervous, fitted well with the company and gave it her all: 'She could do comedy in a way very few people can do it. Nowadays, it's very forced and it tends not to have any sincerity to it, but Beryl was absolutely committed to her work and she portrayed a character with a backstory and a character she knew well, so you got incredibly funny results.'

One to Another would see Beryl perform one of her favourite sketches, revived throughout her career: that of a Spanish maid called Conception who disrupts a dinner party fantastically with her insatiable lust for the man of the house. 'I remember her vividly in this long train, covered in lace, being hilariously funny and the audience loved her for it,' says Eleanor. 'She was very lovable and there was absolutely no side to her; when we went to visit her at Honeypot Cottage during the run, she was exactly the same. She portrayed her character but left that on stage; at home and behind the scenes, she was just Beryl and she made you feel very welcome, she was lovely to be around and was totally unpretentious.'

One to Another was Beryl's first starring appearance in the West End and her eagerness to learn was genuine. As she explained, 'I want to learn more about the stage and how to act. I thought managers would never give me a chance as an actress; they didn't know whether I could act or not, no more than I did myself. One way or another, we had to take a risk and they've got me on the strength of my name, but the plan has worked and I've learned more in the last two years than I have in the first twenty years of my career.'

She confessed that she was terrified of using props but oddly, she also claimed that this was the first time she had been required to address her audience. For a stand-up comedienne, this was almost certainly Beryl's insecurity coming through. From her very first performances on the stage at Bridlington, she'd always welcomed the audience in and made them feel that her performance was unique and specially crafted for them. That warmth made her not only accessible but desirable; as she conceded, 'People won't laugh at you if they don't like you. They simply must like you as well as believe in you.' So what next for Beryl Reid? 'Oh, some nice cameo roles in a film or something,' she mused. 'A comedy part in a straight play… a part which gives me some scope in a musical. Something like that.'

In fact, her first booking after the huge success of *One to Another*, for which she got rave reviews, was an end-of-the-pier show in Hastings. 'I was being rather snobbish,' admits Eleanor Fazan, 'and I went to see it and thought it was just so sad that she'd had all this success at the Lyric and at the Apollo and there she was at the end of the pier in Hastings. And I said, "Oh Beryl, I'm just so sad about all this," and Beryl replied, "Oh don't be sad darling, I'm getting paid far more than anyone else!" ' Her co-stars in Hastings were none other than Morecambe and Wise, not yet the beloved staple of British comedy and who received far less in terms of wages than Beryl owing to her radio fame. Eric and Ernie were still plugging away on the fringes and it would be another ten years before the birth of *The Morecambe and Wise Show* which is now regarded as the stuff of comedy legend.

Because of the rave reviews of *One to Another*, Robert Day, a film director, saw Beryl's work and decided to team her with Peter Sellers in the very typical British farce, *Two Way Stretch*. The film follows the inspired attempt by a group of prisoners to break out of prison to commit a robbery – only to break back in immediately afterwards, according them the best alibi possible. The cast list is a roll call of some of the greatest British names in 1950s cinema including Lionel Jeffries, Bernard Cribbins, Liz Fraser, Irene Handl, Arthur Mullard and Warren Mitchell. Beryl's role was simply a cameo, an elderly lady called Miss Pringle.

With her only other offer of work that year being another pantomime with Ken Dodd, Beryl decided to take a long holiday at a caravan park and to invite Derek along. But when they arrived at the caravan, Beryl had forgotten to mention that she'd invited close friends John Le Mesurier and Hattie Jacques to stay with them for part of the time, along with their small children Robin and Kim. This was a regular occurrence and, whether Derek had expected a reconciliation or not, he didn't get it. Rather than try to rekindle any romance there had once been, Beryl spent the whole time with Hattie and John, and Derek left early.

Beryl had been granted her wish to make a few film cameos here and there; but in 1961, her plea for a role in a play was finally heard – albeit not a straight one. Cedric Messina and Val Gielgud (the writer brother of Sir John) had put together a provisional cast for an abridged version of Shakespeare's *Twelfth Night* to be broadcast on the BBC Home Service. Naturally any comedienne over the age of forty might assume that any roles in Shakespeare would be limited to the Nurse in *Romeo and Juliet* with younger, prettier actresses being given the meatier roles. On this occasion Beryl was cast as Maria, the sharp-tongued, fun-loving maid to Olivia, played in this particular production by none other than the pre-Raphaelite beauty Rachel Gurney (later known to millions as the ill-fated Lady Marjorie in *Upstairs, Downstairs*). Though most of the cast were new to Beryl, she could rely on a lunch companion when Jimmy Edwards was cast as Sir Toby Belch, Olivia's cousin. Whenever Rachel Gurney passed their table, Beryl would sigh and say 'Now there's an angel on earth!' *Twelfth Night* was to be broadcast in January 1962, but now she had a choice to make that put her in an incredibly awkward position.

Robert Luff had suggested to Beryl on many occasions that she should make an appearance on *The Black and White Minstrel Show*, and letters from Luff to Pat Osborne at the BBC suggest that this was never resisted as a booking on the side of the BBC. As far as they were concerned, Beryl was one of their biggest and brightest stars and *The Black and White Minstrel Show* was one of their best and most popular series, so why should the two not cross over? Robert Luff had a vested interest as he was a driving force behind the Minstrel shows and was a huge part of their success, teaming up with George Mitchell who founded the troupe. Whilst other comedians on Luff's books did make appearances, Beryl always resisted. Indeed, she made it known that she 'wasn't available for that particular series' – by which she meant, the concept itself.

Whether she found the programme distasteful or whether she felt it wasn't appropriate for her, if Luff knew of her dislike of the format he can't have made an issue of it. Luckily she had an excuse to leave any confusion behind for a few months and hope that Luff wouldn't find out and take offence in her absence; and Luff was busy working on a new proposal with Tom Sloane, the Head of Light Entertainment at the BBC.

With his brusque military manner, Sloane was known as the man who lost the BBC Tony Hancock; but he was well respected and would later give the BBC one of its most iconic sitcoms, *Dad's Army*. Sloane had a close friendship not only with Luff but also with Jimmy Edwards, and he felt that Beryl and Jimmy should team up again in something more permanent. Beryl was willing, but the entire project had to be put on hold. She had been given an offer to showcase her talents abroad – in South Africa.

At the time, the country had been living under apartheid since 1948; and in an era of student protests, social awareness and equality marches, any star travelling to South Africa was liable for a public shaming. To be seen to be supporting or encouraging the white South African government was risky but, for Beryl, this didn't even factor into the decision-making process. At times, she could be woefully naïve and, despite protests from friends, Beryl was absolutely determined. Public opinion be damned: she had an audience to entertain.

Chapter Five

*'I don't care if you're black, yellow or bright purple. But I do care if
you're a bore.'*

WHEN BERYL STEPPED DOWN FROM THE PLANE into the swelter-
ing heat of Johannesburg in November 1961, she was totally
unaware of the problems she was about to encounter, and yet
she'd left enough problems behind in Britain. Derek had met someone else.
He wanted an annulment of their marriage. Whilst it had broken down
beyond repair, and whilst Beryl too had seen other people in the intervening
years between Derek's departure and his request for a formal dissolution, she
had the added worry that her mother Annie wasn't in the best of health.

Rather than stay put and deal with the crisis, Beryl opted to put as great
a distance as possible between her and the impending media storm around
yet another failed marriage. She was running scared and whilst she never
much cared about what people thought, it was far easier to throw herself
into her work away from Derek, Honeypot and England. But South Africa
was hardly the place to forget one's troubles.

The previous year, apartheid South Africa had experienced one of its
bloodiest struggles against the anti-black regime: the Sharpeville Massacre.
Protesting against the Pass Laws which enforced segregation, around 7,000
black South Africans went to the police station in the town of Sharpeville

in the Transvaal, refusing to carry their passbooks. The government response was brutal. Sabre jets and troops were dispatched in an attempt to disperse the protestors; when this did not succeed, the police, with no warning, opened fire. The majority of those who died were young women and children.

In response to Sharpeville, the government was coming down even more harshly on the black South African population and, in rural areas, there was a strong attitude of resentment to white British people which had resulted in violence and even murder. There was also the issue of a political backlash back home. Many stars were criticised for going to perform in South Africa and this would continue well into the 1970s.

Beryl wasn't terribly political; if she supported anybody it was the underdog. 'She was extremely opinionated,' recalls Siân Phillips. 'If she thought something was wrong, she told the truth and just said. She could be rather rude but always, of course, very witty. She knew everything that was going in the world and she wasn't afraid to speak about it.' Yet she treated this jaunt to Johannesburg as if the Hofmeyr Theatre in Cape Town was the Floral Hall in Birmingham.

Beryl regarded apartheid as 'totally bloody silly' and it wasn't going to stop her putting on a good show. Johannesburg, Cape Town, Durban: Beryl's South African tour saw her appear in a show called *Something New*, a musical revue which the white theatre audiences lapped up, being familiar with Beryl as a result of the BBC Home Service; but Beryl risked the ire of the South African government by also performing for black audiences. 'They were never given the best shows,' Beryl explained, 'because I was never allowed to have white musicians or even white stagehands.'

Beryl couldn't speak Afrikaans, of course, and trying to block an entire two-hour cabaret show in the space of a morning can't have been easy. Yet she took to it all like a duck to water and soaked up the life in South Africa with a typical disregard for the rules. Warned not to buy fruit at the side of the road, Beryl deliberately sought out fresh mangos and sweetcorn from poor black street vendors; and, when she realised that the black South Africans were not allowed to buy alcohol, she took great pride in buying up bottles of brandy and gin to share among them – even though it caused her a personal financial loss and could well have led to her being arrested. She loved watching the black South Africans dance and she was as friendly and jolly with them as she would be with anybody else – and why not?

In Cape Town, she stayed with John Boulter, a British tenor who performed with the ever popular (at the time) Black and White Minstrels and who was to be Beryl's leading man in *Something New*. They shared an agent in Robert Luff, and Boulter had been in South Africa for a run of a production of Lionel Bart's *Lock Up Your Daughters*. Luff must have assumed that Boulter was the man to make sure Beryl behaved, but she was of course a law unto herself. One afternoon, however, she was alone at Boulter's house when a military truck came rattling along the dirt track. The black servants scattered and Beryl was horrified to see militia men with rifles jump out of the lorry and head for the door.

'We want to come in and look at the house,' they said, brandishing their guns.

'I'm sorry, you can't come in!' screeched Beryl. 'I'm an actress from England!'

The militia explained that they had reason to believe Boulter was mixing with coloured servants. Beryl faced the entire incident with total calm and an inspired (if not risky) challenge. 'You call Mr Boulter at his business address and if he says you can come in, you can come in. Now that's fair, isn't it?' And the lorry departed.

Beryl's lifestyle brought her into contact with all kinds of people from all different walks of life; and, though she was a bit of a snob in that she liked to present herself as being slightly more aristocratic than she was at times, she had no room for any kind of discrimination. Indeed, when she was criticised for calling gay men 'pooves' (*sic*), she snapped back: 'I call them pooves because I've only ever known as pooves! And what's wrong with pooves?!'

Whilst Beryl was closing her South African tour in Durban, Robert Luff had managed to get her another film role, her first without the need for an audition. *The Dock Brief* was a legal satire written by John Mortimer who would later create *Rumpole of the Bailey*. Beryl was Doris Fowle, a constant source of irritation to her husband Herbert who was played by none other than the future director of *Gandhi* and mischievous creator of Jurassic Park, Richard Attenborough. Attenborough's character is a meek sort of chap who just wants a little peace and quiet; but his wife, with a galling shriek here and a hacking laugh there, has other ideas. To distract her, Mr Fowle decides to bring in a lodger (played, aptly enough, by David Lodge) in the vain hope she'll fall in love and run away with him. When she doesn't, he finds he has no choice but to murder her. Peter Sellers plays the hapless barrister who ultimately saves his client from being jailed on the grounds of his own incompetence. Richard Attenborough was nominated for a BAFTA award for Best British Actor for his role in the piece while, for Beryl, it was a chance to add another film credit to her CV and to work with her friend Peter Sellers again.

When she returned to Honeypot for a brief rest in between her South African tour and the start of a summer season in Hastings, she finally received a letter from Derek asking her to sign the documents necessary to annul their marriage. On Tuesday 3rd July 1962, Beryl noted in her diary, 'Mummy died at 11.15.' Immediately underneath it featured a full two weeks marked with the word 'play'. Annie Reid had been entirely devoted to her daughter; she had advised her, supported her unconditionally and fought so many battles on Beryl's behalf for which Beryl was eternally grateful.

Annie had died whilst visiting her relatives in Scotland and Beryl's response was typical. 'She would want me to carry on working,' she said. Beryl's family had a tradition that women never attended funerals and this suited Beryl who thought them far too depressing and miserable. As Sue recalls, 'She always found that sort of thing a bit too much for her; she couldn't bear to say goodbye and I think she threw herself into her work and carried on so she didn't have to think about it too much.'

Heartbroken, Beryl telephoned Derek and asked him what she should do. As a parting gift to his wife, Derek said that as he was in Scotland, he would attend the funeral on Beryl's behalf. That evening, Beryl called him to see how things had gone. 'Very sad but a bit odd,' he said. 'They were all a little bit strange and behaved as if they didn't know me.' Which they didn't. Derek had attended the wrong funeral entirely.

Of course, Annie's death brought new responsibilities. It was decided that Beryl's father Leonard should go to live with Roy, Pat and the children with a few weeks a year spent at Honeypot. Not that he ever stayed in the cottage itself. Her father, like most of her overnight guests, was asked if he wouldn't mind sleeping on her houseboat which was moored alongside Honeypot Cottage. It was suitably named *Modesty*. Another followed and was christened *Restfulness*, the last thing it would have offered on a choppy evening on the Thames!

This strange arrangement was partly to do with the size of Honeypot Cottage itself but it was also the result of Beryl's absolute insistence that she must have her own space and that she should be allowed to retain her privacy. The houseboats were comfortable enough but their main function was to enable Beryl to put up a barrier between her and whoever may be staying when she became bored of their company or when she simply wanted to relax, able to pick up the fun and laughter the next morning as if they had just arrived.

A few weeks after the death of her mother, her marriage to Derek was formally dissolved; but the stress of it all hit her hard. Her diary records that she had asked the doctor for help and he prescribed her something to ease the strain. '3.30 a.m., back from show,' she noted. 'Had a pill and it kept me awake but so lovely!'

She wrote to Luff asking him to find her something, anything, to keep her occupied. But her first offer from Luff was once again little more than a begging letter asking her to appear in the tour of *The Black and White Minstrel Show*. Times were changing quickly; this was a new age of liberation and an increased push for tolerance, even if its effects took decades to settle in and become mainstream. The Minstrels were already drawing criticism for their blackface performances, and when Diana Ross saw them in their make-up before a Royal Variety Show, she refused to go on if they did. When the Minstrels began, they could rely on the defence that they were simply continuing the Al Jolson tradition of performing songs from the American South in a traditional way; but now the show had moved away from that and the Minstrels were doing everything from Scottish medleys to a Brazilian extravaganza, which made little sense and which caused the BBC a constant headache. Luff wrote to Patrick Newman in the Variety Department asking if, instead of the tour, Beryl might be slotted into the TV series; but Newman responded, 'I'm not sure this would be entirely helpful for Miss Reid at the moment,' and Luff finally caved in. Beryl sent a thank you card to Newman for getting her out of the awkwardness she'd tried to avoid before heading to South Africa.

In 1967, the Campaign against Racial Discrimination delivered a petition to the BBC to have *The Black and White Minstrel Show* axed. It was ignored and the show went on for far too long, ending eleven years later and forever being regarded as a total embarrassment to the corporation. Thanks to Patrick Newman, Beryl avoided the association entirely.

As Tom Sloane at the BBC had predicted, the public loved the combination of Jimmy Edwards and Beryl Reid so much that there had been requests that they should do more together. A vehicle was found for them, an hour-long comedy about a brass band enthusiast called Ernie Briggs who was obsessed with music. His wife Bessie, of course, couldn't bear it and he was slowly driving her mad. *Man O' Brass* was commissioned as a series without hesitation with a supporting cast including Jill Hyem, Bill Treacher and a young comedian called Ronnie Barker. Everyone agreed that it deserved to be a smash hit and twelve episodes were scheduled in to be broadcast live.

Renamed *Bold as Brass*, the series was a total, unmitigated disaster. Halfway through the run, Tom Sloane went to see Robert Luff at his office in Old Bond Street, and the following day he wrote to confirm what everybody knew: 'It is with a great deal of personal regret that I have decided to finish *Bold as Brass* at the end of six programmes and not to continue it. My reasons for this are that I believe a great deal of pro-fessional harm will be done to both Beryl Reid and Jimmy Edwards by continuing since the vehicle isn't strong enough to support a run of twelve programmes.'

He was deeply apologetic of course, going on to say: 'I am naturally very sorry about all this…' (naturally, because it had been his idea) '… but I am sure that it is in the interests of both the artists and ourselves to come out before any real harm is done.' In the closing line, he extended a personal apology to Beryl, asking Luff to convey his sincere thanks to her at 'what I know has been a very trying time for her'.

The truth of the matter was that this was Beryl's first flop. She was used to a variety audience who didn't laugh in the right places or a film which hadn't done as well as predicted, but this was the first time that a TV series with her in a lead role had been commissioned. The fact that the public didn't take to it was no reflection on her, but Beryl could be oversensitive and take things to heart which is exactly what she did. When a fan wrote to ask if there would be any more outings for *Bold as Brass*, she wrote back furiously, 'There should be, shouldn't there? But there will not be, I'm afraid, and I'm as livid about as you are, dear! Do write to Auntie and let her know your thoughts. She knows mine already!' It didn't sour her relationship with Jimmy Edwards, however – indeed she spent much of 1962 touring with him in a variety show called *Star Time!* – but she certainly felt pained over the experience with *Bold as Brass* and she was in desperate need of a confidence boost.

There was a glimmer of hope. Michael Codron was a producer who was enjoying great success with his productions of the early works of Harold Pinter, Tom Stoppard and Joe Orton. Orton's work was causing quite a stir in theatreland as not only were his pieces rather dark, they invariably came with a threat of legal action against the theatres in which they were performed. Until 1968, any script intended for a public performance had to be scrutinised by the Lord Chamberlain's Office who had the authority to insist on cuts – or even to shut down the performance entirely. Orton got round this by agreeing to stick closely to the approved text but would then tell the cast to perform the original, which led to complaints. The Lord Chamberlain's Office became wise to this little game of deception and began to send police officers to the performances to ensure the censored version was the version the public saw; and, even then, Orton's work had the power to drive sensitive elderly audiences hurtling out of the theatre in tears demanding their money back.

Homosexuality, murder, adultery, even incest: these were the themes which Orton handled with an impish wit. Joe was anti-establishment in every way possible, whereas Beryl was the darling of the BBC. So when Michael Codron approached Beryl in 1964 to consider the role of Kath in *Entertaining Mr Sloane*, she was advised by everyone not to take it. Luff even suggested it might be the end of her career. She graciously declined; but then in 1965, a year after it had opened, Michael Codron invited Beryl to see the play and when she saw it, she thought it marvellous. 'You weren't shocked?' Codron asked. 'In that case, I have a play for you to read.' It was a new piece by Frank Marcus called *The Killing of Sister George*.

The play was almost as controversial as *Mr Sloane* in that its key theme was that of a lesbian relationship. Homosexuality was yet to be decriminalised, and even then a change in the law wouldn't bring an instant change in the public's attitude towards such things. Beryl's role was to be that of June Buckridge, a soap star actress beloved by millions as a kind of district nurse figure on a bicycle. With a Devonshire accent and a butter-wouldn't-melt expression, Sister George couldn't be any further removed from the actress portraying her. Whilst George is sweetness and light, June is a sadistic, paranoid, butch lesbian who is as possessive as she is prone to violent temper tantrums.

The risk of doing the piece was that people may think Beryl too was a lesbian; and indeed, part of the Beryl Reid myth was that she was (as

Beryl's mother termed it) 'a collar and tie job'. When Will Small said he was going to meet Beryl many years later, his mother was adamant that Beryl was a lesbian because 'they always get a real one to play one!' Beryl had no time for homophobia of any kind, but she was firm in pointing out to interviewers that she felt that June should not be thought of as simply a lesbian character. 'She was a lady who happened to be a lesbian,' she said. 'There's more to her than all that business.'

None the less, this was the first time that a lesbian relationship would be played out to the public away from the classics when allowances were made for 'historical representation'; and to have Miss Beryl Reid – the saccharine creator of Monica and Marlene – in the role of a vicious and extremely jealous lesbian was a risk to all concerned. Whilst June fears the axing of her character from the radio soap *Applehurst*, she's further disturbed by the possibility that she may lose her younger lover Childie; and, whilst the word 'lesbian' was never used in the piece and the nature of the relation- ship between June and Childie was never confirmed, this was clearly a lesbian drama in an age ruled by taboo.

Val May was to direct *Sister George* at the Bristol Old Vic which would open in April 1965. Appearing as the rival for Childie's affections in the role of Mercy Croft was a classically trained actress called Lally Bowers who, despite her repertoire in Shakespeare in Stratford-upon-Avon, would later become best known for her role in the 1970s sitcom *You're Only Young Twice* as Dolly Love, a permanently drunk resident of an old people's home, alongside Beryl's old pal Peggy Mount, Pat Coombes and Diana King. For Childie, May had cast a young actress called Eileen Atkins, but initially Eileen wasn't thrilled at the prospect. Like Robert Luff, she had grave doubts about the show and its cast.

'I hadn't really wanted to play the part,' she remembers. 'I thought I was wrongly cast but I was terribly hard up and out of work so I thought I'll do it anyway. And then they told me they'd got Beryl Reid for the lead role and I was so worried. To do a play with a stand-up comic? I knew she'd be raw to it and, quite frankly, I wasn't looking forward to any of it. But I went to Bristol and I met her and I suppose I played a very silly joke on her...'

After being introduced and having coffee in the stalls before the read- through, Dame Eileen went to Beryl and said, 'Miss Reid, where are you living? Because I'm sure that you've heard I'm a method actress and I have to live my part, so I haven't booked in any digs yet because of course I'll be living with you.' Beryl didn't laugh. Instead, she immediately rushed to Val May and said, 'Now you keep that young woman well away from me!'

As rehearsals went on, however, the mood was more relaxed even if Dame Eileen found Beryl's way of working to be rather eccentric. 'When Val May and I would sit down and discuss the implications of a line or the thought process behind it, Beryl would say, "Oh well, if you two are going to have one of your little chats, I'll go and make some phone calls." Most actors would want to be there and hear all that to work out their own role, but not Beryl.'

Despite Beryl's idiosyncrasies, rehearsals proved a great success; and on opening night, the play ran without a hitch… almost. Whilst the actors were word perfect, the audience began to get thinner and thinner. People were actually leaving the theatre, some of them absolutely horrified. Many years later, Paul and Will accompanied Beryl to a party in Bristol at which two elderly ladies approached Beryl. One said incredulously, 'I used to be a fan of yours, Miss Reid, but not since *Sister George*; I was disgusted!' To which Beryl tartly retorted, 'Bit too close to home was it, darling?'

Things didn't get any better as the run went on. There was a polite round of applause from those left seated in the audience when the curtain came down, but there was none of the wild cheering and shouts for 'more' which Beryl was used to. One audience member wrote: 'Well played by Beryl Reid and Eileen Atkins but the last act is cheap and false, I think, and Lally Bowers is a caricature so it all falls to bits in the second half.' The reviewer was none other than Sir John Gielgud who was quite a fan of Beryl's. In later years he would credit her with turning round the success of a play he'd 'loathed on first reading' called *Loot*, another Orton piece which Sir John went to see twice a week during its 1968 run on Broadway at the Biltmore. It seemed that *Sister George* was doomed to failure, but oddly Michael Codron had decided to take the play on tour and the company waited to find out where they'd be heading next.

On the last night in Bristol, things took a bizarre turn. A Dutch actress called Selma Vaz Dias had been brought in to play Madame Xenia, a psychic who advised June in her work and relationships. Vaz Dias had been content with smaller roles in films such as Hitchcock's *The Lady Vanishes*, but her personality was eccentric and somewhat disturbing.

'She was distinctly mad!' Dame Eileen recalls. 'And she and Beryl were not getting on at all; Lally didn't like Selma but I tended to opt out a lot and not get involved. On the last night in Bristol, Beryl was leaving the theatre when she saw flames in this woman's dressing room and got someone to go in. When they went into the room, Selma was found to be sitting there with little figures she'd made and was sticking pins in them and burning things. The curtains had caught fire and the whole dressing room was about to go up!' Beryl later confessed the figures were probably intended to be of her.

Vaz Diaz's foray into voodoo cast a pall and she was asked politely to collect her cards. For the touring production, she was replaced with Margaret Courtenay and *Sister George* went on the road. Things were not improving and by the time the company reached Hull, Beryl and Dame Eileen had become so close that they were sharing digs. Out of sheer frustration at the poor reception they were receiving, Beryl would stand outside the theatre and wait until the last moment to go in, anxious to avoid the inevitable.

'It was pretty desperate,' Dame Eileen laughs, 'and one morning, Beryl came back to the hotel and said, "Oh Eileen, I've found the most wonderful little shop, we must go!" ' Eileen assumed it was a clothes shop ('I'd have found a shop selling second-hand Armani clothes wonderful!') but in fact it sold second-hand false teeth. Not content with just looking in the window, Beryl insisted they go in. 'And she stood there, for about an hour, trying on all the different false teeth and putting on silly voices and gurning, and I just fell about laughing,' Dame Eileen recalls. 'I think we then went back and had something to eat and I suddenly thought, hang on, she's just enormous fun. Enjoy the time with her.'

The tour progressed until it came to London; but on the opening night, Beryl's nerves got the better of her. For someone who had climbed their way to the top via music hall, laughter and applause were a sure sign of success, and Beryl not only craved it but she needed it to give a good performance. *Sister George*'s audiences were giving her none of that and she began to get nervous. After a few kind words from Betty and a brandy or two in the dressing room, Beryl prepared herself for the London audience. She was pleasantly surprised.

'The first night in London was different because Michael Codron decided to hand-pick the audience and it was mostly comprised of gay men,' Dame Eileen remembers. 'Now of course, they laughed because they understood it all. And in the interval Beryl came to me and said, "What are you doing behind my back?" I said, "I'm not doing anything, Beryl; this is a comedy, we've all forgotten that." '

The reviews for the London performance were staggering and took everyone by surprise. Not only did the cast get glowing praise individually, the entire piece was celebrated and, instead of glum faces and empty seats, *The Killing of Sister George* was now the hottest ticket in town. Beryl had found her confidence again; but she channelled this confidence into something dangerous. She decided to improvise. 'She'd got too excited and in the middle of a scene with me, she left the script entirely,' Dame Eileen remembers. 'She went into this long, rambling stand-up set; she was going into Marlene and I was just standing there. The minute the curtain went down, I flew into her dressing room because I was really so angry and I said, "If you ever fucking do that to me again I will walk off stage and leave you on your own. This is a play, not stand-up and I won't have it." ' Beryl folded. She apologised profusely and promised not to do it again.

Indeed, in her memoirs, Beryl noted that Val May had taught her that in a serious play her lines should be delivered to the other actors and not to the audience; the breaking of the fourth wall simply wasn't done. However, whilst she did keep her promise to some, it didn't mean others were not subjected to the same treatment. Weeks later, Beryl challenged Lally Bowers by leaving the script once again, but Lally didn't have the courage to stand up to Beryl. Six months into the run, Lally finally exploded with rage.

'It was the worst row I'd ever heard between two women,' Eileen remembers. 'I think because she hadn't had the guts to say anything the first time it happened, Beryl had kept doing it and it had really stuck with poor old Lally. But that was the thing with Beryl: if you confronted her about something immediately she was just great, but if she felt she could get away with something, and if she could see someone wasn't going to say anything about her behaviour, she'd just keep doing it; and ultimately she came to dislike Lally enormously which didn't make things easy at all.'

It was a rather tense time for all concerned. Not only did Beryl dislike Lally Bowers, but she also came to blows with Margaret Courtenay. Dame Eileen was in the awkward position of getting on well with all of her fellow cast members and recalls how strained everything became: 'I rather championed Beryl because I loved her, but I'd go into her dressing room and she'd tell me how awful Lally was, then I'd go in to see Lally and Lally would tell me how awful Beryl was, then Margaret would chip in and it was just terrible because I had to try not to say anything about any of them which I found rather difficult because, to be frank, I got on with them all.'

Of course, to the public none of this ever filtered through the footlights, and Beryl was so proud of the play's success that she kept every single letter sent to her by colleagues praising her performance. Miriam Karlin wrote: 'I came to your matinee this afternoon and thought you absolutely splendid! I know you have already been showered with loads of well-deserved praise – so let me in all humility – add a little more! It was funny, moving and beautifully performed – many congratulations to you three splendid girls… or is it chaps? Fellows?!' Karlin signed off, 'Bless you, you old cow. You're bloody brilliant!'

Max Bygraves wrote that he had seen the show and adored it. He apologised for not coming round to say hello to Beryl but he explained: 'Our mum has always warned us about your sort!' Sandy Wilson, the writer of the musical *The Boyfriend*, told her that *Sister George* was the best thing she'd ever done; indeed, it was 'the best thing I have ever seen anyone do'. And from California where he was with the touring production of the musical *Pickwick*, Harry Secombe dropped a line to 'dear old lovely Beryl!' to congratulate his friend on her remarkable success. His letter was typical Secombe and is so touching that it deserves to be reproduced here in full:

Hallo buddy! It has just reached us here in God's own country that you have made a great big wonderful hit in your play and I felt I had to write and tell you how wonderful I think it is. I'm as thrilled as if it were me!

I wonder if young Bobby Nesbitt [producer of *Rocking the Town*, 1956] would approve of your working without padding and in those awful pointy shoes! There is one thing though. I'll bet you don't say things to the other members of the cast that you say to me!! We are doing extremely well in this land of hygienic wrapping and jumbo sized shrimp – even the applause seems louder here… but perhaps they have bigger palms. We are moving slowly across country to Cleveland for two weeks, Detroit for four weeks, Washington for three and then Broadway for one!!!

So keep your little fingers crossed for your old mate who loves you and is wildly happy about your success.

God Bless! Lots of love and kisses,

Harry

P.S. – I'm right chuffed (CHUFFED!)

(And a kiss from Myra who is also so very happy for you!)

When the British tour and initial West End run of *Sister George* ended, the four women assumed it was the end of the road. It had been a roller-coaster ride, but surely that was now the end of things? Indeed, Hermione Baddeley was already being lined up to take Beryl's part for a further run of the show; but Beryl's Sister George hadn't been killed off just yet. She may well have the chance to meet up with Harry and thank him personally for his delightful letter. *Sister George* was going to America – on Broadway no less.

Unfortunately for Margaret Courtenay, the American actors' union insisted that at least one of the cast had to be an American citizen and, not being able to part with Beryl, Eileen or Lally, it was on poor Margaret that the axe fell. She was replaced by Polly Rowles who had recently enjoyed a well-received stint as Vera Charles in the 1956 Broadway production of *Auntie Mame* alongside Rosalind Russell who would recreate the role for the big screen with Polly's part taken by Coral Browne. Confusingly, Coral would replace Lally Bowers in the film version of *Sister George* two years later; such is the incestuous nature of casting departments!

When she arrived in America, Beryl was immediately asked about her marriages and not the play itself. She told William Glover of the *Victoria Advocate*, 'It's terribly difficult to have a successful marriage if you are a success in the theatre but I'm not disenchanted, oh dear me no, I'm one who longs for affection and I'm not going to be out of it.' News had just broken in England that Beryl and Derek were now divorced, and he'd just gone on to marry one of the Mackell Twins, a popular 1940s music hall duo. Beryl didn't much mind – she'd already begun a relationship with someone else; though it would never be wedding bells, not least because he was already married. Perhaps there was some security in that?

His name was Peter, a handsome schoolteacher who made her very happy but who didn't expect to move into Honeypot and encroach on her lifestyle or moan when she was late home from an evening performance. The romance was brief and intense and it provided the necessary escape she needed following Annie's death. Beryl was now nearing forty-five years of age and she wasn't at all apologetic that she'd put on weight. She was still attractive, of course, and if her weight gain was mentioned she would simply say, 'It helps me to be butch if I'm carrying bigger parcels!'

Beryl's relationship with Peter began shortly before she flew to New York and she was ridiculously infatuated with him. She was given an apartment on West 72nd Street and Dame Eileen was given an apartment in the same building two floors down, allowing them to spend days going through lines or just enjoying the sights and the stores. But not long into her stay, Beryl began to complain that she missed Peter.

'Almost daily she said she couldn't be without him,' Eileen recalls. 'It was actually a little irritating because she kept saying, "I must have him Eileen, I must have him here," and so finally I think I said, "Oh for goodness' sake Bee, just get him over will you?" and so she did.'

Peter was summoned, Beryl paid for his air fare and for a hotel room; but he was in for a surprise. 'She invited Peter to spend the week with her in New York,' says Eileen, 'but when he got there, she was out. She'd asked if the agent she had out there could get her personal appearances every single bloody day she could, and so she'd call me each morning and say, "Oh darling, will you look after Peter today because I'm terribly busy?" I took Peter round New York that week – Beryl hardly saw him.'

Peter left New York in a huff (understandably) and she never spoke to him again; but interestingly, whenever Beryl spoke of him to friends she would suggest that there had been no way she could have got out of doing the publicity appearances – appearances which she herself had insisted on, thereby sabotaging what seemed like a good thing. Paul Strike suggests that this may have been another case of people poisoning. 'Maybe he just got too close?'

One person who *was* welcomed into the fold in New York was Lally Bowers. She decided to grasp the nettle and reach a truce with Beryl, taking her out drinking and ordering vast quantities of lethal Manhattans, putting the world to rights and holding an impromptu singalong in the bar. They were never going to be bosom buddies, but they were at least able to work together in a civil atmosphere after the embarrassment Lally felt at Beryl's upstaging during the British tour. Ironically, Beryl hated to be upstaged by anyone and, if she felt there was a possibility that she might be, she would misbehave terribly, throwing people off their lines or deliberately missing a cue so that she could (seemingly effortlessly) jump in and save the day to rapturous applause.

She would always find it easier to work with men than women, apart from a very select few; and so she was easily confused by the sudden interest in her private life which had never really been up for discussion before. When an Australian newspaper printed that Beryl was so wonderful in *Sister George* because she was in fact a lesbian, Beryl responded by telephoning the editor directly and firmly denying that she was anything but heterosexual. 'You must keep a level head about it, love,' she urged. 'These are just people and what they do mustn't influence me. All one can do is act out the relationship.' She then reassured readers who may have doubted her saying, 'I'm absolutely feminine, all frilly dressing gowns and I do like the gentlemen!'

Sue explains, 'She played lesbians, and in some roles she was quite butch – in *St Trinian's* for example she wasn't at all feminine – but I can only stress that Beryl was not a lesbian. She loved men far too much to even flirt with that idea!'

And yet the myth continued. One day she had climbed into a yellow taxi on her way home from a matinee when the driver leaned back and said, 'Can I kiss you? I've never kissed a lesbian before,' to which Beryl replied joyfully, 'Well of course you can, if you like, but you still haven't you know!'

Regardless of any long-lasting association, Sister George had become Beryl Reid's part and, whilst it has been done many times since, the play feels wrong without that integral magic which Beryl brought to the role. By stripping away the labels, the prejudice and the assumptions, she tackled George in the same way she did every other role – by reducing her to a pair of shoes. Once she found them (pointed brown brogues, incidentally) she kept them with her and invested every emotion into them, able to slip them on and transform herself from a comedy icon to a ferocious possessive.

*

Four months into the run, the cast were now at the Belasco Theatre on West 44th Street. Beryl was in her dressing room when she received a telegram from Western Union. It read:

> We are pleased to advise you that the Tony Awards Nominating Committee has nominated you for a Tony Award. The Membership of the League of New York Theatres congratulates you and sends best wishes. Richard Barr, President.

Dame Eileen was nominated too but there was no trace of rivalry; indeed, the two friends were more concerned about what they were going to wear. When they'd left England, *Sister George* looked to be an enormous flop and suddenly they were on Broadway facing a night out among the stars at the Shubert Theatre in New York.

'We were furious because we had to wear long dresses,' Beryl remembered, 'and we hadn't anything suitable with us. We went to Bergdorf Goodman's but we didn't want to spend a fortune so we went for all the cheapest rails. Eileen got a beautiful yellow dress which needed no alteration and I bought a long black dress with a long black petticoat and what looked like just skin you saw through the top with a high collar. I never thought I'd get into it but I did and I think we scrubbed up rather well.'

For Beryl Elizabeth Reid, a former shop girl from Manchester, the Twenty-First Annual Tony Awards must have been a dream come true. The event was held on 26th March 1969 and broadcast on ABC, the first time the ceremony had been televised. Mary Martin and Robert Preston hosted the proceedings and the guest list was as glittering and star studded as it could possibly be. Presenters included Lauren Bacall, Carol Burnett, Barbra Streisand, Angela Lansbury and Kirk Douglas.

'And the winner is…' – of course it was.

Beryl climbed the stairs to the stage to accept her award from Kirk Douglas as the orchestra played 'Give My Regards to Broadway' from the musical *Little Jimmy Jones,* her hair perfectly coiffed and the black gown she'd picked up on a bargain rail the day before showing slightly more skin than America was probably used to at the time. She looked wonderful, she felt magnificent and Kirk Douglas thought she was so delightful that he insisted on escorting her personally along the red carpet to the after-party at Sardi's restaurant where he kept his arm around her and insisted the press take photographs of them together.

'It was so unexpected,' Beryl recalled in her memoirs. 'It was so overwhelming that the tears were just running down my face!'

From the music-hall pier in Bridlington to the Broadway stage, being a Tony Award-winning actress had its compensations, and they were not just limited to the attentions of stars like Kirk Douglas. Barbra Streisand threw a cocktail party in her honour; and at home, Robert Luff proudly scribbled a note to the BBC rejecting their latest offer of a small part in yet another variety show. Rather grandly, he wrote, 'I now learn that my client has succumbed to the lure of Hollywood where she is appearing in a film being made about the life of Gertrude Lawrence. This is going to mean a delay in her return of about four weeks or so.' In another missive, Luff confirms, 'Miss Reid is now unable to attend due to her appearance as Gertrude Lawrence in a new Hollywood picture.' The British press ran headlines such as 'Hurrah for Sister Beryl!' and 'Our Beryl: The Hollywood Star!'

Tinseltown wanted Beryl desperately. It was ready to embrace her and make her an international star. And Beryl was only too happy to go along for the ride.

Chapter Six

'Awards are lovely things if they come from your peers. I don't really want the Queen's Award for Industry because that would mean nothing to me but a nice little statue from friends? Oh yes please!'

ALMOST IMMEDIATELY AFTER HER TONY AWARD WIN, Beryl began to be courted by Hollywood producers and stars. There were constant rumours in the gossip columns that a movie version of *Sister George* was to be made but, strangely, none of the rumours cast Beryl in the role she'd made very much her own.

Bette Davis was the popular choice with the Hollywood gossip columns, not so much because of her huge stardom but rather because Bette had led the way in a new genre of films which have become affectionately known as 'biddy horror'. *Whatever Happened to Baby Jane?*; *Hush...Hush, Sweet Charlotte*; *The Nanny*; Davis had played a leading role in what were essentially campy thrillers which now hold no real fear at all, yet in the early 1960s a movie like *Baby Jane* was considered horrifying. Many of these films had been directed by Robert Aldrich, and Aldrich had publicly praised the play, and so it seemed a foregone conclusion that Aldrich would make the picture and Bette Davis would star in it.

Yet Bette had already seen the show and had actually visited Beryl backstage, proclaiming in her unmistakable drawl, 'Nobody must do the movie but you! You're the only person to do it!' As far as Beryl knew, there were no such plans to make a film and she didn't understand the buzz in Tinseltown that resulted from her staying at the Chateau Marmont where she was being visited regularly by Hollywood legends such as Barbara Stanwyck and Lauren Bacall. The Marmont, on the world-famous Sunset Boulevard, had hosted all kinds of MGM stars including Ingrid Bergman, Audrey Hepburn and Greta Garbo, who had resided in the apartment in which Beryl was now staying. All of this was too much for the gossip columnists who declared, 'Who is Miss Reid?'

Truth is always more disappointing than fiction. The reality was that Beryl had been approached by Twentieth Century Fox to make one picture whilst she was in America, but there was absolutely no suggestion that she might move there or that she was being given a five-year contract by Warner Brothers… or that she was having a wild affair with Kirk Douglas!

The picture offered by Fox was called *Star!*, pitched as a biopic of the actress Gertrude Lawrence. Somewhere along the line, things had become a little muddled and, whilst Luff proudly told the BBC to take a step back to allow his client to fulfil her potential as the lead in a Hollywood motion picture, Fox were not offering the part of Gertrude Lawrence to Beryl at all. Ironically, the actress Beryl had replaced as Archie Andrews' girlfriend way back in the early 1950s had been fairly busy in the intervening years and it was she who got the lead. It was, of course, Dame Julie Andrews.

The making of *Star!* was unremarkable, though Sir Bruce Forsyth has spoken of Beryl's reticence to rehearse a complicated dance number to be performed with him and Dame Julie. She arrived late and not particularly in the best of moods. 'You'll ache tomorrow, Beryl,' he warned. 'No I won't!' she snapped back. And of course she was practically bedridden with terrible cramps all night which made the following day's shoot almost impossible.

The film was not very well received with Renata Adler in the *New York Times* suggesting, 'Miss Andrews is not at her best in this one. There is some sort of clash between her special niceness and innocence and the attitude of the film. Miss Lawrence is portrayed as a kind of monster with none of the crispness or glamour or wit that would give her ambition style.'

Beryl dutifully stuck it out and lived out her visa, attending parties she thought she might like and picking up knick-knacks and souvenirs for friends back home; but her first thought upon arriving back at Honeypot was not, 'Oh dear, they didn't want me'; rather it was, 'I'm so glad to be home again!'

Naturally she did feel some disappointment, however. Though she never bemoaned her fate and was enormously proud of the work she had done during her long career, she perhaps wondered whether she was destined to be stuck with panel shows and variety bills.

With Beryl a little lost and with the BBC offering nothing on account of Luff's rather grandiose letters, an old friend stepped in to help. Peter Sellers suggested her for the role of Mrs Weaver in *Inspector Clouseau*, the latest film in the Pink Panther series. The character was a Scots eccentric which Beryl could do standing on her head, and she took the role thrilled at the prospect of working with Peter again. However, while Sellers had made an institution of the inept French detective in the two previous Pink Panther films made with director Blake Edwards, on this occasion both star and director had already begun work on another film, *The Party*, and Alan Arkin was instead cast in the title role. Sellers was conspicuous by his absence; and, lacking the familiarity of the unique talent and warmth he brought to the franchise, *Clouseau* was Beryl's second flop of the year.

In the mid-1960s, Beryl met two men who would change her life completely – for entirely different reasons. The first was Norman Newell. Newell was a record producer for EMI and had not only compiled albums for singers such as Vera Lynn, Shirley Bassey and Dorothy Squires but had also put together comedy albums with Kenneth Williams, Jake Thackray and Terry Scott. It had become quite the thing for comedians to show off their talents with specially written novelty songs and everyone from Joan Sims to Benny Hill had a bash, with some of the tracks becoming cult classics (such as Joan's 'Spring Song' or Bernard Bresslaw's 'I Only Arsked'). Newell was also a talented songwriter; he'd even penned 'Portrait of My Love' for Matt Monro, composed in (of all places) Peggy Mount's front room. He had a flair for spotting talent and even if the vocals were not particularly strong, he had a way of taking comedy from the stage or television and retaining its magic on vinyl. But it was his recordings of West End musicals that really made him an integral part of Beryl's post-Hollywood success because, whilst work was slow to come after the disaster of *Star!*, Newell's ideas for a few records with Beryl as the lead performer were the best audition she could possibly have to show off her range and versatility again.

Norman Newell took the decision to produce four albums with Beryl. The first was made in 1965 in between the London and New York productions of *The Killing of Sister George* and was very much a dummy run. *Alice in Wonderland* was narrated by Dirk Bogarde and the cast was quite impressive. Kenneth Connor, Peggy Mount, Tommy Cooper, Fenella Fielding, Bruce Forsyth, Karen Dotrice, Harry H. Corbett – these were the biggest names of the age; and Newell (always loyal to his dearest friends) teamed Beryl with Dorothy Squires, Beryl as the Duchess and Dot as the Cook. The recording seemed to capture the topsy-turvy world of Lewis Carroll perfectly, and with so many of the artists having unique voices and superb timing, *Alice in Wonderland* was a big success with children who could lose themselves in what was essentially an LP pantomime.

So taken with Beryl was Newell that he managed to secure the recording rights to a musical which was extremely new to British audiences and offered it exclusively to her. *Hello Dolly!* had just hit Broadway the previous summer and, as with many of Jerry Herman's musicals, the tunes became firm favourites; indeed, Louis Armstrong had topped the *Billboard* album chart with his rendition of the title song. Whilst the Broadway stage had looked to Carol Channing to take on the role of the widowed Dolly Levi, for Norman there could only ever be one Dolly: Beryl Reid. (Much later, Danny La Rue would take on the role, the first man to play a leading female role on the British stage. When Beryl heard about the casting she said, 'Well, at least my tits are real!')

Beryl's recording of *Dolly* was released a month before the show opened at the Theatre Royal Drury Lane but, bizarrely, nobody thought to cast her in the live production. That role went to Mary Martin. It would happen again with Beryl's recording of *Mame*, made in 1969: when the curtain went up at the Theatre Royal Drury Lane, it wasn't Beryl Reid the audience welcomed as Mame Dennis, but Ginger Rogers. Admittedly Beryl had spent a year in New York and Robert Luff had rejected certain offers in the misguided belief that bigger things were around the corner, but there can be little doubt that *Mame* in the West End would have been not merely a chance for Beryl to keep her name up in lights but also the ideal role for her: that of an eccentric middle-aged woman full of energy and fun but who actually has a tender and loving heart beneath the madcap antics. It could have been written for Beryl.

One doesn't have to look too far for the oversight. George Cole told this author: 'Beryl's problem was that she was grouped together with the "variety bandbox" performers of the day. She was a comedienne; they didn't know she could do anything else and so she was always overlooked, which was a crying shame because certainly in that sort of big West End musical role, she'd have been delightful.'

Norman Newell clearly had faith in her, but if the EMI records she made with him were intended to be auditions for stage roles, it didn't work. They were slightly ridiculed and unfairly compared to the efforts of Mary Martin and Ginger Rogers – and so Beryl lost out.

However, by far Beryl's favourite project optioned specially for her by Norman Newell was a recording of *Bedknobs and Broomsticks*, but this was less to do with the material and more to do with the male lead. Again, the LP didn't transfer to a stage version (despite a particularly delightful rendition of 'Substitutiary Locomotion'); but it did begin a friendship that, for Beryl, was the best possible reward for her efforts.

In her later years, Beryl would often speak of an actor to whom she'd lost her heart. Since Bill and Derek, there had been nobody whom she would seriously consider as a third husband; indeed, she had come to love the liberating feeling of the fun without the foundations. 'It wouldn't be fair of me to reveal his name,' came the standard response, 'but he was the love of my life and I dearly wanted to make a life with him.' If Beryl hadn't chosen wisely in love thus far, she was about to make a truly foolish decision but with the best intentions in mind.

For many, the greatest BBC radio comedy of all time remains *Round the Horne*. A zany revue full of Britain's best, it would make stars of Betty Marsden, Bill Pertwee, Kenneth Williams and Hugh Paddick who provided the voices of various characters from the outrageously camp Julian and Sandy to Fanny Haddock, Gruntfuttock and Rambling Syd Rumpo. They were all kept in check by the sober-voiced but incredibly funny Kenneth Horne. Each week, millions would sit around the wireless and wait for that unmistakeable catchphrase, 'Oh hello! I'm Julian and this is my friend Sandy!' and the two characters would converse in Polari, a hidden language used by the gay community to avoid detection at a time when homosexuality was still very much illegal.

Hugh Paddick's career had mostly been limited to small theatre roles but his ability to take direction, to stick to a script and to tackle more serious roles meant that, unlike co-star Kenneth Williams, Paddick was regarded as the ideal leading man, having already worked with Tommy Cooper and Morecambe and Wise. When he finally met Beryl at a party given by Norman Newell in the late 1960s, the pair became firm friends and Hugh was a regular visitor to Honeypot. But was it a romance?

Actress and co-star Dame Barbara Windsor knew nothing of the situation at the time, neither did Beryl speak of it to her in later years; but Dame Barbara's reaction to Beryl's infatuation with Paddick was probably the reaction of everyone in the business who came to hear of it. 'Hugh Paddick?!' she exclaims. 'No darling, if she really did love him then I'm afraid she was absolutely barking up the wrong tree and I think Kenneth Williams would have put her right on that one. He was known for playing a gay man; he wasn't as camp as Kenny but we all knew and so she must have known too.'

Sue remembers meeting Paddick at a party at Honeypot that year, the first of many visits which would make Hugh a regular fixture: 'He was very tall, very thin and I didn't think he was all that attractive but you could tell she liked him. I thought he was a bit strange because he didn't really talk to anyone, certainly not me; he just stood there in these two leather jackets, one of them zipped up and the other one open to show the second one.' Close friends knew of her interest in Hugh but, as they got closer, nobody dared broach the subject that Hugh was clearly homosexual.

Beryl is very insistent in her memoirs that her love affair with Hugh was exactly that, and in interviews given later she hinted that they'd been intimate together, always with the mention of 'a homosexual actor' but with names and places omitted to protect Hugh's identity. 'I was on the wrong wicket,' she said. 'I was a hopeless case and I would never win. There was no question of winning; we both loved each other very much and my whole life was satisfactory at the time, physically and emotionally and in every way but of course I had to accept what people had told me. Homosexuality did win. I was the loser but I did have a very, very happy time and so many laughs with this lovely man.' Beryl claimed that Hugh warned her not to accept a marriage proposal if he offered one; and, by her own admission, she fell hard and fast. As she said herself, 'The only sad thing is that I was left at the end with a heart that was knocked about a bit. But not for the first time. All through my life I've had knocks – who hasn't? – but that's all part of living and it's all part of your character make-up.'

During the relationship, Beryl had an unofficial 'rider' in her contract, proof of her devotion. Whatever piece she did, whatever role she took, there had to be a role for Hugh; and, for someone whose success had been mostly confined to radio thus far, Beryl's generosity couldn't have been more welcome.

If the immediate aftermath of Hollywood had been a bit of a let-down, the latter part of 1968 brought two great opportunities. The first was the news that the BBC had finally decided to give Beryl her own sketch show based on the radio series *Good Evening Each* which she had enjoyed working on almost a decade earlier. Just as Lucille Ball was breaking down barriers for women in American comedy, so Beryl Reid did in the United Kingdom. Whereas performers such as Joyce Grenfell or Pat Kirkwood had delivered a very classical programme, perhaps an hour of light music with a few monologues, this was anarchic, Pythonesque comedy and the first example of the modern-day sketch show in the format we've come to know and love.

The production notes for the 1968 series *Beryl Reid Says Good Evening* have been lost to time. Sadly they do not appear in the BBC Archives and the only mention of Beryl's series comes in the form of the pilot episode which was called 'Beryl Reid and Friends'. The friends were Sheila Hancock, Patrick Cargill, Mary Kenton, Joan Sims and, of course, Hugh Paddick. The sketches were typically revue scenarios with Beryl as the protagonist; many of the routines had been performed before to theatre audiences but never on television.

Written by Alan Melville, Arthur Macrae, P. H. Robinson and N. F. Simpson, the show always opened with a musical number. In one episode, for example, a glamorous-looking Beryl appeared in a sequinned gold cocktail dress with a blonde bouffant. As 'Policewoman Doris', she sang the song 'I Shall Hate Myself in the Morning', which tells the tale of an undercover policewoman who can't catch the criminal she's supposed to be observing because she's got far too tiddly on toff's lemonade. Beryl threw herself around the floor, delivering her most salacious lines directly down the lens of the camera and the live audience shrieked with laughter as she fell over a table and laid back seductively on a chair kicking her heels up.

In another, she's the Midlands housewife (the closest the series came to including Marlene) alongside next-door neighbour Joan Sims. 'Nothing but Percussion' is a surreal sketch which sees the two women lending musical instruments to each other as if a bassoon was a cup of sugar. Beryl and Joan are perfectly in tune, each complementing the other but with Sims allowing Beryl to take the lead. To watch them together is not only joyous but is a poignant reminder that they shared many of the same struggles in their private lives. Devoted to her career, Joan hadn't formed any long-lasting relationships and had become a little too fond of alcohol and, whilst she relied upon it in a very different way to Beryl, the parallels give the two woman a chemistry which comes across wonderfully on screen.

But by far the best sketches were those with Hugh Paddick. 'Inland Revenue' sees Beryl as a wealthy widow who is completely appalled at the notion that she has to pay income tax, and Hugh Paddick is the civil service martinet who must threaten her with a bailiff. When he finally calls one in, the bailiff is of course very tall, very dark and very handsome and the elderly lady is thrilled with her prize.

Another sketch, 'Crossword', sees Beryl at her finest but, behind the characterisation, there's a hint of something more. Beryl plays a cockney widow resplendent in a large hat and with endless shopping bags. She plonks herself down in a railway carriage between two very starchy, very stern bowler-hatted gentlemen (played by Hugh Paddick and Peter Reeves) who are busy with their crosswords. In the beginning of the sketch, Beryl is desperate to make conversation with them. 'Nothing worse than someone trying to talk to you when you're doing a crossword, is there?' she says, doing just that. She eats a cream cake, managing to dab it all over Hugh's lapel, and then brings out a gossip rag: 'Look at that. Harold Wilson with Cilla Black. That'll get 'em all talking.' Professing no interest in crosswords at all ('Bingo's my game'), she then proves to be a marvel at them, getting all kinds of obscure clues which the snobbish bowlered men would never dream a little lady from the East End would figure out.

It's a wonderful example of the class system being exploited for comedy; and Beryl puts in tiny ad libs, which of course get the biggest laughs. 'Tickets please!' is met with, 'Oh, that's all we're short of, I love him, tickets please!' and whilst you can tell that Beryl is indeed off script, she's on the money as far as working the audience is concerned. Not once does Hugh Paddick dare to corpse, but the warmth in their work shines through; and, whilst they were often cast as opposites, they worked extremely well together.

However, by 1969 it was all over. Her diaries, once filled with references to him, rarely include him any longer; and certainly friends knew that things had reached their natural decline, which was incredibly difficult for

Beryl to bear. Hugh had settled down with his partner Francis with whom he shared his life until his death in 2000. He was no longer invited to Honeypot, and he and Beryl rarely saw each other socially; but she remained devoted to the memory of those years they had spent together.

When Beryl appeared on Roy Plomley's *Desert Island Discs* in 1983, her first choice was a record which was clearly chosen to remind her of her love affair with Hugh Paddick. Julio Iglesias' 'So Close to Me' could have been written to describe it. 'So close to me, I wish that you could spend forever close to me, but there is someone else and this can never be, for you and me.' It's a record which was played many times at Honeypot when Beryl found herself alone and perhaps a little wistful. Glass of brandy in hand, Beryl would reflect on how Hugh could have been husband number three; and, had he not been homosexual, Beryl may well have lived happy and contented with Hugh at Honeypot for the rest of her life.

But as her previous marriages show, eventually her affections would have come second to the greasepaint; and so a two-year love affair with many happy memories ended and, with it, a close friendship that couldn't be salvaged. She kept Hugh's identity a secret for the next twenty-five years; in revealing his name in this biography, it is to set the record straight and to celebrate what must have been a truly wonderful time for Beryl rather than to offer 1960s celebrity tittle-tattle.

*

The television series had been a huge success and, in a life of extremes, Hollywood was once again tapping at Beryl's door, much to her delight and surprise. Bette Davis' prophecy was coming true. Bob Aldrich was indeed making a film version of *Sister George* and what's more, he agreed with Miss Davis: only Beryl could play that part.

There was no doubt in anyone's mind that Bette Davis had been considered first; after all, she had a bigger name than Beryl in the United States, but naturally that came at a price and Aldrich had to keep production costs down. It's also been suggested that Angela Lansbury was considered for the role, but there's no evidence for this and it seems that, after Davis was ruled out, Beryl was the only possible choice. Dame Eileen Atkins didn't wish to return to the role of Childie, and instead the part was given to Susannah York.

Lally Bowers was not approached to reprise her role of Mercy Croft which she forever remained bitter about and quite understandably so, having toured with the production both in the UK and America. Aware that Beryl Reid was unknown to American audiences and accepting that Susannah York was very much the ingénue, Aldrich needed a big name, a Hollywood actress who could slip into the role with ease; and knowing the dangers of an all-female cast (he had just about survived Bette Davis and Joan Crawford in *Whatever Happened to Baby Jane?*), he opted for Coral Browne whom he knew Beryl liked. Coral had appeared in the big-screen production of *Auntie Mame* alongside Rosalind Russell but she was also much loved in the industry, not least because of her talent but also because of her rather colourful personality. Although she was deeply religious, this didn't extend to her vocabulary. When someone accused her of sleeping with someone else's husband as she left the Brompton Oratory in London, Coral was heard to declare: 'I don't want to hear this filth, not with me standing here in a state of fucking grace.' Beryl thought her delicious and certainly she got along far more easily with Coral than with Lally.

The film changed some of the key elements of the play allowing for a more visual storyline. The radio drama *Applehurst* became a television soap opera and this allowed the cast to grow. Whilst the role of the psychic was cut, others were introduced and were played by Hugh Paddick, Ronald Fraser and Patricia Medina among others. Hugh Paddick's role was Freddie, a TV executive; his performance was really no different to those fey, posh types he'd played before, but that didn't matter to Beryl – she was just thrilled to have him on set with her and to be able to spend as much time as possible with him. It was the last time they would work together before going their separate ways.

Known for courting controversy with his pictures, Robert Aldrich had decided to emphasise the lesbian elements of the play so that nobody was left in any doubt that the two characters were an item. Whilst Britain had decriminalised homosexuality the year before (homosexuality between two women never actually being a crime, however), the public mood regarding such things was still strictly Vita Sackville-West: 'I don't care what people do in their own home, just don't do it in the street and frighten the horses.' Initially, Beryl was uncomfortable with the changes being so explicit and the characters being so much more intimate. 'I'm terribly sorry but I can't do that,' Beryl explained. 'I have no intention of making a sex film.'

Luckily, Coral Browne and Susannah York both agreed with Beryl to tone things down a little and, after an assurance that this was her only stipulation, she'd agreed to increased sexual references provided these did not compromise her decency. Aldrich was concerned, but in her usual no-nonsense way Beryl made it clear that she had to have a clause in her contract which wouldn't require her to kiss Childie 'passionately' or to appear naked.

The budget for *Sister George* was set at $2.5m and, as he had done with *Baby Jane* back in 1962, Aldrich chose to use the studio last used by Mary Pickford for her own independent films in the early days of cinema. Beryl was happy to be back in America and her confidence was slightly restored after the *Star!* debacle, but this could also be attributed to the fact that she knew the part of George inside out. With no need to prove herself, she deferred entirely to Bob Aldrich's direction as she had promised to after the initial assurance that he wouldn't demand too much of her. One scene even saw her molest two nuns in a minicab, but Beryl was true to her word. As long as she wasn't required to take her clothes off or engage in anything too salacious, she was happy to do what Aldrich wanted.

'If he'd have said to me, "I want you to fall off a cliff," I would have done it in one take,' she said. 'I was devoted to him.' And when his request for a kiss between Beryl and Susannah came, there was nothing of the animal passion about it at all. 'You did that so gently that you've just caused six million conversions!' he cried happily. The film was wrapped, toasted with a few brandies and Beryl waited to see the final result. But the movie adaptation of *Sister George* almost never made it to the big screen at all.

Slap bang in the middle of filming, the Motion Picture Association of America instituted its brand new film rating system. Intended to rid the business of overbearing censorship, it brought in four ratings: G, meaning a film was suitable for general audiences; M, which advised parental guidance; R, which meant only those older than sixteen could see the film unless accompanied by an adult; and X, which allowed nobody under sixteen entry, whether with a parent or not. Because of the increased sexual content of the film, *Sister George* was given an X rating whereas Aldrich had felt it was likely to get an R rating. It mattered terribly to him, as an X rating impacted on where it could be advertised and how often it could be screened and at what time of day. In effect, *Sister George*'s success was doomed before it was even completed. Aldrich spent $75,000 trying to get the X rating lowered to an R but it didn't work.

At the same time the British Board of Film Censors was applying its own X rating with the chief of the board, John Trevelyan, insisting that dialogue be changed and that the seduction scene be removed. His reasoning was that the play hadn't required such a scene, so why should the film? Again, Aldrich lost. With money short, he now needed *Sister George* to be a big success.

The Killing of Sister George has since become a cult classic and indeed, the original version has now been restored and released on DVD. It is often held up as a perfect example of early gay cinema and yet, even today, the so-called seduction scene (as tender and innocent as it is for the time) is omitted. Beryl's performance stunned critics so much that she was nominated for a Golden Globe for Best Actress in a Motion Picture. Beryl didn't attend the awards ceremony but said she was deeply honoured to be nominated – as well she might be. Fellow contenders in the category were Joanne Woodward (who won the award that night), Mia Farrow, Vanessa Redgrave and four-time Academy Award-winner Katharine Hepburn (who, like Beryl, didn't see the point in attending).

Ironically, *Sister George*'s financial success was entirely down to the fact that it *did* get an X rating. All over the country, men in raincoats flocked to the few cinemas in which it was shown, and one cinema reported being knee-deep in fivers from men demanding a second and third showing. Aldrich made a few million dollars on the picture but he was never happy with it; and, despite giving Beryl Reid the credit she deserved, everyone accepted that censorship had contributed to the film not doing as well as it could do at the box office.

Almost immediately, Beryl was offered another film, which had a connection to *Sister George*. *Entertaining Mr Sloane* had been the test of Beryl's shockability for Michael Codron; now they were making a film adaptation of *Sloane* and Beryl was clearly the first choice to play Kath. She was veering into territory as far removed from Monica the schoolgirl as one could possibly get – but she loved it.

Yes, it was comedy, but it was also dramatic, dark and meaty; as Beryl said, 'It's a play to pick the bones out of.' And Joe Orton's plays had a certain reputation. Tragically, Orton was murdered by his lover Kenneth Halliwell in August 1967. An insanely jealous Halliwell had battered Orton to death with a hammer before taking his own life, stunning the theatre world, in particular Kenneth Williams, who had been a very close friend of

Orton and Halliwell, even going on holidays with them to the far more liberated climes of Tangier.

With Orton's death came a revival of his work and Williams was asked several times to direct productions of *Loot* and *Entertaining Mr Sloane*, but he wasn't asked to direct the film version. This rankled with Williams who had (until that point) been very complimentary about Beryl's work. Now he was irritated. A few years after the film of *Sloane* was made, Williams was putting together a stage production which he wanted Barbara Windsor to appear in. 'I don't know, Kenny: Kath is Beryl's role – everyone knows that she did it and she did it so well,' Dame Barbara protested. Williams was scornful. 'Look, I knew Joe,' he ranted, 'and I know what he wanted Kath to be. Kath should be played by a woman you want to fuck. And nobody wants to fuck Beryl Reid.' Did Dame Barbara agree? 'No, I didn't. I did the role, but Beryl's version was brilliant and it's the one everyone remembers. Too bloody right as well,' she says.

Entertaining Mr Sloane is as dark as Orton could possibly be without the Lord Chamberlain banning the piece. The story surrounds the young Mr Sloane, a pretty bisexual with a chequered past who meets adult baby Kath in the grounds of the cemetery where her almost totally blind father is groundskeeper. Surrounded by graves, Kath is clearly in her mid-fifties but spends the entire film desperately trying to bed Sloane. Her rival for his affections is none other than her brother (played by Harry Andrews) who makes Sloane his chauffeur, complete with leather uniform, driving him around in a large pink Cadillac. Whilst their father warns them of Sloane's murderous intentions, neither cares in the pursuit of love and, finally, the poor old man is done to death by Sloane who then only escapes justice by 'marrying' both Kath and her brother in a macabre ceremony held in the front room of the chapel house where the corpse of Kath's father is laid out ready for burial.

Dame Siân Phillips was not the only one to raise an eyebrow at the notion of Beryl taking on such a sensational role. 'For someone of her standing at the time, that part (Kath) was truly a departure from what she was used to,' she explains. 'But she was so versatile. She was a shoo-in for heightened English speech, period speech, which most actors find terribly difficult to do but it just came naturally to her; she had an incredible sense of rhythm. She had an instinctive ability to change her delivery to suit the different periods and I envied her that so much. It's a thing you don't hear all that often from actors and, aside from her diction, her sense of language was acute because her delivery of Joe Orton's lines was magical.'

As with *Sister George*, Beryl had a few requirements to lay down before filming began, and as usual these concerned the practicalities of making the film rather than any wish to spare her vanity. She had put on weight and so when the costume department produced a sheer multi-coloured chiffon dress that barely covered her thigh, she could have been terribly precious; but with Beryl, it wasn't how she looked that mattered to her (at least not professionally). She cared about the lines and her delivery; every minute detail was considered before she attempted a performance. As mentioned previously, she stalked the 'tart shops' in Soho to find just the right sort of stockings and thigh-length boots; and when her make-up was applied, she complained it was far too subtle for Kath and played the part through thick false eyelashes, her rosy cheeks plastered with bright pink rouge.

Fresh from Hollywood, it would have been easy to assume that Beryl had become a little grand. One story suggests that she refused accommodation in Marmora Road opposite Brockley cemetery where *Mr Sloane*'s outside shots were filmed because she didn't want to 'lower herself'. Whilst there is no doubt that Beryl loved to play the star and to be treated well, it simply wasn't within her nature to be overly demanding and she never forget her roots or her struggle to get to the top. She knew the value of a penny and, whilst she always liked the finer things in life, it's unlikely that her Winnebago in the grounds was for any other reason than that she didn't particularly want to cross a busy road each morning dressed in next to nothing.

Susan Penhaligon recalls that during the filming of *No Sex Please, We're British*, Beryl asked for a chair to sit on whilst on location in Windsor High Street in between takes. 'It was the end of the day and she was tired, so they brought a mattress and plonked it in a shop doorway. I looked back and saw Beryl crouched on this mattress like a homeless person, sobbing. She needed to feel special and appreciated.' As close friend Jan Linden explains, 'That had nothing to do with Beryl wanting to be a star: she just wanted to be recognised for what she was – a hard-working, successful actress.'

Of course, she loved the attention and the adoration of the fans too and, if she could play the star, she would. 'We'd go to Berwick Street market where Beryl would buy fish for her cats,' Jan remembers, 'and she'd be there in a fur coat, a gorgeous hat and white gloves and all the stallholders would cry out to her, "Morning Beryl!" and she was like the Queen Mother, sailing through it all and loving every moment.'

Whilst she was now fully aware that Hollywood was a closed door, and though being stuck in a rut of endless panel-show appearances bothered her, Beryl hoped that *Sloane* would bring similar success to that of *Sister George* and once again push her forward for dramatic roles rather than comedy pieces. But it would be another decade before anything similar to *George* would be laid at her feet.

*

In April of 1970, Beryl was contacted by the Master. Sir Noël was personally directing a revival of his most beloved work *Blithe Spirit* and he wanted Beryl to take on the role of Madame Arcati. At first she declined. 'The problem was that it had been done so brilliantly by Margaret Rutherford and I didn't want to go and give them Beryl Reid as Margaret Rutherford,' Beryl explained. 'But then I came up with a few changes and put them to Noël and he fell about with laughter and, graciously, he let me do it my way.' Beryl's way was to play Madame Arcati with a thick Scottish accent and to give her vivid red hair and clumpy steel-toe-capped boots with bright yellow socks pulled up to her knees. She mixed her jewellery so that her earrings didn't match each other, let alone her necklace or the chainmail of bracelets on her wrists.

The show opened on 2nd June at the Yvonne Arnaud Theatre in Guildford before moving to the Globe the following month. Coward was nothing but complimentary about Beryl's performance, and it was in this production (which ran an entire year) that Beryl cemented her friendship with Patrick Cargill, the actor best known for his role in the sitcom *Father Dear Father*. In the 1960s and seventies, Cargill lived a few minutes away from Honeypot Cottage with his partner Vernon… and his pet monkey. He was roughly the same age as Beryl, but his homosexuality was well known and, however tempted she may have been, she'd learned her lesson from the Hugh Paddick affair and the two simply remained just good friends.

In the January of 1971, the cast were asked if they would consider performing one last time in Toronto at the O'Keefe Centre. It took a personal telephone call and endless flowers sent from Sir Noël Coward himself in Jamaica to convince Beryl to fly to Canada and give her Arcati one final time; but she did so and a new audience opened up to her, the newspapers being full of lovely reviews (though she would never return to Canada for work or for leisure).

As soon as she returned home, she was asked to appear on Radio 4's *Choice of Paperbacks*. Produced by Rosemary Hart, the series was a kind of literary version of *Desert Island Discs*, a precursor to *My Life in Books* currently presented by Anne Robinson. *Choice of Paperbacks* saw famous faces present a passionate introduction to their favourite books. (When Barbara Cartland appeared, she naturally chose her own works.)

Beryl was booked to appear with the composer Richard Rodney Bennett and Norman St John-Stevas MP, a future Minister of the Arts in Margaret Thatcher's government who clearly knew nothing about how to handle a star of Beryl's calibre. Beryl was of course a Conservative supporter and she wouldn't hear a word against Mrs Thatcher or her top team, but something about St John-Stevas didn't sit well with her.

Beryl chose *Kiss Kiss*, a book by Roald Dahl which she felt confident she could discuss; but St John-Stevas tried to play a rather dirty trick on her. He had come to blows with Beryl a year or so before, asking her rather rudely, 'So who are you supposed to be married to now?' just after her marriage to Derek Franklin had come to an end. St John-Stevas held back his selection (a biography of St Teresa of Avila) until the day before recording. Perhaps he knew that Beryl struggled with her reading and wouldn't be able to make sense of it in time? Whatever his motives, it upset Beryl hugely to be presented with a huge tome on a subject she had no interest in with just twenty-four hours to read it.

Before stepping into the studio, there was a light lunch at which Rosemary Hart, Beryl, Norman and Richard could get to know each other a little. The row could be heard all over the canteen. St John-Stevas was consistently rude to Beryl, not allowing her to talk and saying things like 'You haven't actually read my choice, have you dear?' By the time the recording was under way, the air was blue and a ferocious argument erupted when Beryl said of St Teresa, 'I can't understand it at all. If she wanted to do so much good she should have got out and done meals on wheels and mixed with a lot of people, not just shut herself away in a nunnery.' To the ire of St John-Stevas, she went on: 'Surely [she was] pandering to what she wanted to do. I felt her work would have been wonderful if, like Jesus, she had gone among the people and fed them and cared for them outside of the nunnery.'

St John-Stevas was a devout Roman Catholic who had once enrolled in a seminary in Rome. Eventually he gave up on the idea but, despite his homosexuality which must have conflicted deeply with the official line the Catholic Church took in those days, he remained staunchly loyal to his religion. A knock at St Teresa was a knock at him personally and he responded by being terribly obstinate. 'You don't have to be so Joe Dogmatic!' Beryl fired at him, to which St John-Stevas kept replying, 'You do not understand this book my dear, you clearly haven't read it.' In truth, Beryl had sat up all night desperately trying to make sense of it and she was left hurt by the entire experience.

The following day, Rosemary Hart offered a profound apology for the whole affair but Beryl quickly forgave her for putting her in such an uncomfortable position. When it was broadcast, a Tory colleague of St John-Stevas' wrote Beryl a letter inviting her to the House of Commons for lunch by way of consolation. His name was Sir Fergus Montgomery, the MP for Altrincham and Sale and known for his love of the theatre. The two became devoted friends, remaining so for the rest of their lives; Beryl even named a small china frog after him. If anybody criticised the Thatcher government in her company, Beryl would snatch it up and say, 'Now you say sorry and kiss Sir Fergus!'

In choosing her selection for *Choice of Paperbacks*, Beryl had discovered the *Mapp and Lucia* series by E. F. Benson. She was now seriously pitching the idea of an adaptation for the BBC and regarded it as a sound vehicle for her, providing they could get the casting right. In a letter to Rosemary Hart, she wrote, 'Fingers crossed dear because I MUST PLAY MAPP!' Rosemary replied and said, 'I do hope you find someone who will take *Mapp and Lucia* as a television adaptation for you and I hope we can work together in the near future.'

The idea came to nothing, and clearly Hart was in no position at the time to make it a reality. It is a crying shame that nobody at the BBC spotted the enormous potential of such a series and *Mapp and Lucia* would remain on the shelves of second-hand bookshops until 1985, when it was adapted by Channel 4 with Prunella Scales as Miss Mapp and Geraldine McEwan as Lucia.

Whilst *Mapp and Lucia* was out of reach with the BBC, Thames Television had formed a working partnership with two new writers who had Beryl in mind for a sitcom they were writing. Brian Cooke and Johnnie Mortimer were the brains behind *Man About the House* (starring Richard O'Sullivan) and its eventual spin-offs *Robin's Nest* and *George & Mildred*. Cooke had got his start in comedy by writing for *Round the Horne* whilst Mortimer had penned a series called *The Men From the Ministry* (a radio sitcom based around the goings-on of the Civil Service) starring Wilfrid Hyde-White and Richard Murdoch before joining Cooke. Beryl's flirtation with sitcom had been tentative since her radio days. In 1968, she had taken a risk on a sitcom called *Wink to Me Only* written by Jennifer Phillips for the BBC, but in truth had only agreed to it (despite her misgivings about the script) as it offered her a chance to work with Hugh Paddick, her love affair with him not yet in its death throes.

For comedians who had started their working lives on the music-hall stage, sitcom had replaced the summer season, and in the 1970s anyone who was anyone had given it a go. Some were more successful than others, of course. Hylda Baker was revelling in glory having made a massive hit as Nellie Pledge in the pickle-factory-based sitcom *Nearest and Dearest* whilst Peggy Mount had won a new legion of adoring fans thanks to the long-running British forerunner to *The Golden Girls, You're Only Young Twice* alongside Pat Coombes and Beryl's old sparring partner Lally Bowers. Yootha Joyce was now a household name having appeared in *Man About the House*, and so beloved was she by the public as sex-starved Mildred Roper that she secured the success of her own spin-off.

It seemed that the combination of Thames Television (where the most popular sitcoms of the decade were being made) and writers Cooke and Mortimer was a magical one, and to sweeten the pot just a little further they had an extremely close working relationship (which almost amounted to exclusivity) with the actor Richard O'Sullivan. Their offer to Beryl was a series of six half-hour episodes called *Alcock and Gander* and, whilst O'Sullivan was by now a big name, it was very much pitched as being Beryl's show. Indeed, the opening credits feature Beryl wandering through Berwick Street market shopping with neither of her regular co-stars (O'Sullivan and the actor John Cater) even mentioned. This was her vehicle and she liked the idea that it may well become a long-running success, even though she was still loath to get stuck in a part. 'They'll never typecast me!' she insisted.

Just before the making of *Alcock and Gander,* Beryl took the decision to find a London base and chose two small apartments in a smart red-brick Victorian building called Montague Mansions just off Baker Street. Her financial advisor, Innes Hamilton, suggested it may be better for Beryl to actually buy an apartment rather than to rent two, but the company which owned the lease refused to let Beryl buy the apartments she was already resident in and so she had to settle for taking the one on the top floor. She stayed there as often as was practical, but it in no way rivalled Honeypot in her affections; and, whilst Sue stayed there whenever she was in London, it was offered more and more to friends for their use until Beryl eventually sold it as she made Honeypot her permanent and only base.

Beryl's character in the new sitcom was a widow, Marigold Alcock, whose husband had left her a chain of dodgy businesses in Soho, all run from an office above a strip club. These ranged from dodgy pills and potions to a coach-tour company which was disastrous and left a bookish young man called Richard Gander (played by O'Sullivan) so shaken that he demanded a refund. Rather than part with the cash, Marigold offers him the chance to become her business partner. Naturally they know nothing about business and, over six episodes, Alcock and Gander get into various scrapes with the law and with the Soho scene.

It didn't quite work. Beryl felt the scripts were good, and when she began work at the Teddington Studios in August 1971 she had high hopes for it, but the audience response wasn't exactly a thunderous demand for a second series. A review which appeared in *The Stage* was kind but clear: 'Beryl Reid is undoubtedly one of our most appealing and compelling comedy actresses and anyone who questions this only has to watch the opening episode of *Alcock and Gander* to be convinced that she has the ability to make an unbelievable character become entirely plausible. A situation comedy would be doomed in less experienced hands but immediately comes to life when undertaken by an artist of her calibre. It is hardly surprising therefore that Miss Reid should walk away with the comedy honours.' In other words, it was a joy to see Beryl doing what Beryl did best but the script was 'poor and laboured' and 'whilst everyone else is falling over themselves, she alone maintains her composure and lets the laughs fall into her lap.' A second series of *Alcock and Gander* was not commissioned.

Working with Cooke and Mortimer brought two film roles which could be deemed compensation for the Alcock and Gander flop. *No Sex Please, We're British* was a farce written by Alistair Foot and Anthony Marriot for the stage and was now being considered for a film adaptation. A nervous bank clerk accidentally takes delivery of a stash of European pornography, which his conservative boss is trying to ban in the local town, and thus ensues a convoluted plot to remove the offending porn before the poor bank clerk loses his job. The stage version had been touring since 1967 to packed houses, but when it premiered in the West End on 3rd June 1971 the critics found it 'over-exaggerated' and 'too complex to be considered amusing'. American audiences didn't take to it either, and a Broadway run in 1973 closed after just sixteen performances. Clearly believing it would be a success, John R. Sloan decided to produce a film version but with the script adapted by Brian Cooke and Johnnie Mortimer, making several plot changes that would be more appealing to audiences.

Michael Crawford had originally played the protagonist, Brian Runnicles, in the stage version but, with the critics less than complimentary about the play, he declined a role in the movie version. The part went instead to Ronnie Corbett. Playing David and Penny Hunter, the newlyweds living above the bank, were Ian Ogilvy (who had just enjoyed great fame as the Bohemian poet Lawrence Kirbridge in *Upstairs, Downstairs*) and Susan Penhaligon (another graduate from 165 Eaton Place and by no means new to films having just appeared in *Under Milk Wood*). Arthur Lowe was brought in to play the fusty bank manager (who ultimately turned out to be Captain Mainwaring out of uniform and without his moustache), and there were supporting roles for Brian Wilde (*Last of the Summer Wine*), Michael Bates (*It Ain't Half Hot Mum*) and Deryck Guyler (*Sykes*).

The part of Bertha Hunter (renamed from Eleanor) was offered to Beryl but, with the successes of *Sister George* and *Mr Sloane* still fresh in her mind, it was hardly the sort of challenge she'd come to relish. Cooke and Mortimer also included her in an adaptation of the sitcom *Father Dear Father* on the advice of Patrick Cargill but it was very much of its time, the seemingly inevitable extension of any successful sitcom of the day which always meant a feature film – and a flop.

No Sex Please was different. Beryl's character was adapted to play to her strengths and she was deliciously camp as the snooty vegetarian dowager, clearly not thrilled with her son's choice of bride. Bertha descends on David and Penny announcing that she might be able to stay for three weeks, if she feels up to it – in the middle of the aforesaid pornography invasion of downtown Windsor.

Arthur Lowe's character, a prudish bank manager, has something of a romantic interest in Bertha and their scenes together are tender and charming as well as giggle-worthy. As her co-star Susan Penhaligon recalls, 'I remember seeing her and Arthur playing a scene together and it was a masterclass in comedy technique, particularly to watch Beryl's timing and charm and the way she delivered a line.'

She adored Ronnie Corbett, and in one particular scene the pair represent British farce at its very best. Poor Runnicles has tried to dispose of the pictures by throwing them in the Thames, by burying them, burning them and even attempting to flush them down the lavatory. Putting the offending images into Penny's handbag, he dives into the kitchen to force the smutty pictures down the waste disposal unit, making such a racket that Bertha enquires as to what on earth is wrong with the poor boy. 'Is he… funny?', she asks, full of *double entendre*. Despite Penny's protestations that he isn't 'funny', Runnicles suddenly appears from the kitchen, handbag over his wrist, declaring, 'I'm so sorry. I've just been in the kitchen. Mincing.' Beryl's raised eyebrow is a joy to behold.

It was hardly Joe Orton calibre stuff; and during the making of the film she seemed to be a little out of sorts at times, even though there were happy moments. 'She would bring a hamper for lunch to her dressing room at Pinewood Studios where we shot *No Sex Please, We're British*, always with a bottle or two of wine,' Penhaligon remembers. 'I'd pass her dressing room door and she'd furtively beckon me in saying, "Come and have a spot of lunch!" We'd chat, consume far too much wine (for me anyway) and she'd make me laugh, tell me about her cats, seven of them I think, and her cottage.' But films didn't have the warm embrace of the theatre: there was no camaraderie, no audience… and of course, no Betty.

The infrastructure of Beryl's life was changing and she was becoming a little more wistful. 'She'd tell me about her marriages and how she had no time for men now,' says Susan Penhaligon. 'She had a great sense of humour but sometimes I felt she was lonely. We kind of bonded because I think I was somewhat lost at that time, and she sensed it and befriended me.'

Beryl's brother Roy was in poor health; and then came the terrible blow of the death of Joan Bissett, her friend and confidante for over two decades. She'd come to rely heavily on Joan who arranged Beryl's diary, helped with fan mail and kept the cottage just as she knew Beryl liked it. When she died suddenly in 1974, Beryl was devastated. 'We never had a wrong word. We had a great lot of laughs together, a great deal of fun and we enjoyed ourselves something rotten in the time we had,' Beryl said.

Joan had always treated her as a friend, never as 'the star'; but the 1970s would confirm that Beryl Reid was exactly that. Producers had woken up to Beryl's extraordinary range and, finally, the nerves she often spoke about had begun to dissipate as she took confidence from the remarkable body of work she had achieved over the previous thirty years. She was now over fifty, an age at which many women (let alone actresses) look to what they have done rather than what is left to come. Beryl, on the other hand, insisted that she wouldn't 'go soggy'. She'd keep on working, she'd keep on building on a career that many would kill to have had up until that point alone. But it was far from over and the best was yet to come.

Chapter Seven

'If you don't work, your brain goes soggy. And mine is soggy enough to begin with. If I think I can do it, I'll give it a go because what's the alternative? To get old and silly? That's not for me.'

To the outside world, Beryl had everything she could possibly want. She lived a charmed life; her career had traversed the rocky path of music hall, radio, television and the stage; and she'd accumulated awards and countless positive reviews as well as gaining the undying respect of her peers. Beryl never regarded work as a means to an end and, whilst there was an element of not wanting to be forgotten, she worked as much as she did because she truly adored the work she did. Scripts flooded into Honeypot Cottage and each one was reviewed and then passed to a friend who could give her advice on whether she was right for that part. 'But does it suit me?' she'd ponder.

Whilst Beryl had become a little obsessive about taking on more dramatic roles at this point and badgered Robert Luff terribly for them, two big stumbling blocks had thumped themselves down before her. The first was out of her control entirely: frustrating for someone who by all accounts needed to be in control of herself and those around her. Casting agents still regarded her as Beryl Reid the comedienne and not Beryl Reid the actress. She had a Tony award to prove that she was very much an actress; but to many, however wonderful her performances were, she could only ever be a comic. This was a source of constant irritation to Beryl and to her agent who tried his best to find roles for her that he thought she'd enjoy and which would best show off her unique and vast range. But the second issue came directly from Beryl's character, and it is revealing because it says so much about her approach to her own life and not just the parts she considered worthy of her time.

'She loved working, she adored working and if something stopped her from doing that then she would get quite low,' remembers close friend Paul Strike. 'She would get scripts in all the time, huge stacks of them, and she'd make me stay awake until two or three in the morning reading through them to see if they were what she called "sympathetic". You see, Beryl didn't like a sad ending. She didn't want a sad ending. She wanted something happy.'

The theatrical profession is traditionally represented by the two masks of comedy and tragedy. For so many performers of Beryl's generation, the comic mask was usually representative of their working life and public face, full of fun and laughter, whilst the tragic symbolised their terrible private battles with brutal personal demons and hang-ups. Beryl's personality was not as clear-cut as that; but Stephen Boxer's image of her as a not-quite-grown-up little girl, tiptoeing through the bluebells at Honeypot Cottage in this self-created fantasy world to which she could escape, does lend itself to the way that she refused to take on roles in pieces which would end tearfully or catastrophically. She couldn't bear too much sadness in her life, and perhaps that's the real reason she didn't attend funerals.

People commented that Beryl changed after her surgery with Dr McIndoe; and certainly, around this time, the stories and anecdotes people share about her take on a very different flavour. Beryl had found her confidence and her courage – but also her temper. If there was one thing she could never stand, it was laziness, and it was not uncommon for stagehands who chattered away in the wings whilst she was on stage giving her all in rehearsal to find props thrown at them. By the same token, some crew members were given a firm (and very public) lecture on professionalism if they didn't give her the respect she felt she deserved.

At times, she could be ferocious for what seemed to be sport. Each morning, Beryl would have her coffee and toast whilst sitting on a little three-legged stool in the cottage; and, if friends Paul and Will were staying

Beryl's parents, Leonard and Annie

Beryl, aged four, with older brother Roy

An early incarnation of Monica, c. 1935
(Photo © Strithon Ltd)

Educating Archie with (*left to right*)
James Robertson Justice, Beryl,
Archie Andrews and Peter Brough

Monica, the naughty schoolgirl

Beryl marries BBC producer Bill Worsley, 1949

Beryl's second wedding, 1954, with
Derek Franklin

Weston-super-Mare, c. 1960 with
Frank Ifield, Dorothy Squires and
Russ Conway

Beryl with Hugh Paddick, 1966

The Killing of Sister George in London, 1966, with Lally Bowers (*left*) and Dame Eileen Atkins (*centre*) in Carnaby Street

This page and opposite: Honeypot Cottage, inside and out, pictured in the 1960s

In front of the Queen Mary to promote *The Killing of Sister George* in New York, 1967, with Lally Bowers (*left*) and Dame Eileen Atkins (*centre*)

With Kirk Douglas after winning the Tony Award for *The Killing of Sister George*, 1967

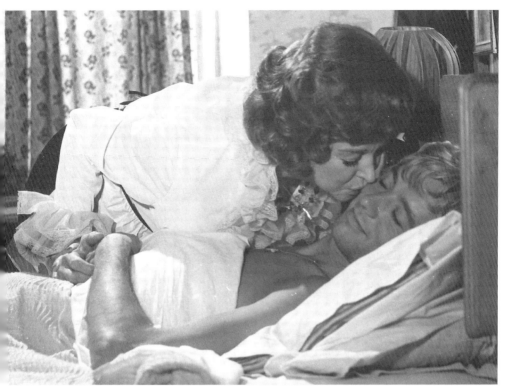

Entertaining Mr Sloane
(in bed!): Beryl as Kath
with Peter McEnery, 1970

She's Burlington Bertie from Bow!

With brother Roy, c. 1968

The Beast in the Cellar with Dame Flora Robson, 1970

Blankety Blank with (*left to right*) Sir Lenny Henry, Liza Goddard, Sir Terry Wogan, Beryl, Larry Grayson, Lorraine Chase and Jimmy Tarbuck

As Sarah Pigswill in 'Mother's Day', *Worzel Gummidge*, 1981

By Royal Appointment: meeting HRH Princess Margaret, Countess of Snowdon, c. 1973

And again! Meeting Her Majesty the Queen after the Royal Variety Performance. Others being presented that night were Rula Lenska, Dennis Waterman and Sir Norman Wisdom

With Peggy Mount at the National in *Il Campiello*, 1976

Get Up and Go! with Mooncat (David Claridge) and Stephen Boxer, who kindly submitted this photograph (Photo © Thames Television)

A right royal knees-up! As Grandma Mole in *The Secret Diary of Adrian Mole*, 1985

Beryl relaxes at Honeypot Cottage with a feline friend, c. 1988

The place she loved best. Beryl at Honeypot Cottage, 1984

After collecting her OBE, accompanied by agent Robert Luff, 1986

Beryl Reid OBE, as painted by the portrait artist June Mendoza (Photo © June Mendoza)

the night (being allowed to actually sleep inside Honeypot and not relegated to the houseboats), they would join her.

'Good morning Beryl, how are you today?' asked Will on one occasion.

'Oh, I'm not at my best today, darling,' Beryl said. 'I'll be all right when I've had a good row with someone, and I don't want it to be you so let's just be quiet shall we?'

The victim was her friend Muriel Carey who worked for the Cats Protection League and provided Beryl with many of her feline companions. 'Oh Muriel, you've brought a big black cloud in with you today!' Beryl soothed. 'What on earth is the matter?' Muriel protested that she was fine but Beryl kept goading her, needling her until both were ratty and frustrated with the other. She meant no harm by it of course; Beryl was never vindictive and she also never sulked. Quick to rage at times, she could strip a person down to the bones with her acid tongue but, after the apologies were shared, it was never mentioned again.

Paul and Will both had personal experience of this in different ways. Once, when Beryl had been away working in the mid-eighties, she asked them to stay at the cottage and to keep an eye on the place. Will had naturally used the kitchen and taken great care to wash everything up and leave it well-ordered and clean for when Beryl returned. On the Monday morning, he went into the office and began work when the receptionist suddenly appeared asking if he knew a Miss Beryl Reid and, if so, was it really *the* Beryl Reid? Will took the call.

'Where's my fucking plate? Where is my black oval plate Will? I want it. Now I don't care if you've broken it but if you've hidden it from me, I want to know where it is *now*!' The plate was found, an apology was given and it was never mentioned again.

Much later when Beryl was having the paving surrounding the cottage replaced, she was getting into a dreadful state trying to juggle house guests and workmen all at the same time. Paul was headed to Scotland for an acting engagement and flying from Heathrow, not that far a drive from Wraysbury. Beryl suggested that Paul leave his car at the cottage for the two weeks he'd be away and she would get her chauffeur, Rick, to drive him to and from the airport as he needed. Paul arrived to find the cottage in chaos; he told Beryl that he'd leave his car tucked away safely out of the lane and away from the workmen so that it wouldn't cause any problems, but she wanted his car keys just in case.

'You won't need them, Beryl,' Paul patiently explained. 'The car isn't in the lane and it isn't near the cottage; it won't be a problem.' A game of tennis began where the keys were brought out and put back, brought out and put back. Eventually, fearful of missing his flight, Paul left with Rick to go to Heathrow.

A few days later, a furious Beryl was on the telephone: 'You haven't left us your keys and I can't move your fucking car! You have ruined *everything*!' And she slammed the telephone down. When Paul returned to Heathrow, Rick was nowhere to be found to collect him; but, after a little coaxing and some flowers, Beryl let the matter rest and it was never raised again.

But if Beryl was short-tempered with crew, friends and family, she was never so with her fans. Indeed, the door to Honeypot Cottage was left permanently unlocked, and from the angle of her bed Beryl could see who was coming up the path. If it was a fan who had found out where she lived, she was thrilled and would invite them in and talk to them for hours at a time. When Beryl called actress and close friend Jan Linden and found that there was a party line, she made friends with the man in the flat above Jan's and Jan had to wait patiently until Beryl had finished her chat.

In later years, she absolutely adored visits from Jehovah's Witnesses, not because she had any intention of converting but because it was an unexpected audience. They came back time after time and Beryl entertained them. In her personal archive, there are stacks of books given to her by the missionaries who must have found the whole experience an absolute delight, even if they didn't manage to share their message with her in the way they might have liked!

When barges or houseboats floated down the Thames through Old Windsor Lock and past Honeypot, Beryl would dash out and give them a wave. She would spend far too long at the stage door making sure she had signed everything she was being asked to; and fan mail responses got longer and longer, more and more personal, with some correspondence flying back and forth for over thirty years. She sent photographs, she sent gifts and she even sent birthday cards, all to fans she had never met but to whom she felt she owed a debt of gratitude.

She was once dining in a London restaurant with a friend who was becoming a little irritated that the conversation kept being halted because of eager fans asking her to sign menus.

'Oh Beryl, can't you just tell them to go away?'

Beryl was livid. 'They're paying for your dinner this evening,' she raged. 'Show them some thanks for it!'

*

In the first three years of the 1970s, Beryl had focused almost entirely on films. These included the sitcom spin-off *Father Dear Father* (with close friend Patrick Cargill) and of course *No Sex Please, We're British*; but two films she made around this time remain cult classics and are very much in the Robert Aldrich mould, even though Aldrich himself had nothing to do with their production or direction.

The Beast in the Cellar was written by James Kelley for Tigon British Film Productions which specialised in Hammer House of Horror style shockers. Most have dated terribly, but *The Beast in the Cellar* remains popular. The film stars Dame Flora Robson and Beryl Reid as spinster sisters living in a small military town who notice that there is a sudden spate of brutal murders in the neighbouring barracks, the police suspecting a large wild cat to be the culprit. But Joyce and Ellie Ballantyne know better. It is of course, their brother, who has been locked in the cellar for thirty years, totally deranged and out for blood. The film was marketed as 'a chill-filled festival of horror!' and was an unlikely but limited success. The parallels with *Baby Jane* were not unnoticeable, Dame Flora spending most of her time in bed whilst the child-like Beryl buried bodies in the garden.

At times, Beryl could clash with female co-stars who were of the same stature she knew herself to be but, for the most part, she seemed to get on well with Robson. When an assistant accidentally called for 'Dame Flora, Dame Beryl,' Flora remarked: 'Oh, Beryl's not a Dame,' to which Beryl retorted, 'No, but I have got all my own teeth,' and the two collapsed into giggles.

Financially, Beryl wasn't in the best shape. Her flat in Montague Mansions, which had served as a permanent base when the journey back to Windsor was too much, was now sold and Beryl had assumed that royalty cheques (which she'd always ensured paid slightly more than those of her colleagues) would be coming in thick and fast, but the BBC simply weren't repeating the things she'd been paid well for. Films such as *Beast in the*

Cellar and *No Sex Please* were not exactly box office smashes and, despite the accolades and the increased demand for her services, money was tight. Of course, Beryl did like to flash the cash when she could. A new car every year, constant renovations to the cottage and gifts for friends came at a price – not to mention the ever increasing bill for the cats' dinners. (Stephen Boxer recalls visiting Beryl to find that the cats were being fed on prime steak.) Her clothes were custom made, her phone bill was always astronomical and she began to struggle slightly. So when she was offered a part in the 1973 film *Psychomania*, it was for the money and not the script that she signed up.

The film centres on Tom Latham (played by Nicky Henson), the leader of a biker gang who dabbles in black magic. His mother, played by Beryl of course, holds séances with her butler; and the pair make a pact with the devil so that, if they die, they'll be able to come back to life and torment the villagers.

One cast member of note was the Hollywood actor George Sanders who was by no means small fry. Not only had he appeared in such classic movies as *All About Eve* and *The Jungle Book* but he'd also been married to two of the Gabor sisters, Zsa Zsa and Magda (though not at the same time of course). Because the budget for the film was so small, a message was sent from on high instructing the props department that, to cut costs, there should be no 'named chairs' for artists. 'This was probably to save about twelve pounds or something,' Nicky jokes, 'but George Sanders was a huge international star and he was only in the production for ten days, that's all they could afford him for. A couple of guys in the props department at Shepperton were so ashamed that they brought this chair out and written on the back, in biro, was… "George *Saunders*".'

Nicky Henson had worked with Beryl before ten years earlier in a revue called *All Square*. It was Nicky's first West End appearance and Beryl made a lasting impression. 'It was a silly revue really; it was our attempt at a parody of *That Was the Week That Was* but we thought we were much funnier of course,' says Nicky. 'And I hadn't really got much experience of that sort of thing but I learned absolutely everything from Beryl. I was a young starving actor, I'd had no training whatsoever and I learned my trade on the shop floor from her, my comic timing, you name it, everything I learned from Beryl.' Noticing that Nicky and fellow starving actor Julian Holloway were always hungry, Beryl insisted on bringing cakes and pastries she'd baked at Honeypot to the theatre for them and quickly christened Nicky and Julian 'Stuffed Guts' and 'Rumblebelly'. In the ten years between *All Square* and *Psychomania*, Nicky had been focusing on music in a rock-and-roll band, but when he found he was working with Beryl again, he was delighted. The script was, in his own words, 'an absolute embarrassment' and most of the time Beryl and Nicky were doubled up with laughter at the absurdity of it all. 'I'm afraid *Psychomania* was ridiculous,' he laughs. 'I know it's become a cult now and I still get offers of work off the back of it because young filmmakers see it and they like it very much, but we couldn't keep a straight face. George Sanders too, actually; we just absolutely howled with laughter the whole time.'

Beryl wasn't the first choice for the part of Mrs Latham, it having been offered originally to Maureen O'Sullivan; but, whilst it wasn't terribly well paid, Beryl made the best of a bad job. 'It fitted in with her schedule, she behaved impeccably and it made the thing bearable,' Nicky recalls, 'but our relationship? It was flirty. We flirted with each other all the time but she never pushed the limits. And she never played the star with me; then again, the whole project was so ridiculous that she couldn't really. She didn't behave in a lah-di-dah way at all.'

Beryl and Nicky put the entire thing down to experience, battling through *Psychomania* with professionalism and leaving it firmly behind them. But for George Sanders, there would be more tragic consequences. For some time he had been suffering from depression and dementia and, whilst visiting Castelldefels in Barcelona, he was shown the rushes of *Psychomania* to see what he thought. That night, he went back to his hotel room and wrote a note: 'Dear World, I am leaving because I am bored. I feel I have lived long enough. I am leaving you with your worries in this sweet cesspool. Good luck.' He swallowed the contents of five bottles of the barbiturate Nembutal and was dead within hours.

Beryl and Nicky never kept in touch after production closed but, whenever she saw him at an awards ceremony or a 'do', she'd always call out 'Hallo Stuffed Guts!' and giggle all over again at the bizarre experience *Psychomania* had been.

'It was a crap film,' Nicky says. 'I'll never understand the fascination with it, but the chance to work with Beryl again made it for me. I think I actually appreciate the time I spent with Beryl more than I appreciate the film.'

*

The early 1970s saw a subtle change in the way Beryl was regarded professionally. Now considered a stalwart who could turn her hand to anything, she couldn't have been more surprised – but delighted – at being asked to join one of the most prestigious theatre companies in the country: the Royal Shakespeare Company.

For women of a certain age, an offer to play the Nurse in *Romeo and Juliet* was inevitable and many of her counterparts regarded it as something of a death knell, an unmistakable reminder of age. But for Beryl, there was a certain niche within the classics that made her a firm favourite with companies like the RSC. Restoration comedy is naughty, exaggerated, eccentric and camp; its 17th century bawdy humour and play on English stereotypes provided the perfect release from the grim Puritan regime which had banned all public stage performances since the time of the English Civil War. When Charles II was restored to the throne in 1660, this dour and miserable approach to theatre was cast off and everyone from aristocrats to the peasantry could enjoy what essentially was the satire of the day.

Most plays in the genre had a stock set of characters: the fop, a witty but obsequious gentleman who cares more about fashion and style than he does about learning; the drunken aristocrat; the rake, a womanising young man of means who wastes his fortune on wine, women and song; and the aged *grande dame*, an elderly spinster or widow with more money than sense and an insistence on the old values being upheld. Arguably, much of Noël Coward's work had included these stock characters and Beryl had proved to be a popular Madam Arcati in *Blithe Spirit*, even managing to make the role her own when everybody regarded it very much as Margaret Rutherford's part. It was the perfect audition for taking on the Restoration comedies of Sheridan and Congreve.

In January 1978, the Royal Shakespeare Company began rehearsing Congreve's *The Way of the World* to open later that month at the Aldwych Theatre. The play tells the tale of Mirabell and Millamant, two young lovers who want to marry but who need first to obtain the blessing of Millamant's imperious and bitter widowed aunt, Lady Wishfort – a play on the words 'wish for forty', the character being fifty-five, man-hungry and somewhat vain. Brash, bawdy and loud, the part called for an actress who could storm the stage and make her presence known, and so when Beryl was offered the role it thrilled the entire company who saw the genius behind the casting. As actor Michael Pennington explains, 'It was a golden time at the RSC and we'd developed a style which was very "in-house", which was a big part of its success, but it wasn't half a shot in the arm to have someone from outside as a guest, especially Beryl. I was delighted because I'd loved *Educating Archie*, Monica and Marlene; and I'd also marvelled at how someone often thought of mainly as a revue performer could turn her hand to *The Killing of Sister George* and *Entertaining Mr Sloane*.' Her variety days stood her in good stead for this particular production, as Lady Wishfort's part had been slightly reworked into a sketch format which Beryl was no stranger to and could easily learn – almost.

Michael Pennington remembers, 'There were wildly funny two-page scenes which of course caused Beryl no trouble, and then a sustained long one at the end when she was deeply implicated in this impossibly complicated plot. This is where Beryl and I struck a deal.' Michael had become aware of Beryl using an old trouper's trick. 'If she did dry, she would put in an abrupt full stop, as in "What I wanted to say is…" And then she'd look enquiringly at you, so of course it made it seem that it was you who had missed a cue. But she was pleased I'd found her out and we made a plan. I would hold her hand firmly, which was fine for the scene and then contained a message. If I felt her grip tighten, I knew she was beginning to forget something and I should be ready to improvise for a bit.'

As well as Michael Pennington, Beryl was to share the stage with a young Judi Dench and an even younger Ruby Wax. Ruby was cast as Lady Wishfort's servant and recalls her time working with Beryl as being rather nerve-wracking: 'I remember waiting in the wings to be her serving wench and thinking I had never seen anything so brilliantly funny and charismatic at the same time,' Ruby explains. 'She took that stage and made it her own. I was sick to my stomach that I had to go on stage to serve such a Goddess!'

When it came to opening night, Beryl waited nervously in the wings. Whilst she was not prone to stage fright as some obituaries suggested, whenever she undertook a new form of theatre she did become incredibly fastidious and her attention to detail was legendary. Of course the shoes had to be right but, for this particular role, she had very much gone to town on her overall appearance, squeezing herself into an 18th century gown that pushed her boobs up, powdered white with a beauty spot or two painted on. With lashings of rouge and a red wig piled high with feathers and flowers, she bustled onto the stage in lace and silk giving her lines with an impeccable timing that was all her own.

The reviewers agreed with Ruby Wax: she was a goddess. John Peter in the *Sunday Times* said, 'The other jewel of the production is Beryl Reid's Lady Wishfort. Congreve was cruel to this woman: there's something almost brutal in the way he ridicules the desires of someone ageing and undesirable. Yet Miss Reid gives a performance that might have shamed him: she plays her not as a shrieking grotesque but as a simple, gullible, fretful creature, silly but brave, and not without dignity.'

For Ruby, Beryl left an indelible impression: 'She was probably one of the first women I ever saw that made me think, we can be even more brilliant than men in comedy.' Restoration comedy was clearly a medium Beryl was perfect for and the production was hugely successful, but for Beryl personally there was an even more important aspect to her time with the Royal Shakespeare Company. She was finally being taken seriously as an actress. Whilst her foray into Hollywood had flopped a little, this was not only the zenith of respectability but she was also working with the biggest names of the day; and she loved that feeling of being seen as a 'real actress' and not just that silly girl who spilt the ink.

So when a gossip columnist thought he would invent a little drama of his own and attribute it to ill feeling backstage between the cast, Beryl was quick to stamp it out. Writing for the *News of the World*, the journalist suggested that Beryl had taken against Judi Dench and was making her life a misery, bullying her and alienating her from the rest of the cast. Beryl was furious and, whilst it took a lot to make her lose her temper, once she'd given way to it there was no turning back; you simply had to wait for the storm to pass. The journalist found himself sat on the other end of the telephone as Beryl let fly with a tirade, fuelled by a trip to buy fruit at a greengrocer's in Covent Garden that afternoon when someone had shouted, ' 'Allo Beryl! You been duffin' up poor Judi again then?' Beryl insisted on being told where the story had come from; and, if someone in the company had fabricated rumours, she wanted to know exactly who it was. With Judi Dench and the company manager at her side, Beryl said, 'It must be dreadful to be a third-rate citizen who has to make up lies about people to earn a living!' A retraction was quickly printed.

From Congreve, the next logical step was another great Restoration master, Richard Brinsley Sheridan, and this meant moving from the RSC to the Old Vic. The first of these productions was *The Rivals*, once again a familiar theme of young lovers who find their road to romance impeded by the interference of an elderly widow. This time, the role was that of Mrs Malaprop whose habit of muddling her words has become a staple of British comedy. The malapropism has since become associated with Hylda Baker who perhaps gave the best examples of the kind: 'I can say without fear of contraception…', 'I'm prostate with grief!' and 'I'll inhale that remark!' Beryl had incorporated many malapropisms into Marlene ('When I make up me eyes, I like to use lots of massacre on 'em!') but learning the script for *The Rivals* was going to be hard enough without getting to grips with the rather confused contributions Mrs Malaprop makes throughout the play. Beryl said of her dyslexia (or whatever term would be appropriate for her struggle with reading), 'It isn't just that I don't see sentences; I don't really see words, it's all a jumble to me and I have to get it all in the right order before I commit it all to memory.'

Beryl had come to insist on another actor from the company being assigned to help her learn her lines and she was especially keen to find just the right person before she went to the Old Vic. A young actress called Jan Linden was asked if she wouldn't mind helping Beryl. 'I was thrilled to be asked,' Jan remembers. 'I'd sit in her dressing room with her and we'd try to get the lines, but Beryl often came out with malapropisms that were actually far funnier than Sheridan's original lines!' As Beryl and Jan got the script in order, Betty made the place feel like home and, before long, her command of the part was well established.

Beryl had met the rest of the cast which included Anthony Quayle, Christopher Neame, James Aubrey, Enn Reitel and Isla Blair; but as rehearsals began in a draughty old church hall behind Waterloo station, a problem arose which would threaten the entire production. The director was Sir John Clements, a former favourite of Noël Coward's who had worked with some of the biggest names in the business including Robert Donat and Marlene Dietrich. And he didn't like Beryl one bit.

'One sensed that something magical was going to happen in terms of the play but there had been, from the beginning, an underlying tension between Bee and Sir John,' Jan explains. 'I'm afraid he really did not like her and though it was never spoken of or brought into the rehearsal room,

I do recall one incident that should never have happened – and I'm sure it wouldn't have done had Anthony Quayle been present that morning.' In Act Three, Beryl was to be hidden behind a long screen where Mrs Malaprop can eavesdrop on the two lovers, Lydia and Jack. Sir John wanted Beryl to poke her head around the end of the screen, a different end of it for each reaction. Of course, this meant Beryl running backwards and forwards which she found extremely difficult. 'It was an impossibility in one particular instance as there were only about half a dozen words before she had to appear at the other end of the screen to deliver her line! After a second or third unsuccessful attempt, two waving hands appeared above the middle of the screen and a whispered, but very audible, "Knickers!" wafted through the canvas!' It didn't go down well with Sir John.

When it came to the usual note-giving at the end of rehearsal, the full company assembled and were forced to watch in an embarrassed silence as Sir John humiliated Beryl very loudly in front of the entire cast and crew. 'It was horrible, embarrassing and, I think we all felt, totally unjustified,' says Jan. 'Above all, it was humiliating to Beryl; but I remember her so clearly, standing there alone, in the middle of the room and just taking it in, saying nothing.' When he had finished, she got up from her chair and walked away quietly back to her dressing room, breaking the silence with 'Squish squash!' Everyone erupted into laughter; and, whilst Beryl recovered from the incident (not being prone to sulking), Sir John Clements left the production entirely and was replaced by Anthony Quayle who absolutely adored her.

This happened rarely throughout Beryl's later career, but when it did the die was cast and, once out of Beryl's affections, it was almost impossible to get back in. She could instantly take a dislike to somebody simply for what she perceived as rudeness but which may have been a threat. This insecurity always came most to the fore when she was working in theatre and, as more reputable companies sought to include her, she discovered an inferiority complex which she insisted was because the rest of the company had been trained at RADA and not at the end of the pier in Bridlington. Nobody else, at least nobody who put such thoughts to paper, felt this way about Beryl and they regarded her as extremely talented and skilled; but, for Beryl, this insecurity could breed tension and it was coupled with a brutal honesty that some found hard to bear.

As Sue explains, 'If Bee didn't like you, she would tell you. She believed in total honesty which sometimes meant she came across as a little bit blunt or difficult, but she wasn't at all: she just wanted everyone to know where they stood.' She had a very low boredom threshold and, whilst always keen to be polite, she could only stand so much. One afternoon as she left the BBC, Beryl noticed a well-known presenter with a bit of a reputation for being something of a misery, whom we'll call Frank for anonymity's sake.

'Hallo Frank!' she said cheerily. 'How are you?'

Frank then proceeded to tell her exactly how he was with a long and rather depressing tale about how rotten things were. Beryl stood and listened, occasionally saying, 'Yes, but…' or 'Well, the thing is…' only to be cut off by yet more tedium. When he was finished, the presenter simply wandered off without so much as a 'And how are you Beryl?'

Not one to let such an oversight go without comment, Beryl called out, 'Frank dear?!'

He turned. And hitching up her fur coat, adjusting her white feathered hat and pulling on her driving gloves, Beryl said, 'I don't really give a fuck how you are, darling,' and returned to her car. She hadn't intended to be rude; she was simply bored.

It is also true that Beryl had something of a big ego: a comedian has to have a certain amount of gumption to think that they can stand on a stage and entertain an audience, and this confidence only increases with success. And, of course, she loved to be deliberately naughty when the mood took her. Her financial advisor, Innes Hamilton, often visited Beryl at the cottage with his wife who had the unfortunate habit of twitching when she got nervous. Beryl had pointed this out to Will Small, who hadn't noticed it at all; but when the Hamiltons arrived, Beryl began to needle the poor woman so much that she became anxious and twitched. A gleeful Beryl kept winking at Will, who had to excuse himself to avoid embarrassing the poor lady with his giggles. It was all part of Beryl's complex make-up; and, in times of real crisis or stress, her natural safe haven was comedy which she used to dispel tension. Sadly this had not worked with Sir John Clements and she made it clear what her feelings were. Sir John left the production.

With Sir John out of the picture, Beryl could get back to rehearsals with Anthony Quayle as the director and this was a happy coincidence in that the pair had a natural rapport. They worked well together and Beryl always spoke of him with fondness. The play began to take shape and with just ten days to opening night, everyone was quite confident that the unpleasant-ness of the past week had been the only blip in proceedings.

Then Jan got a telephone call. Beryl had tripped over one of the cats at Honeypot and broken her arm. She arrived at rehearsals bound up in a sling and soldiered on. During this time Beryl was word perfect and on top form, doing her best with the physical side of things despite her injury.

'She managed perfectly,' says Jan, 'but then... she tripped over a chair behind her and fell heavily on the broken arm. We all just froze in horror and disbelief and I remember Anthony and I just stared at each other – we knew it was most likely the end of things.'

The second break had compounded the first; and, though Beryl insisted that she would be well enough to go on, it dawned on everyone that she simply couldn't manage. 'It was a sad and disappointing end to so much hard work and graft,' says Jan, 'and I know how much of a blow it was for her to have to give up the role, but never once, either during those weeks or afterwards, did I ever hear her complain or bewail her fate.'

When Anthony Quayle saw some of the original press photographs for the production, he looked at them and said wistfully, 'Ah Jan. That was the production that never was.' Beryl's next foray into Restoration comedy would have to wait until 1983, and all plans for a second Sheridan play were postponed to allow her to recover.

The weeks at Honeypot recuperating were agony for Beryl, not because of any physical pain but because she knew she was missing out on a good thing. By May, she was well enough to make a brief appearance in another *Play for Today* along with a cameo in the Elaine Stritch and Donald Sinden comedy, *Two's Company*. Stritch was notoriously difficult, battling with alcoholism and prone to fits of rage, but if there was any rift or animosity between the two women it hasn't been documented; and when Elaine visited London in 1983 to see Donald Sinden in *A School for Scandal* which also featured Beryl as Mrs Cantour, Elaine was glowing with praise for Beryl in the dressing room.

Two's Company was a brief role, but a memorable one. It was followed by an offer from Peter Rogers and Gerald Thomas to make her only appearance in a *Carry On* film. It may seem that Beryl had been previously well placed to take a role in the series. After all, she was extremely close to

Hattie Jacques from her *Archie* days. It was even suggested that the two replace the Baddeley Sisters, Angela and Hermione, in *Island Fling* for the BBC Home Service in the early fifties. Beryl would always speak kindly of Hattie saying, 'I felt much richer by working with her, a lovely, lovely lady. Dead sexy!'

Likewise, Beryl had been delighted to work with Joan Sims in *Beryl Reid Says Good Evening* and always said that Joan was 'a fuzzy funny little peach' whom she greatly admired. She was no stranger to Kenneth Connor or Jack Douglas either; and so it seemed that Beryl would have fitted very easily into the *Carry On* team. The truth of the matter was that Beryl had been asked to appear in them before, but she was loath to become caught in a serial, a constant bugbear of hers; and, whilst the roles were subtly changed or renamed with each foray into the *Carry On* franchise, towards the end they had simply become vehicles for the company to portray a version of themselves around a theme and, sometimes, a rather poor script.

Emmannuelle was the thirtieth film in the *Carry On* series and was also destined to be the last of the genre in the true sense of the word. Whilst *Carry on Columbus* was released in 1992, even those who appeared in it are dismissive of it, regarding it as a disastrous attempt to revive the familiarity of a much-loved format but which lacked the warmth of the regular cast, most of whom had died the previous decade. *Emmannuelle* was intended to be a parody of the X-rated soft porn films of the same name and lead the *Carry Ons* out of seaside postcard humour and more into the *Confessions* style. Whilst we think of the *Carry Ons* as family-friendly today, *Emmannuelle* was branded with a double-A rating because the female lead, Suzanne Danielle, showed considerably more flesh than was considered suitable for children, and only those over the age of fourteen were allowed into the cinema to see it.

Emmannuelle featured a few of the original *Carry On* cast but, of the usual band of players, only Peter Butterworth, Kenneth Williams, Jack Douglas, Kenneth Connor and Joan Sims appeared, and as Joan Sims later said, 'It was really out of loyalty by that point I'm afraid; the guts had gone out of it.' Beryl was cast as Mrs Valentine, the mother of a man seduced on Concorde by Emmannuelle who then becomes obsessed with her. Mrs Valentine tries to convince her son Theodore to forget all about it, but her pleas fall on deaf ears and he takes Emmannuelle's story to the newspapers.

Whilst it sounds a reasonable plot on which to hang a *Carry On*, most of the film was focused on Suzanne Danielle jumping into bed with the majority of the cast.

Carry On Emmannuelle has since been dubbed 'the worst movie ever', 'embarrassingly feeble' and 'the death sentence for *Carry On*'; the reviewer Philip French said of it: 'This relentless sequence of badly written, badly timed dirty jokes is surely one of the most morally and aesthetically offensive pictures to emerge from a British studio.' Particularly cringeworthy is a scene in which a naked parachuting Kenneth Williams descends into the path of a weather vane on a church roof. It felt wrong, a betrayal almost, and Beryl was rather relieved that her role had been a tiny one. She felt the entire project vulgar; though her sense of humour could be naughty, Beryl did take issue with anything she felt too blue and this was very much in keeping with the national mood of the time among women of Beryl's generation. Times were changing and Britain was being assaulted by the lady in the winged specs and the bird's-nest hat: Mary Whitehouse.

Mrs Whitehouse and her famous group of moral maidens, the National Viewers' and Listeners' Association, were now policing everything on stage and screen and rattling off furious letters, petitions, even launching court cases against that which they deemed to be filth – and *Emmannuelle* was most definitely in their sights. But the success of Mrs Whitehouse was attributable to more than just a generation of appalled older viewers. Britain was about to elect its first female Prime Minister; and, ironically, Beryl (who had done her fair share of pushing the limits in comedy) became a firm supporter of both Mary Whitehouse and Margaret Thatcher.

Although Conservative with a big C, Beryl wasn't a very political person and this made it all the more bizarre when some bright spark at the BBC thought her the perfect guest for *Any Questions* with Enoch Powell as a fellow panellist. It sounds to be the most unlikely clash of personalities, and yet Beryl's conservatism was born of two things: a kind of inverted snobbery and her rather picture-book view of how the world should be. For someone who had challenged apartheid, broken barriers in lesbian and gay cinema and had more than once been castigated by the BBC for going too far in a live broadcast, Beryl wasn't exactly a poster girl for the Tories; but, like many women of the age, she was extremely taken with Mrs Thatcher – perhaps because she was a mother, perhaps because she dressed well. Either way, Beryl's one appearance on *Any Questions* has disappeared from the BBC radio archives and one can only imagine the nature of the discussion between Miss Beryl Reid, actress and comedienne, and Enoch Powell, renowned right-winger with a passion for Wagner.

Unlike many in her industry, Beryl never felt that she needed to involve herself with Equity meetings or protests; she didn't take on causes other than to support local children's charities and, of course, the Cats Protection League or the RSPCA. She had very little time for or interest in 'issues', and whilst many celebrities of the time felt it necessary on chat shows to comment on the way things were, often siding with or against the government, Beryl took on a regal attitude towards it all and kept herself above it. She would rather be liked than challenged; and in 1979, shortly after Mrs Thatcher's landslide victory, Beryl made her first appearance on a show which became indelibly associated with her.

In the ever-present fondness for nostalgia, people look back at *Blankety Blank* and remember the hideously tacky prizes and Sir Terry's wand-like microphone being bent out of all recognition by Kenny Everett. But for many, the centre spot on the top row provides another memory. This was Beryl's seat and, from her first appearance to her last, she reigned supreme from the special place always reserved just for her.

Blankety Blank was based on the American quiz show *Match Game* created by Frank Wayne. The Australian Network Ten had changed the format and the BBC bought it as a vehicle for Sir Terry Wogan. As the host, Sir Terry posed questions to contestants who had to fill in the missing blank or blanks in a sentence and hope that the panel of six celebrities had reached the same conclusion. Whilst other quiz shows of the time offered a cash prize or a holiday, the offerings on *Blankety Blank* were famously poor with a hostess trolley or a sunlounger being considered a big win.

The celebrities chosen were always of the same blend to ensure the perfect pace of the show, with an older male comedian on the top row nearest to Sir Terry for initial patter to warm up the audience (and the panel), an older lady next to him and, on the bottom row, a pretty starlet seated next to a younger comedian. The remaining two spaces were taken by those who may or may not have been as well known as the others.

For Beryl, *Blankety Blank* allowed her to create a few running jokes such as 'the little man under the desk'. After writing their answer on a card, each celebrity would dispose of it by dropping it through a slot, and so Beryl invented a little man whose job it was to sit there and catch the cards as they fell. When she felt things were getting a little quiet, she'd exclaim, 'Oh stop it dear! We're on the telly you know!' and wriggle around with a naughty grin. Sir Terry would descend into giggles and the audience roared as she came out with the answers which were usually the most risqué.

Sir Terry recalled: 'Her heart was in light entertainment which is why she became the lynchpin of *Blankety Blank*. It was the perfect setting for her quick wit, sharp tongue and the warmth the viewing public loved. We struck a responsive chord from the very first show and, although others came and went, she was always my special guest. I always felt she was more than that. Beryl was my dear friend.'

Beryl felt Sir Terry could have been slightly more than that. Though he was very happily married and though she was much older than him, Beryl was so sweet on Wogan that, whenever she was asked to make an appearance on his chat show, she would insist that other engagements be cancelled to allow her to do it. She was fiercely loyal to him and their close friendship shone through.

Sometimes, Beryl could aggravate a host. If the cameras were rolling, she was 'on' and she would occasionally step on someone else's punchline or interrupt a story, which often happened on *Blankety Blank*. In one episode where Paul Daniels is being particularly trying, Beryl comes to the rescue of a clearly frustrated Terry Wogan by shouting loudly, 'Oh knickers! I've left the immersion on!' Daniels looks upwards with daggers, but Beryl simply smiles and feigns ignorance of the fact that she's just upstaged him, a typically Beryl tactic for deflating an ego bigger than her own.

She wasn't well paid for *Blankety Blank*, taking home just £100 an episode in contrast to the two or three thousand pounds fee she could expect from a feature film. Yet Beryl had a loyalty to the programme and to Sir Terry himself. 'I instantly had a great feeling of being at home with him,' she wrote in her memoirs. 'I have a great feeling of safety with him too.' She was full of gratitude for the opportunity and, though many frowned upon the show and tried to paint it as lowest-common-denominator light entertainment, Beryl understood that the public loved it and that it was extremely funny if the magic was right and the panellists showed off their talents.

'I play so many parts that it's wonderful to be given that kind of chance for a minute and be totally abandoned,' she said. 'You know it can all be cut out if you say the wrong thing.' And yet she never did.

Contestants almost always chose her as the panellist they wanted to be matched up with in the final head-to-head round, but it came at a cost to Beryl. If she gave an answer which saw the contestant lose, she would feel so guilty that she'd insist on paying for the top prize herself and handing it over. If you chose Beryl, you had a decent chance of going home with something!

Her success on *Blankety Blank* put her in constant demand for other game shows – *Celebrity Squares*, *Give Us a Clue*, *Looks Familiar* – and, whilst poorly paid by comparison, she did enjoy the social side of them and felt that they provided a constant showcase. Lurching around a set miming the word 'goat' wasn't exactly dignified, but doing these regularly meant that people would remember her and her body of work would never be forgotten, a constant theme in Beryl's life.

Beryl's appearances on *Blankety Blank* came to an end in 1984 when Sir Terry was replaced as the host by Les Dawson. It had been Wogan's own decision to leave and the producers assumed that Beryl would be happy to stay; but, whilst she respected his skill, Beryl was not very keen on Les Dawson's approach. 'He laughs at you, not with you,' she insisted, and this was disagreeable for Beryl who could be oversensitive at times.

In the mornings, Beryl would put on a face 'from memory' with a little powder and lipstick before tucking her hair under a straw hat and taking a turn in the garden. One summer's afternoon, a handsome young man in a canoe was coming along the river when he noticed her and stopped.

'Didn't you used to be a famous actress?' he said.

From behind her large dark sunglasses, Beryl said with a touch of steel in her voice: 'Well I rather hope I still am, dear.'

*

Beryl was never snobbish about *Blankety Blank* or indeed any of the parts she took on which her contemporaries may have shied away from. But for those involved with producing the television adaptation of John le Carré's novel *Tinker Tailor Soldier Spy*, Beryl Reid would not have been an immediate choice. Indeed, the day before her audition, Beryl had made a brief appearance on a Ronnie Corbett BBC comedy special and this only emphasised her music-hall background. *Tinker* was an extremely serious piece, exploiting the very real fears of the time that the USSR was secretly infiltrating the British Secret Service. It tells the story of retired spy George Smiley who makes it his mission to discover the truth about a suspected double agent; in the third episode, he seeks the advice of his old boss and ally in the service, Connie Sachs.

The part of Connie was totally incongruous with the sort of thing Beryl was taking on at the time and there was absolutely no trace of comedy in it. Whilst *Sister George* and *Mr Sloane* are considered modern classics, they were of course supposed to be rather funny despite some extremely bleak moments; in contrast, this role would demand an absolute abandonment of everything Beryl was. Chased out of the service, Sachs is a lonely spinster consumed by guilt, longing and rejection. She misses the agents whom she refers to as 'her boys' and she is crippled by arthritis. Living in a basement flat, she gives lessons to students ('the blockheads') and her only companions are a mangy dog and a bottle of whisky. She is tearful and broken, desperate for one last kiss from George Smiley as validation that her struggles have all been worthwhile.

Measure this against one of Beryl's more recent performances as a female plumber dressed as a bee in a Peter Sellers sketch and you begin to understand the original reticence the production team must have had, but Beryl's audition showed promise and she was given the part. She was especially keen to work with Sir Alec Guinness and, whilst he frightened her a little, she set to work on trying to prove herself capable.

Guinness had trained at the Old Vic and was primarily known as a great Shakespearean actor before his foray into Ealing comedies. But by the time Beryl came to work with him, he had acquired the same mysterious reverence that accompanied Sir John Gielgud or Sir John Mills. *Star Wars* had made him a megastar throughout the world; and, though he was generally regarded as a genial man, he was naturally dedicated to his craft and demanded the very best from his colleagues. He was known to work actors to death in pursuit of the perfect scene and, knowing full well that this was the case, Beryl diligently rehearsed her appearance at Honeypot. For weeks on end she tried to find the essence of the character but her confidence faltered slightly.

'I thought [that] part was something totally beyond me but I tend to think that before I get to grips with them,' she wrote in her memoirs. 'There was no rehearsal for Connie; I was asked to go to Oxford and it was completely up to me to do the learning before I went.'

Not having run the lines with Sir Alec, she was a little flustered as she readied herself for the one scene she had with him which would run to just over seven minutes in total. The make-up department removed every scrap of make-up from her face and ruddied her complexion with red stipple paint to suggest that Connie was an alcoholic. Noting that she was arthritic, Beryl went as far into the character as she could and came up with a staggered walk. She even crooked her hands so that when she raised her whisky glass, she had to do so holding it between her thumbs, attention to detail easily overlooked but which gives an insight into the mind of Beryl as a serious actress who wanted to inhabit her character totally in a way she wasn't often able to do.

The scene was filmed in a tiny house in Oxford. The first time Beryl met Sir Alec was minutes before the take and, overcome with it all, she immediately fluffed her lines shrieking, 'Oh knickers! I've forgotten your bloody name!' as soon as she opened the door of Connie's flat to reveal George Smiley standing behind it. An added complication was a rather eager dog which refused to lie quietly on the couch and went mad every time Sir Alec rang the doorbell. It was given a tranquilliser and thereafter lay quietly – if not a little too quietly – next to Beryl as the scene continued.

Author John le Carré, whose brainchild *Tinker Tailor* was, has always defending the casting and insisted that Beryl was the right choice for Connie. 'She played her magically, bringing a maverick pathos and beauty to the part of a retired vestal of the British Secret Service,' he said. 'She shamelessly upstaged Alec Guinness, but he was wise enough and large enough to let it happen, knowing that the comedienne's imp in her would never let her go. She was in her fifties when I met her, rakish and twinkly, very quick to sum you up and if necessary, put you down! She was a wonderful mix of a *bête intellectuelle* and a boozy fairground fortune-teller, and in rehearsal she never did the same thing twice. I suspect she was much the same in life.'

There has been a suggestion that Alec Guinness didn't care for Beryl or that he found her difficult. Whilst it's true that he put her through her paces during the filming, both Guinness and Beryl took direction from John Irvin who wanted to bring out the bitterness in Connie rather than just the sadness and regret, and there are no grounds to the suggestion that Guinness overworked Beryl or made her feel unwelcome on the set. She had doubts about her own performance as Connie, but she was only too happy to reprise the role four years later for *Smiley's People*; and so, had there been any animosity between Beryl and Sir Alec, it certainly didn't find its way into their working relationship. She would casually remark that she didn't like Guinness at all, but again this seems to have been born of that same inferiority complex she had. If messages were left by certain illustrious names, Beryl refused to call them back, not as a snub but rather because she couldn't possibly think what to say to them – or why they wanted to speak to her.

When production closed on *Tinker*, Beryl immediately travelled to Bristol where she'd agreed to join the company of a new Peter Nichols play which was to open at the Bristol Old Vic. She would play Maud in *Born in the Gardens*, an eccentric mother who lives in a crumbling Victorian house with her son. As he bashes away on his drumkit, Maud offers advice to a mute television set with an almost Baby Jane-like eccentricity.

Beryl was not the first choice for the part, as Peter Nichols explains: 'My thoughts only went so far as a local production so I wanted the Bristolian actress Constance Chapman to play Maud. She'd already been in several TV plays of mine and knew how to do the local accent, but she was unavailable so it was a case of a far more famous star being a second choice.'

It was whilst in rehearsals for *Born in the Gardens* that Beryl got a phone call to tell her that she'd been nominated for a BAFTA Award. She was suitably pleased and called her brother Roy in Greasby to tell him her news; but she quickly became aware that Roy wasn't a well man.

For some time, Roy's family had been concerned that he was working too hard, and his wife Pat and children Sue and Peter tried to convince him to take early retirement. But like Beryl, his work ethic was so strong that he felt he'd be letting the company and his family down if he did so; and he continued to work long hours, certain that he had to provide for his family for as long as possible. Beryl knew of their concerns but she was unable to visit Roy and discuss the matter in person. She was simply too busy, and she'd even declined an invitation to the BAFTA Awards ceremony, stuck as she was in Bristol learning her lines and blocking her scenes. (In the event, the BAFTA went to Cheryl Campbell for her portrayal of Vera Brittain in *Testament of Youth*.)

The cast of *Born in the Gardens* was a small one and included Barry Foster (better known as 'Van der Valk'), Peter Bowles and the actress Jennie

Linden. Nichols recalls: 'My memory is of a happy month rehearsing, just the four actors and an acting stage manager and sometimes, their understudies. They were a sparky quartet and I wasn't the sort of director who gave them the support and affection actors always need.'

It's fair to say that Beryl could sometimes demand enormous attention from her directors, but this was generally if she didn't like them very much. If she was co-operative, it meant that she trusted them and shrugged off the temptation to test them; but, as ever, her ego could be fragile and easily bruised. In the middle of rehearsals, the BBC debuted its latest sitcom, *To the Manor Born*, starring Dame Penelope Keith and Peter Bowles. Audiences lapped it up from the very first episode, and so the following morning as Peter and Beryl walked through Bristol, it wasn't calls of 'Hallo Beryl!' which filled the streets; rather, the public wanted to shake hands with Richard DeVere.

This grated with Beryl but Peter Bowles insists that he never noted any real animosity between them. 'I never felt that Beryl didn't like me, and I certainly liked her: she was brilliant, amusing and kind. I was going from Somerset where we were filming *To the Manor Born* and then up to Leeds where we were recording *Only When I Laugh* and Bristol was in the middle of it all, so if there was any tension between Beryl and me, I didn't really have the time to notice it.'

But Beryl did retain a bee in her bonnet. At a drinks party to celebrate the hundredth performance of the show after it had transferred to the Globe Theatre in Shaftesbury Avenue, Beryl confided to Peter Nichols: 'If you'd tried to cast the most difficult and troublesome couple of men in the world, you couldn't have done better... oh! Hullo Peter!' Of course, Peter Bowles had arrived just in time to overhear Beryl's last remark.

Sometimes, Beryl could be withering without realising how it may be taken by her victim. During rehearsals in Bristol, Beryl decided that she'd flick a feather duster across the drum kit during one of Barry Foster's major speeches. It quickly distracted him.

'Are you going to be doing that on the night, dear?' he asked.

'Oh no, darling, not if you don't like it!' Beryl cooed, adding sternly, 'I'll just stand here stock still.'

Barry pictured it. 'No... don't do that either.'

Whilst staying in Bristol, Beryl was to meet someone who would become an important friend and confidant for the rest of her life. Paul

Strike was a young actor living in Bristol studying at drama school, and one day the actor David Trevena contacted him to ask if he might like to help an actress out with her lines for an upcoming play at the Old Vic. It would be good experience and, whilst Trevena didn't tell Paul who the actress was at first, eventually he relented and Paul agreed.

Beryl's digs were located at the top of several flights of stairs and when Paul arrived, she cooed down, 'I'm up here darling! Where the carpet ends!' Over a bottle of wine, the two went through Beryl's lines for *Born in the Gardens*; and as the evening went on, they realised that they enjoyed each other's company enormously.

He invited her for Sunday lunch, much to the horror of his partner Will. 'Paul told me that he'd invited somebody for lunch and then he told me it was Beryl Reid. That didn't faze me, but the night before she came, she was on local television plugging the play and when she was asked what she'd have been had she not been an actress, she said, "A chef! I love to cook," and that filled me with absolute dread and panic. I kept it very simple and when Beryl arrived, all in black, I was terrified of her; but when we went through to the dining room and she saw the effort I'd gone to, she said, "Oh, I was expecting lunch! This is a five-act drama!" and that really broke the ice.'

Paul continues: 'We kept it simple, we made her feel welcome and we didn't treat her like a big star, we didn't fawn over her. At the end of the dinner, I brought in coffee and she pulled out a little hip flask and had a brandy and the whole evening was really very lovely.' The three spent a lot of time together preparing for the opening night, but nobody could have predicted what happened next.

On the morning of the day the show was due to open, Beryl got a call from her sister-in-law Pat. Roy had died suddenly at the age of sixty-four. Beryl was absolutely distraught and she considered pulling out of the run entirely. Immediately the company went into a panic. 'I asked the producer if he could possibly postpone the opening as it looked likely she wouldn't make it through the play,' says Peter Nichols, 'but he said he couldn't. The London critics had all been invited down.' Beryl had no choice.

Nichols warned the other actors to give her any support she needed, but in the end, 'Beryl, star that she was, sailed through it like a three-masted clipper.' No easy task considering that the play opened with a coffin on stage. Just as she didn't make an exception to her 'no funerals' rule for her mother or her father, Beryl chose to remain with the production rather than attend Roy's burial. That night, she bravely attended the after-show party, but she was clearly in low spirits and all she really wanted to do was to go back to her digs and wrap herself around a brandy bottle. She sent flowers for the funeral and offered support to Roy's wife on the telephone; and thus began daily calls to Pat to ensure that everything was as it should be. When Pat died, the calls came instead to their daughter Sue. There wasn't even time to visit the family after the run in Bristol ended as the play immediately transferred to London's Globe Theatre for an extended run.

Peter Nichols suggests that the success of the piece owed more to the cast than to his play. 'Beryl was a wonderful actress,' he explains. 'She was a born performer with a contagious twinkle that made audiences love her to bits.' And of course, she constantly entertained the company with funny stories. In the play, Beryl had to mistake the word 'duplex' for 'Durex' which brought a roar of laughter from the audience. When a New York producer enthused that the play might go to Broadway, he asked Beryl what she felt about the possibility.

'Do you know what a Durex is, dear?' she said, full of innocence.

'No.'

'Then I don't think it could.'

Born in the Gardens had been an extremely difficult run, not because Beryl hadn't enjoyed the piece but because she'd had to soldier through it ever aware that she had now lost both of her parents and her brother. She was the only member of the original Reid family left, and sadly the recognition Beryl was now receiving for her roles had come that little bit too late to be shared with those who had been there at the start.

To offer a little light at the end of the tunnel, she was nominated for an award for Best Comedy Performance of the Year by the Society of West End Theatres for her role as Maud. Maureen Lipman remembers seeing the performance she gave and insists it was the best thing Beryl had ever done, a view shared by an old friend and colleague Sir Norman Wisdom who wrote to Beryl saying, 'All lovely things are born in the garden – which rose bush did your mother find you under? Beryl, I love you.'

At the awards ceremony, her name was read out alongside those of Edward Duke, Ben Kingsley and a young actress from Birmingham called Julie Walters, starring in a Willie Russell play, *Educating Rita*. Beryl won.

In 1984, the Society of West End Theatre Awards changed their name. Now, they are simply known best as the Oliviers.

Chapter Eight

'Life's not all violinists and pigeons, is it?'

WHEN PAUL AND WILL SAID GOODBYE TO BERYL before they departed for a two-week holiday, they assumed that their association with her had reached its natural end; but now invitations to Honeypot turned into a more semi-permanent arrangement with the pair being invited to spend the night there and to fit into the furniture of Beryl's life.

It afforded them the privilege of seeing Beryl at her best and most quirky. By the front door to Honeypot were two shotguns (and a third kept by her bed just in case) and, thanks to her 'open-door' policy, they were stolen. 'Get me two more would you, Paul darling?' she asked, not taking into account that she would actually need a licence. Paul was forced to trawl through the *Exchange and Mart* looking for a pair.

And then there was another of Beryl's strange little phrases: 'walling it'. Beryl was an adventurous cook, but it didn't always work out as she'd planned. 'Oh, that's terrible,' she'd wail. 'Wall it!' – by which she meant, take the frying pan outside and literally hurl it at the wall. A few months after Beryl's death, Will had the task of going through the kitchen cupboards to clear them and found that every single frying pan was bent and buckled, the result of frequent 'wallings'!

Honeypot was rarely silent. As well as Paul and Will, there were visits from Sue and her husband Michael; colleagues and co-stars such as Harry Secombe and Patrick Cargill came for lunches and dinners, and there was a succession of housekeepers, a regular chauffeur (Rick) and Muriel who inevitably arrived with talk of an injured kitten who would be just perfect for Beryl. The idea that Beryl lived a lonely existence by the river is one of the many myths surrounding her life that have been incorporated into the legend.

Taxi drivers in Wraysbury specialised in Reid lore, recounting tales such as: 'The dining room is round and turns round to follow the sun you know,' and the most bizarre, 'Under the living room is a round crypt and when a cat dies, she has it mummified and puts it on a shelf down there!'

Beryl's eccentricity was never regarded as such by those closest to her, and neither did Beryl consider herself to be in any way unusual, a point she made ferociously to Russell Harty: 'I'm really not eccentric at all, I just play eccentrics. My life is perfectly normal… whatever that is. Is your life normal?'

By 1975, her career veered either towards the frilly and silly or the serious and straight. For example, in the afternoon she might record an episode of *Blankety Blank* or *Give Us a Clue*, pretending to be a parrot for Lionel Blair, before rushing off to the National Theatre to appear as Donna Katherina in Bill Bryden's adaptation of *Il Campiello*, an 18th century Venetian comedy by Carlo Goldoni. During one of Beryl's daily chats to Sue, Sue remarked, 'It's all about striking a happy medium, isn't it Beryl?' to which Beryl replied, 'Yes. And when I find one, I'll strike it!'

Beryl already had a devoted legion of fans under her belt; and though theatreland was once again in awe of her, she was about to take on something quite different. Many children who had marvelled at Monica in the 1950s had now grown up and were equally amazed as adults by her dramatic talents which had just been displayed in *Tinker Tailor Soldier Spy*. A return to a children's series may not have been a logical step, but when Beryl was offered the chance to appear in a run of programmes for Yorkshire Television specifically designed for children in 1981, she jumped at it.

This was slightly ironic as Beryl really couldn't get along with small children at all. It wasn't that she had a 'Mommie Dearest' attitude; it was simply that, until they could have a conversation with her and until she could entertain them, she had very little interest in them. (Despite this, it's worth noting that she never wavered in her support for a local school for children with learning difficulties; so adored was she at Birchfield School that the children even made a brief appearance on Beryl's *This is Your Life* in 1976, presenting her with a painting of Honeypot Cottage.)

The premise of the show (given a working title of *Mooncat*) was that a green cat from another planet had beamed down to earth and had to be educated in the ways of the world. This gave the presenters an ideal opportunity to raise important themes in each episode, such as 'Sorry', an episode about apologies. Originally a vehicle for Beryl and the comedian and musician Neil Innes, it was now renamed *Get Up and Go!* with Mooncat the puppet operated by David Claridge who later had huge success as the man behind Roland Rat. Beryl was offered twenty-six episodes, to be filmed over three months in Leeds; the twenty-six would be repeated so as to ensure that every week, Mooncat was being shown somewhere in the country.

By the time filming began, Neil Innes had been replaced with a younger actor and songwriter called Stephen Boxer. Beryl and Stephen lived in a brightly coloured house with Mooncat; as well as their dialogue with him, there were songs (written by Stephen), a cartoon (voiced by them both), a little VT about the topic of the day (making use of the crew as extras), and of course a story read in *Jackanory* fashion, usually by Beryl. The characters were always the same and allowed Beryl to show off her vocal talents – though it was perhaps a little difficult to bring any sincerity to an elephant called Mrs Pinkerton-Trunks so soon after her success as Connie Sachs.

That said, Beryl never regarded *Get Up and Go!* as a step down the ladder. It was no secret what sort of work she preferred, and the target audience may not have been the one she wanted; but when she arrived for work on the first day, everyone was certain that she was happy to be there.

Stephen Boxer remembers that first meeting: 'I hadn't done a lot of telly before, and I remember I turned up for the first episode and I hadn't washed my hair which was quite long in those days. The wigs department immediately went into a spin and gave me this dry shampoo stuff that just made it worse and so I looked like I'd just got out of bed; and there was Beryl, beautifully turned out and very smart. To me, she was the star of *Sister George* and the Joe Orton plays, so I was very excited to work with her and she and I got on fine. She had a big ego of course, but based on her talent, not unjustifiably. She had a lot of confidence; age was probably beginning to be a bit of an issue and so we made sure we rehearsed as much as we could, but we were absolutely fine together.' Of course, there was one issue which nobody had considered and perhaps emphasises the naivety of the time. What on earth was a sixty-year-old woman doing living alone with a young, handsome thirty-year-old and a big green extraterrestrial cat?

The filming for *Get Up and Go!* was quite an arduous business. Time was of the essence and most scenes were done with one take, meaning that there was little manoeuvring room for mistake or improvisation. This suited Beryl, who preferred to get things done quickly; but her recent successes had brought out something of the diva in her, a side of Beryl not usually seen on a set. As the only female and very much as Queen Bee of the lot, she could pretty much do as she pleased and that suited her enormously. This sometimes meant a clash with David Claridge who operated (and voiced) Mooncat.

'Mooncat needed quite a lot of camera time,' explains Stephen. 'David Claridge would have to film all his things separately and then we'd film the background into which Mooncat was placed, and so it was a very high-maintenance thing and David was very much a perfectionist who wanted to get things right and all this took time. On this particular day, we were recording an episode called "Circus" which had Mooncat as the ringmaster and Beryl and me as clowns. Beryl was wearing a pierrot costume she'd designed specifically for it and she'd spent a long time putting on this clown make-up, and we were hanging around quite a lot. The director, Len Lurcuck, was very sweet and kept saying, "Not long now, not long now," but it was too much for Beryl and suddenly, she shot up out of her chair and burst into tears. "It seems Mooncat is getting all the close-ups!" she said and then stomped off to her dressing room and wouldn't come out. Len had to go down and mollify her and soothe her ego a little and then she came back; but in the take, there's mascara smudged down her face and it's really quite poignant, quite literally the tears of a clown.'

Sometimes, however, it was her training (and not her ego) which kicked in as a second instinct. As Stephen remembers: 'I will never forget the day that we were in the studio, in this extremely colourful set, waiting to start work and we'd have a little meeting before we began. "Morning Beryl!", "Morning Stephen!" and then we'd get down to the script. Now, there were banks of lights in this studio but she'd decided that one was her key light which is so music hall – it was her spotlight. We started filming, I walked onto the set, "Morning Beryl!", "Morning Stephen!" as usual and then *bang!* – she elbowed me hard in the ribs! Now that was Beryl saying, "Get out of my light!" But I could understand that, it was a different school she came from; and she was very lovely about my songs and things, she was complimentary, so I could forgive anything like that if it happened.' Anyone who dared take her on would be greeted with the familiar warning, 'I've seen off two husbands, I can see you off as well!'

During filming, Beryl stayed in a smart suite at the Queen's Hotel whilst the rest of the cast and crew shared small flats they'd rented. After a day in the studio, they'd often decamp to a local restaurant and it was there that Stephen saw the best of her. 'She would hold court, she'd have a few drinks, and she'd tell stories and anecdotes, some of them quite rude and racy but always funny. She was never cruel; she could be catty, but it was funny. And that made her a joy to be with.'

Beryl's acid tongue is legendary and people who mistook her for a sweet old lady living in a cottage by the river with her cats were sometimes in for a shock. When Beryl was starring in *Born in the Gardens* at the Bristol Old Vic in 1979, she arrived at the theatre resplendent in fur coat and pillbox hat, her dimpled smile and twinkly eyes giving her that 'Queen Mother' effect which people recognised her by. An innocent box office assistant rushed to greet her but asked if she would mind coming in not through the main door but, rather, by the stage door at the side of building.

'You mean the servants' entrance?' Beryl questioned dangerously.

'Oh, no no, I didn't mean…'

'I've been thrown out of better digs than this before; fuck you, I'm going back to London!' And off she swept.

Even those she adored were not spared a gentle ribbing. When Peter Brough was feeling a little sore over comments made about his skills as a ventriloquist he asked her, 'Beryl, tell me honestly, can you see my lips move?' to which Beryl replied, 'Only when Archie's talking, dear.'

But her diva moments were rare on the set of *Get Up and Go!* and Beryl struck up a close friendship with Stephen. 'I didn't compete with her,' he says. 'Beryl was a star and she knew it. She was loud about it and she was very much "Look at me!" I was saying "Look at me!" as well – but quietly. So I wasn't a threat to her and I wasn't going to take any of the spotlight from her which meant we were well matched. Beryl was brought up in a style that demanded attention, I wasn't, so we could really overcome that battle for the camera quite quickly.'

Her practical side showed itself one afternoon when she simply couldn't get the hang of the chromakey (the name given to the green-screen technique). Sometimes, Stephen and Beryl would find themselves performing to a masking-tape cross on the floor where Mooncat would later be, but this meant that Beryl had no eyeline and so sometimes she'd look directly into the camera or over Stephen's shoulder when she should have been looking at Mooncat. Finally, she marched out of the studio to her car and came back with an enormous hat box. She fished out a pink hat with silk flowers on it, plonked it on the top of the box and declared, 'Now that's Mooncat!'

Beginning in 1981, *Get Up and Go!* meant that Beryl had a permanent fixture in her diary and everything else had to be worked around it for those three months of the year. Now in her sixties, she had decided that pantomime was not only too exhausting but slightly humiliating. When she heard that friend and co-star Peggy Mount was to play the Good Fairy in a pantomime in 1986, Beryl said, 'I should shoot myself if that happened to me at my time of life.'

Bizarrely, Beryl was now fitting in Mooncat around appearances in Restoration comedies, poetry recordings and even a drama series about pre-Home Rule Ireland. And there was something lurking in the background, initially passed off as arthritis but which would soon make things somewhat impossible. Nothing seemed to fit or to flow; Beryl's working life was becoming very haphazard and whilst, in the past, she might focus on a serious role for a few months before returning to comedy, now it was a mixture of everything and anything.

By 1983, she was finding it harder to commit to *Get Up and Go!* and, with new offers of work coming in, she decided that it was time for her to move on. The show was redesigned with Stephen taking up residence with Mooncat in a junk shop. The 'Beryl Reid voice' was provided by a variety of female stars of the day who appeared in each episode to narrate the story and to take part in the sketches, most notably Pat Coombes as a haphazard WPC! But naturally the legacy of her association with children's television had won her a new legion of fans, and for years to come she'd be approached by teenagers who were incredibly fond of her, something she couldn't quite understand.

'I think they're going to mug me,' she'd say, 'and then they ask me where Mooncat is!'

At the same time there was another whole new audience who were only too willing to celebrate Beryl's work in a unique way. Beryl had cemented her place as a gay icon; but when this was put to her in later years, she said, 'That's Sister George, of course. They think I'm like her but I'm really not.' Yet she welcomed the love of the gay community wholeheartedly: 'The homosexual boys are always so sweet with me, they are such darlings; but I do explain that I'm not a lesbian, and that doesn't seem to upset them too much. I always feel they'll be terribly disappointed when they find out!'

It was more than Sister George. Beryl's story was identifiable: an eccentric, colourful, confident single lady who had fought her battles and won. She was funny, she was extravagant – but also she was extremely camp. This led to confusion when she was asked if she might consider doing 'An Evening with Beryl Reid' in Manchester in 1985. Since 1978, ITV had put on gala specials for comedians including Jasper Carrot, Dame Edna Everage, Kenneth Williams and Joan Rivers who had given an hour's set, usually in the context of a look back at their career, with a star-studded audience. For weeks Beryl spoke of nothing else. She travelled from Wraysbury to Manchester by car, never once questioning why there hadn't been a rehearsal or a meeting; and not knowing what to expect, she was stunned when the car pulled up outside a nightclub. She hadn't been booked for *An Audience With...* at all. She'd been asked to tell a few jokes and stories in a gay bar in Canal Street. 'I take it Peter Ustinov isn't here then?' she mused. Luff was given a strong dressing-down and told to ask as many questions as possible in the future. It was the only bump in the road of their long association and friendship.

As a seasoned actress and music-hall comedienne, very little fazed Beryl; but occasionally the new way of doing things did appear to be altogether too much. In 1982, she agreed to make a cameo appearance in the *Doctor Who* story 'Earthshock' with fifth doctor, Peter Davison. It was producer John Nathan-Turner who suggested Beryl for the role of Briggs, but nobody could quite have foreseen what would actually happen. For a dyslexic who found scripts difficult to decipher anyway, the sci-fi lingo threw her off and Nathan-Turner was not best pleased when Beryl pondered loudly: 'Warp Drive? That's just off Earl's Court, isn't it dear?' For some bizarre reason, the costume department decided to give Beryl a bright red bouffant and to stuff her into a skintight black PVC catsuit with thigh-length boots. The world may not have expected to see Monica the Naughty Schoolgirl in bondage attire giving a karate chop, but there it was.

Beryl Reid was fighting the Cybermen and trying desperately to be sincere; but, as Peter Davison remembers, 'She had absolutely no idea what was going on. She'd turn round after a take and say, "I have no idea what I just said darling!" She never quite understood the zeal of the *Doctor Who* fans either. She dutifully signed things as "Captain Briggs" but said, "They're quite bizarre people, you know. They think it's all real!" '

In 1981, the popular sitcom *Agony* was in its third series. Maureen Lipman played Jane Lucas, a successful agony aunt who is an expert at giving advice to others but who can't really keep her own private life in order. The series was written by Stan Hey and Andrew Nickolds, based on an idea by real-life agony aunt Anna Raeburn, and Maureen Lipman was thrilled when she first heard that Beryl was being given a role. Beryl would play Cherry Lightfoot, an eccentric midwife; and for Maureen, the chance to work with her was an opportunity she'd never forget. 'I was in awe of her!' she told this author. 'This was my show and here was Beryl Reid! For me it was like having Maggie Smith on the set.'

Beryl's health was not all it might be and, when she arrived at London Weekend to record her episode of *Agony* (which she described as 'Agony for all concerned!'), she wasn't at her best. 'It was a hard thing for her because she'd had a bad night and she came in a little bit all over the place,' Maureen remembers. 'She dropped the ball a few times and of course this was in front of cameras and a studio audience which made it stressful; but she was very practical, she didn't seem to want fuss about her.'

The bad night concerned was another sign that something wasn't all as it should be. She had fallen over a few times, unsteady on her feet and feeling a little achy here and there, but doctors continued to put it down to arthritis. It would take some time before a doctor realised that there was something more to it all and that there had to be a reason for these falls and the serious repercussions of them. Beryl was not yet sixty-five and every fall seemed to incur a broken bone. She battled on, taking a little extra nip of brandy here and there to help her, and threw herself into her work.

Southern Television asked if she might like to pop along to discuss a slightly strange proposition but one which enthralled Beryl from the word go. Worzel Gummidge, the walking, talking, lisping scarecrow, was created by Barbara Euphan Todd in the 1930s and was an ideal role for the fabulously eccentric actor Jon Pertwee. The character lived on Scatterbrook Farm, standing in the ten-acre field. Naughty and full of fun, Worzel was aided and abetted by Aunt Sally (played by Una Stubbs), a rosy-cheeked life-size dolly whom Worzel was in love with. The television adaptation allowed writers Keith Waterhouse and Willis Hall to create cameos for some of the biggest TV stars of the time which would widen its popularity to parents as well as children. Joan Sims was brought in to play Mrs Bloomsbury-Barton, a local aristocrat, whilst Barbara Windsor came in as a ship's figurehead called Saucy Nancy. But for Beryl, there could only be one part: Worzel's mother, who had the delightful name of Sarah Pigswill.

When it came to costumes and make-up, Beryl was hardly vain but Worzel was never going to mean anything glamorous. Whilst Joan Sims got away with Barbara Cartland-style gowns, poor Beryl was put in torn cotton blouses, a ratty old cardigan with huge holes in it, a crushed farmer's hat and a wig made entirely from wheat and straw. Two ears of corn were spirit-gummed over her eyebrows and a little latex carrot nose was stuck on, after which the make-up department said, 'Stand over there and close your eyes and mouth Beryl.' Wondering what on earth was going on, she was pelted with mud and dirt which she immediately took to, rubbing her fingers into the bucket of wet earth and painting her face with it. She was happy to pose for photographs and later recalled that working on *Worzel Gummidge* had been an absolute delight, frequently asking if she could pop back for another episode.

Her role in *Tinker Tailor Soldier Spy* had not been forgotten and so in 1982 when the BBC commissioned a sequel, *Smiley's People*, Beryl was asked to reprise her role as Connie. Although unsure as to whether or not she should take it on, she agreed; but this time she struggled far more – no doubt aware of the expectation there would be upon her. She prepared in the same way she had for *Tinker Tailor*, diligently learning her lines at Honeypot which gave endless pleasure to the boaters rowing down the river from Old Windsor Lock. In the middle of a scene played out in her dining room, she'd suddenly find that all eyes were upon her and so she quickly feigned dusting before giving a polite little wave to the passers-by!

Connie's death scene was even more moving and even more poignant than her first appearance in the role. Even before the nominations were announced, theatreland was abuzz with talk of Beryl's performance and it came as no great surprise when Beryl was again nominated for the Best Actress award at the BAFTAS. Though she always maintained she'd never seen her second appearance as Connie because she felt she hadn't done a particularly good job, the judging panel clearly disagreed and Beryl won.

She took to the podium in a low-cut silver gown which twinkled under the lights as Anthony Andrews presented her with the award and the audience rose as one to give her a standing ovation. Beryl's only comment was, 'Why must these things be so heavy?!' – which delighted the audience all the more – before turning to Anthony Andrews and saying, 'Could I check that envelope darling? There's been a terrible mistake!' But everyone was in firm agreement. Connie Sachs was now the defining role of her career: not Monica, nor Marlene. If Beryl had yearned for recognition as a serious actress, she'd finally got it.

A BAFTA, an Olivier, a Tony Award, even a Golden Globe nomination. For Beryl, awards meant very little but when George Cole telephoned to congratulate her on her achievement, she did allow herself a little moment of pride: 'Not bad for an old stick!' she said, 'not bad at all.' Unlike many of her contemporaries, Beryl never felt the rather morbid desire to keel over on stage in the middle of a hit production; and, while not particularly vain, she did undergo a minor facelift and lost weight so that she'd be considered for parts other than mad old ladies.

In 1983, Beryl was cast away on *Desert Island Discs* for a second time by Roy Plomley. A staple of BBC Radio 4 that's as much a British institution as the Queen, the programme features prominent people who are shipped off to an imaginary desert island with a meagre allowance of eight records, a book and a luxury item. In between the records, there's a chance for the castaway to talk about their life and their career, ably guided by the host of the programme.

Beryl had been to the desert island once before, twenty years earlier in fact, when her choices had included 'Nessun Dorma' (performed by Sir Harry Secombe) and her luxury item had been a variety of lipsticks. But so much had happened in the intervening years that the BBC asked if Beryl might like to repeat the experience, hinting that the presenter Roy Plomley had specifically asked for Beryl and that he'd be delighted to see her for a light lunch before the recording – the lunch to include a bottle or two of toff's lemonade to get her warmed up. A quick wander through the BBC

Record Library and she was in front of the microphone doing what she did best: simply being Beryl.

Her choices were deliciously her: the light relief came from Jimmy Durante singing 'Monte Carlo or Bust', Gerard Hoffnung at the Oxford Union and Jake Thackray performing 'Leopold Alcox' whilst a couple of romantic ballads courtesy of Julio Iglesias and Charles Aznavour rekindled her memories of love affairs past.

Beryl was a master of the chat-show format and the rise of the television talk show, led by Michael Parkinson but embraced by almost every network with interviewers such as Sir Terry Wogan and Russell Harty, provided an ideal outlet for Beryl's unique charm. Sir Terry recalled, 'You only needed one question for Beryl. That was it. She'd use it as a springboard and she'd just go off into a thousand stories; the audience loved her and I would just sit and marvel at it all. She was the chat show host's dream and that's a rare thing to find.'

By now, she was growing into the role of a national treasure, though she was never very fond of that particular label. Indeed, when a journalist used the phrase in front of her she snapped, 'What am I then? A bloody mummy?!' But people were genuinely interested to hear more of Beryl's story; the chat show format didn't give her long enough and, whilst fellow guests were more than happy to let Beryl steal some of their limelight, Robert Luff felt that there was a market for Beryl's reminiscences. And why shouldn't Beryl write her memoirs? Surely it was the right time?

At first she was loath to do so, her literacy problems forming a potential barrier. To undertake the writing of an entire book was a daunting task, and so she came to an agreement with Hutchinson, her publishers, which seemed to work for everyone. Beryl would take delivery of a tape recorder, talk into it recalling the memories she had as best she could and then an editor called Eric Braun would be brought in to make some sense out of the chaos until they had a manuscript. Unfortunately, in the process Braun would sit with a bottle of whisky and Beryl with a bottle of brandy and, between the two of them, some key dates or names were lost or confused. Still, *So Much Love* as it was called brought Beryl huge joy, and she began to refer to it as 'The Bible' because of Braun's truly wonderful appendices which listed every play, TV appearance and film to date in chronological order. There were of course some glaring omissions (either by design or by error), which have now been corrected in this book.

Beryl found this writing business quite a lark and she suddenly got the taste for it. Her next foray into the publishing world was *Food and Friends*, a cookbook interspersed with memories of friends; and then came *The Cat's Whiskers*, a glorified photo album of Beryl's cats, each with their own little story below and the history of the moggy as a pet.

Sadly, Beryl then came to blows with Eric Braun. Beryl had chatted to a reporter from *The Stage* at a party when she had perhaps been hitting the brandy a little too hard. 'Oh, Eric does nothing you know,' Beryl said. 'I do it all myself, he just edits the things and takes the money.' This wasn't strictly true and probably wasn't ever intended to diminish Braun's role in the process, but he took it to heart; and, following a most dreadful row, most of which was carried out in the gossip columns with each one sniping at the other, the two parted ways. Beryl did try to make amends and Braun offered to come and visit her occasionally, but she refused to allow him to come to the cottage for fear that he'd pass on something she'd said to a journalist. It was not quite the end of Beryl's publishing career but, as far as the Braun association went, things were considered to have reached a mutually beneficial close.

*

In 1985, Beryl mentioned to the *Radio Times* that she was 'falling to bits' and that she was riddled with arthritis. In reality, things were far worse. It was now impossible to ignore the aches and pains in her bones, and the falls and fractures had concerned her doctors enough for them to carry out X-rays. Beryl was suffering from osteoporosis, a disease that makes the bones brittle and prone to break easily. For some time she had been losing weight, but she was trying to and so put it down to the fact that her diet was going rather well. In many of her television appearances from around this time, her mobility seems to be an issue and her shoulders had begun to round slightly. She walked boldly but with a slight stoop.

It was a cruel twist of fate, directly brought on by her decision taken with Dr McIndoe to have an early hysterectomy to avoid the possibility of having children. In trying to avoid any disruption to her career, she had actually brought about just that, through no fault of her own. Immediately after her surgery she had been put on a daily dose of hormone replacement therapy, but this was not the tried and tested HRT which many women rely on today post-menopause. This was a synthetic hormone, made from horse urine. The long-term side effects were unknown; but now more and more women were coming forward with similar symptoms. Osteoporosis was diagnosed but, as far as Beryl was concerned, endless trips to a GP or a physiotherapist would put a drain on her time and then she might have to turn work down. She turned to something far quicker and more easily accessible: alcohol.

The stories of Beryl's drinking are legendary. They range from the demand for a bottle of Courvoisier in her dressing room to offering her co-stars a drink at insanely early times in the morning. As the actress Barbara Flynn recalls, 'I loved working with Beryl and she was a delight but I will never forget being offered a gin at 8.30 in the morning; that had never happened before... and it's never happened since!' The bottle of brandy became a common fixture, always in her dressing room and, more often than not, a hip flask in her handbag.

Eleanor Fazan says that the amount Beryl drank was in no way unusual. 'It was rather like smoking,' she says. 'We all did it even though we knew it probably wasn't good for us, and there was a lot of heavy drinking going on. It was everywhere and it was part of the culture so Beryl was not at all like some of her contemporaries where she needed it – I think she just liked it.'

Beryl hated to lose control, she didn't like anything that would cloud her judgement; but there were occasions at Honeypot Cottage where she would drink to excess and become a little weepy, spending hours on the telephone talking to friends and listening to records, looking through old photograph albums and performing to the cats. It was by no means a regular thing – and what Beryl did in the privacy of her own home was nobody's affair but her own – but some friends did notice that, around this time, the drinking did increase.

Dame Eileen Atkins says that she began to time her phone calls around the drinking, just in case. 'I realised she was probably drinking too much, but Beryl had always been a big drinker. I spoke to her every day but then I began to make sure that I never phoned after five because I knew she'd probably be incoherent,' she says.

Certainly there was never any sign of Beryl's drinking interfering with her work. 'She did drink before a performance and she had her brandy in the interval, champagne in the dressing room at the end and I knew she'd been drinking when we were on stage together,' Dame Eileen says, 'but the audience would never know. She was on the ball and she knew her lines and delivered them perfectly.'

Susan Penhaligon says, 'I think she probably drank too much to compensate for something sad inside her, but her public face was always twinkly, quick and funny,' and this is a sentiment everyone seems to agree with.

Beryl did not drink every day, neither did she drink to escape reality as co-stars Yootha Joyce and Joan Sims did. As Sue says, 'It wasn't that she was lonely, though I'm sure that contributed sometimes. She didn't like a fuss about illness, she wouldn't go to hospital if she could absolutely help it, so a lot of the drinking was self-medicating. And yes, she got bored and drink helped to pass the time.'

Paul Strike confirms this. 'Yes, she liked a drink, but this talk about her sitting in front of the telly with a bottle watching herself and sobbing has absolutely no basis in fact whatsoever. It was partly habit, it was partly boredom and yes, sometimes loneliness but she was only ever lonely if she chose to be. Mostly it was self-medication, which I'm sure of.'

Actor Steve Nallon (who would have a rather unique association with Beryl much later) explains, 'Many women of her generation drank for "medicinal" reasons. You see elderly ladies in Tesco with a bottle of sherry in their basket, and they may have a little drink in the morning because they don't regard it as booze – it's not, it's medicinal, to ease the aches and pains; and it certainly seems to me that Beryl was doing just that.'

Tabloid reports since Beryl's death have suggested that she was an alcoholic; and indeed, some anecdotes related by those who maybe met her once or twice have been embroidered by upping the ante and insisting that she was an eccentric old drunk – but, though she was undoubtedly unconventional, she was never a drunk.

Despite the new challenges ahead, she refused to slow down. Work had been fairly consistent and in 1983, she was reunited with Peter Bowles in the series *The Irish RM* set in 18th century Ireland. Rosemary Ann Sisson was the writer of the series and she recalls how surprised she was when Beryl was cast as the elderly landowner, Mrs Knox: 'I know some people felt that she was wrong for the role because she was a comedian, but in the end she really was very good indeed and so funny. I liked her very much and, even though I know she had problems at that time, it didn't show. I just loved the series so much; I still think of it so fondly and she ended up being just right for that role.'

The series was a risk, not because of any doubts over casting or concerns that Beryl may once again feel her spotlight shared with others but because it was made in Ireland at a time when the IRA were at their busiest. Indeed, when a ship had to fly the Union Jack in one scene, there were threats made that they'd take action if they saw it. In the end, the Union Jack was quickly hoisted, recorded and then brought down again in a huge hurry to avoid incurring any unnecessary risk to the cast and crew.

The diagnosis of osteoporosis didn't mean an immediate shutdown of the diary; for Beryl that would have been absolute death, and as long as she could, she would. Luckily, casting agents were never far from Honeypot – though one young playwright was taken aback when he sent Beryl a script which he hoped she'd like and waited patiently for a telephone call with a yes or a no. He heard nothing back from her but when he was visiting the BBC canteen some time later, he saw Beryl in the queue who immediately put down her tray, kissed him and said, 'Oh darlings, you must meet this wonderful young writer whose play I'm not going to do!'

When Robert Luff told her that she was being considered for a part in a revival of the Lerner and Loewe musical *Gigi*, Beryl assumed it would come to nothing. Not since the LPs she'd made for Norman Newell had she been required to sing much; she had what might be called a music-hall voice, and indeed she once recorded a singalong album complete with the clanging and crashing of a till and the clanking of glasses as a crowded Edmonton pub provided the chorus. She was also a popular regular in the hit TV series *The Good Old Days* which saw her whip the audience into a frenzy with renditions of popular songs from the turn of the century, and once included a beautiful duet with Roy Castle in which the pair sang 'We Live in Trafalgar Square'.

She was willing to at least try for *Gigi*, though she knew little about it. Set in Paris, the musical presents the story of a girl who falls for an older man despite the best efforts of two imperious aunts to push her into the arms of a respectable young man. Whilst the film with Leslie Caron in 1958 had been a success, it was considered far too similar to *My Fair Lady* and so never really enjoyed the lasting reputation that some of the other musicals of the 1950s and sixties had enjoyed. Still, the numbers were memorable and included 'Thank Heaven for Little Girls', 'The Night They

Invented Champagne' and 'I Remember it Well'. Beryl's career had now come full circle. At the BBC in the late 1940s, she was spoken of as a possible replacement for Hermione Gingold; now she was being offered the part of Madame Alvarez, the role Hermione had not only played in the film adaptation but also won great acclaim for on Broadway, despite Broadway audiences not really embracing *Gigi* as a show.

Madame Alvarez was a far more physical role than Beryl was now used to and she did have some reservations about what that might mean. She hadn't taken on a long run in the theatre since *Born in the Gardens*; and, though there had been brief stints in plays, these were usually roles that allowed her to take it easy, physically if not mentally. The show was to be directed by John Dexter, a well-respected name in theatre and television but a man who could be extremely acerbic. When Beryl said she might not be up to anything too physical, Dexter quipped, 'We're not asking you to carry *Gigi* dear, just to be on stage with her.' And so, not without hesitation but with a certain degree of confidence, Beryl signed up.

Aunt Alicia was to be played by Dame Siân Phillips whilst the role of Honoré, originally brought to life by Maurice Chevalier, was taken by Jean-Pierre Aumont; and starring as Gigi was a young actress who would be treading the boards for the first time in a West End musical: Amanda Waring. When she learned that she was to be working with Beryl Reid, Amanda was thrilled. 'I'd seen her in various things and I knew of her through my parents as well who thought she was an absolute legend,' she recalls. 'I was a bit in awe of her, but it was perfect casting of course and I couldn't wait to get started.'

The production was not without its tensions. 'In some ways, she was absolutely lovely and professional but in other ways, she was very vulnerable,' Amanda Waring remembers. 'She didn't really see eye to eye with the director and I remember her sitting on a chair crying because John Dexter had said something vile to her. I just held her hand and she really did seem lost at that point. She just looked like a child.' Beryl told everybody that Dexter was bullying her and the only two cast members she really enjoyed working with were Dame Siân and Amanda. Even the stagehands irritated her, and – even with the show in full swing – if they were larking about in the wings she would throw something heavy at them to keep them quiet.

'There were times when I was on stage singing one of my more poignant love songs and she'd suddenly come in at the back of the stage and start doing something or other, and that could be a bit tricky to deal with. I think it was hard for her not to be centre of attention and so yes, she would quite get diva-ish at times,' says Amanda.

Dame Siân remembers objects being thrown into the wings to wake up stagehands, but she was also a victim to Beryl's occasional flights of fancy halfway through a scene. As she explains in the foreword to this book, Beryl's improvisation never wrong-footed her and the audience adored it all so much that it didn't seem a problem. But, much like Dame Eileen Atkins' twenty years earlier, for Amanda Waring Beryl's onstage tricks could sometimes cause frustration.

'We had the hundredth performance of *Gigi* that year,' she explains. 'Every kind of Hollywood star going was there, it was a huge event; and during that show, Beryl often came to blows with the musical director because she could never seem to get the timing. For example, when it came to "The Night They Invented Champagne", she wouldn't do it in time which didn't bother me but it of course threw off the orchestra. The musical director was desperately trying to get it together and so he started to bash this small triangle when Beryl suddenly just stopped. It stopped the entire show, mid performance, on the hundredth anniversary night. And I was left there singing, just carrying on! I was so young I'd thought I'd just do my best, but I don't think Beryl was too happy.'

On the same occasion, Beryl had enjoyed rather more than her usual one or two interval brandies. 'The Night They Invented Champagne' was to be performed on a revolve, a large moving disc in the middle of the stage which wasn't that easy to master sober. 'The whole revolve got stuck that night, the hatstand and everything fell over and the entire thing got jammed. Beryl just disappeared and I was left standing there so I quickly improvised and said, "I didn't know you could get earthquakes in Paris!" '

But backstage, Beryl was facing a problem she'd never encountered before. Most of her friends insist that Beryl never forgot a play she'd been in: she could quote large sections of Orton and Sheridan, and she retained lyrics amazingly well. When she did watch herself on television in a film, she would recite the words along with it because she still remembered them. But now, Beryl couldn't seem to remember the lines that she had in the here and now; and, several times, she dried on stage.

'She would struggle for the words, she'd dry on stage and she'd sort of look at me and I knew I had to then come up with a way to feed her lines in the most imaginative way I could,' Amanda says, 'which did I'm afraid make me quite stressed and quite nervous; I even developed a bit of a nervous thing where I'd pick at the skin on my fingers because it was such a baptism of fire. You never relaxed into the show because we never knew what was coming next with her. It was very much "Can I survive another show?!" '

Whether down to age or whether she was simply bored by the saga of it all (not being liked by the director always turned Beryl against a piece), she tried to inject her usual fun and naughtiness to keep things jolly. As Amanda remembers with a giggle, 'There was a big scene at the end with a spotlight on me as Gigi was getting married, and so sometimes she'd just hold my head down into her bosom so I couldn't actually lift myself up. Sometimes she'd tweak my boobs, sometimes she'd let me be! She was extraordinary, so watchable and endearing; but at that time, fresh out of drama school, I wanted to get everything right and so it was difficult. She had two understudies and they did things very differently to her when she wasn't on stage, so I'd get settled with them and suddenly, Beryl was back and being a little bit cheeky which now I can appreciate but then, it really did terrify me a little.'

Musicals that had just arrived in the West End were given a helping hand by the Royal Variety Performance, organised each year by the Entertainment Artistes' Benevolent Fund, for which the cast would be invited to perform a scene from the show in the presence of a royal personage – in this case, the Queen accompanied by the Duke of Edinburgh. Beryl was thrilled: she loved the chance to rub shoulders with members of the Royal Family, her invitations to Windsor Castle by now bizarrely frequent! But this time, she decided to give the Queen a special treat. The scene chosen was 'The Night They Invented Champagne' and this saw Amanda Waring, Beryl Reid and Jean-Pierre Aumont dancing on a table and generally being very enthusiastic and energetic. Dressed in a long white silk Edwardian gown with huge straw hat tied about her neck with a chiffon scarf, Beryl looked every inch the imposing dowager until she leaned back on the table, full of the joys of the music. This got a decent giggle at the Lyric, but Beryl decided to step things up a little for this very special appearance. As Amanda Waring recalls, 'She'd asked the set people to give her an extra high block so that when she went back on the table, she could show her bloomers. But nobody had thought to tell me that that's what had happened so when I had to jump off the table after doing the can can, I fell onto the block and broke my ankle. So I then had to do the Royal Variety Show with a broken ankle! She wasn't my favourite person that day but she got a massive laugh, and I think that's how she got away with so much: she had something so magical about her that you just forgave her anything.'

The show must have been equally as memorable for Her Majesty. In the line-up backstage, Beryl was introduced, dutifully curtsied and said, 'You know, I do live just up the road from you, Your Majesty.'

The Queen replied kindly, 'Yes of course, Wraysbury I believe?'

'Yes Ma'am, just near to Old Windsor Lock.'

'How fascinating,' said the Queen, eager to move on. And then with all sincerity and seriousness, Beryl warned, 'If you do come, don't bring the corgis. The cats wouldn't get on with them at all.'

At the Lyric, the cast fawned over Beryl, making her feel very welcome and loved; but as Dame Siân remembers, 'She came from a very different time in the theatre when there was a lot of socialising after the performance. So she always had her dressing room door open and she wanted people to go in and see her and have a drink and a bit of a party, but that sort of thing was dying out and I think she missed all that.'

Beryl was beginning to show signs that the backstage bitching was taking its toll, and one day she got so upset that she ended up in floods of tears. Amanda Waring comforted her and Beryl was grateful for a young ingénue trying to cheer her up; but suddenly, she became distant. 'I'd felt really close to her in that moment, but then there was a block,' Amanda says. 'She did put a distance between us, not that she was anything other than charming and lovely and there was never any bullying or unpleasantness; she just didn't seem to want me to get close. And I think she then got bored.' A case of people poisoning once again.

The reviews for *Gigi* were varied. Whilst some felt it was a charming revival of a popular classic, one review in *The Stage* said, 'Thank God they invented champagne, for the only possible way to enjoy this night is to down huge quantities of it before entering the theatre.' As so often happened, Beryl made the best of it; and though she left with her head held high, the only thing she felt she had gained from the experience was a close friendship with Dame Siân which she treasured for the rest of her life.

In the midst of *Gigi*, Beryl received a letter from the Prime Minister's Office. Margaret Thatcher had been to see *Gigi* and she had it in mind to put Beryl's name forward to the Queen for an honour. Would she accept one? Honours are always offered in this rather cloak-and-dagger fashion so that if the intended recipient does decline, the offence is taken by the Cabinet Office and not by the Queen. Beryl accepted, of course; but part of the deal with such things is that the recipient keeps totally silent about the impending honour until it's officially gazetted on either the Queen's Birthday or the New Year's Honours List. Beryl only made one tiny slip. In an interview with Russell Harty, she said, 'The Queen came to see *Gigi* you know. I might sing her a bit when I go to the Palace.'

'Are you going to the Palace?' Harty said excitedly.

Laughing and desperately trying to cover, Beryl quipped, 'Darling, I'm always at the Palace!'

On New Year's Day 1985, the New Year's Honours List announced that Miss Beryl Reid, Actress, was to be made an Officer of the Order of the British Empire. For Beryl, this wasn't the icing on the cake – it was *the* cake. A staunch monarchist, a fierce patriot, she thought her award overdue but she was thrilled when it finally came. She decided that it was time to begin to relax her commitment to *Gigi* and she asked to be released from the show early. It was agreed that she would alternate performances for a few weeks with *Bless this House* actress Diana Coupland, but Beryl eventually managed to persuade Dexter that she really wasn't enjoying the show and she'd rather leave. Diana Coupland replaced Beryl permanently, but within a few weeks *Gigi* left the Lyric entirely.

With each passing decade, Beryl had been handed a new challenge, a challenge she always met with superb professionalism, gathering fans and friends along the way. Every decade brought a new accolade, an ever-growing timeline on which the awards became the hallmarks of a great career. Unbeknown to Beryl, the latter half of the 1980s would see three years of 'lasts' as her health began to decline and it became more difficult for her to accept the roles she'd really like to take. Beryl knew the limitations her condition would place on her but she wasn't ready to fall off the perch just yet. For Beryl Reid, it was time for one last push.

Chapter Nine

*'I'm very good at sitting down jobs. If you want any sitting down
done, I'll do it!'*

O N 18ᵀᴴ MARCH 1986, AN INVESTITURE WAS HELD at Buckingham
Palace by Her Majesty the Queen. Beryl was driven from
Honeypot by her (now permanently employed) chauffeur, Rick;
and in the forecourt of the Palace she met her agent Robert Luff, looking
handsome and smart in his grey morning suit. The two had been firm
friends for forty years and Beryl would always credit Luff with finding her
the very best work. Luff was now nearing retirement and so Beryl took on
another agent, James Sharkey; but Luff always came first.

Beryl, glad of a chance to dress up a little, donned a made-to-measure
fuchsia pink suit with a matching pink bowler hat covered in netting and
little silk flowers. The Queen recalled seeing Beryl in her role in *Gigi* at the
Royal Variety Performance just a few months earlier.

'How's the show going?' she asked kindly.

'Actually, at the moment, I'm not in it,' Beryl said. 'I've been rather ill.'

'Well, it was very energetic, wasn't it?' the Queen said, perhaps recalling
the sight of Beryl's bloomers as she flew across a table!

Robert Luff arranged a private celebratory lunch at the Garrick Club,
and then it was back to Honeypot Cottage where Beryl proudly showed off

her OBE to everyone and anyone who came to call – she even modelled it proudly for the cats.

Despite her success and her iconic status as a groundbreaking comedienne, Beryl would never be given the accolade of a damehood, something she resented. Now she believed she'd found out the reason why the precious gong had been withheld: she'd offended the Queen Mother.

In fact, she hadn't done any such thing. In 1984, the satirical puppet show *Spitting Image* had begun its ruthless parodies of prominent British politicians, celebrities and of course, members of the Royal Family. The Queen's voice was provided by Jan Ravens, and initially Jan was to provide a slightly similar voice for the Queen Mother; but it didn't sound quite right. As Steve Nallon recalls, 'The problem was that nobody knew what the Queen Mother sounded like, and her public image was that of this sort of grandmother of the nation. Beryl Reid had that same quality, the little hats and the posh frocks and things, but there was no real character to the Queen Mother and so we had to invent one.' Steve went to the producer John Lloyd and said, 'I can do quite a good Beryl Reid impression.' Lloyd was puzzled. 'I thought it would be really funny to give the Queen Mother Beryl's voice and mannerisms and allow her to take on that aspect of Beryl which could be very posh but could also be, when she did Marlene for example, really quite common. There was an idea that the Queen Mother hadn't been a royal princess or anything and they hid her away and stopped her talking to the public because she was a bit rough around the edges. So I did it for John and he loved it and that was that.'

Steve had long been a fan of Beryl Reid and, whilst most people clearly knew that this was another uncanny impression provided by a very skilled actor, Beryl was horrified. Whilst she wasn't offended, when she saw the programme she declared: 'Well, that's my damehood down Duck's Lane isn't it?!' – Beryl believed that the Queen Mother (no doubt an avid viewer of *Spitting Image*) would think that it was Beryl herself behind the puppet and that she'd be blacklisted from royal events. A year later, she would perform for the Queen Mother and Princess Margaret. Presumably, neither one complained about the portrayal, no doubt having not actually seen it.

Her reaction to *Spitting Image* reveals a side of Beryl that was becoming more prevalent as she got older, and it came directly from fear. When she was asked if she was at all confident, Beryl gushed, 'Oh, I've never been confident doing anything! Miss No Confidence of 1975, 1976, any year you care to name.' She even had a code word for performances she felt had been poor: BRING, or Beryl Reid Is No Good. 'It's all a great adventure,' she insisted, 'but I wish sometimes that I had a little more confidence because I'd be less hurt by the process of feeling inadequate during rehearsal which I do… but I don't think I'll ever change now. I'm stuck with it.' And now she began to feel inadequate more and more. Her age bothered her, her illness worried her, and this could make her slightly more bad-tempered and prone to behaving badly.

When Dame Siân Phillips spoke to her on the telephone one day, Beryl said, 'Oh, I must work, Siân; they'll forget me if I don't. I must do a television or something, stay in their minds.' From around 1985 onward, Beryl's appearances were either in series which have entered the Hall of Fame as classic television or in dross which she instantly regretted doing. Every now and then, though, something truly magical came her way, and this was the case with the popular TV series, *Minder*.

Beryl was given a cameo as Ruby Hubbard, a kind of cockney Barbara Cartland, in an episode called 'The Second Time Around'. The character is a slightly tipsy novelist, with a running joke that she has written endless novels but all of them within a month, and she staggers about the various locations in a floor-length mink coat and dainty little hats, suggesting that she's still on Capri time… which happily makes it cocktail hour. Ruby's ex-husband (Bill Maynard) has sold her house behind her back and Arthur Daley has assigned Terry (played by Dennis Waterman) to look after her.

Beryl's interpretation of Ruby was the first in a long line of eccentric old ladies which would very much become 'Beryl Reid types' for the rest of her career, but this was no bad thing; Beryl took the script and made a brief cameo memorable. Lines which some actors may see as one-dimensional became hilarious and quotable. For example, as Ruby sits dictating her latest novel into a tape recorder (a sad tale of a widow nursing two young children), she suddenly drops her posh accent and reminds Terry in her best East End: 'I'm 'avin' the beef!'

By far the best thing about *Minder* as far as Beryl was concerned was the chance to work once more with George Cole, and she sent him a letter a few weeks before filming began telling him how excited she was to see him again. 'I hadn't seen Beryl for a few years and I was little bit taken aback,' George recalled. 'She seemed quite frail and shaky, and her lines didn't come to her very easily in rehearsal; but as soon as the camera was on her, she seemed to grow a few inches and that was it. She was throwing her weight around, she was full of energy and that old Beryl twinkle was still there. I don't think the character she had to play was that far removed from who she really was and, once she settled into it all, she was a joy to work with.' She did speak frankly and openly about her illness and the problems it was causing. 'It's not just a pain in the arse, George,' she said, 'it's a pain everywhere.'

When Will asked her how she was feeling during a visit to Honeypot, she confided that she'd seen the X-rays after a recent visit to Wexham Park Hospital in Slough and said grimly, 'My spine looks like an old fishbone the cats have dug up and had a go at in the garden.' A physiotherapist, Anne Mitchell, was brought in regularly to try and improve Beryl's mobility; and, though she had good days and bad days, she would never dream of cancelling a job. However bad things were, nothing was bad enough to let an audience down.

The filming of Beryl's episode of *Minder* took place, for the most part, on location at a manor house in the country. 'There was this little kitten that kept appearing,' George Cole remembered. 'We all assumed it belonged to the owner of the house, but they hadn't a clue where it had come from. Beryl was obsessed with it and sent a runner out to buy some fish for it. I think the boy wasn't really all there because he came back with battered cod and chips! So Beryl sat there with newspaper laid across her lap, picking all the batter off, and then she fed the kitten the fish and cooed away to it. I think she took it home at the end of the day.' It's more than likely that she did.

Whilst cameos were now Beryl's stock-in-trade, there was one that she loved more than the rest because it allowed her to revive a trace of Marlene. *The Secret Diary of Adrian Mole* was a television adaptation of the popular Sue Townsend classic about a teenager and his struggles through adolescence. Naturally Beryl was cast as Grandma Mole; and, whilst most of her scenes allowed for her to sit down, in one memorable episode she sailed around trestle tables set up for the Royal Wedding of the Prince of Wales and Diana Spencer getting more and more merry, cooing to everyone in a modulated Marlene accent, decked out in lurid purple.

Grandma Mole was slightly snobbish but in an endearing way, a firm believer that the Royal Family were to be greeted from her armchair with a royal wave; and of course, she always had a kind word for Mrs Thatcher.

Grandma Mole became a much loved character in a cast that included Julie Walters as Adrian's mother and a young Gian Sammarco in the title role.

The series was filmed in Leicester, and this was the last time that Beryl would accept a role that took her so far from home. Honeypot itself had a dedicated team of carers who looked after Beryl, the cottage and the cats but she now instructed Robert Luff only to find her roles which were 'sit downs'. 'I'm very good at sitting down jobs!' she explained determinedly. 'If you want any sitting down done, I'll do it!'

Her chauffeur, Rick, now came into his own. As Beryl struggled to walk long distances, she always worried about attending functions or awards ceremonies because, if she was to receive anything (and she usually did), stairs were an issue. Looking smart and handsome in his dinner jacket, Rick found a way to discreetly escort Beryl to the stage without making it appear obvious that she needed the help; and, far from thinking that she was in any way ill, most believed Rick to be her toy boy, a mistake Beryl didn't mind being made in the slightest!

In 1987, Beryl agreed to play Sylvia in *The Beiderbecke Tapes* as the part allowed her to stay in a wheelchair throughout. Whilst it was a brief appearance, actress Barbara Flynn who played Jill Swinburne remembers Beryl fondly. 'It was a real experience working with her,' she recalls. 'She was gloriously mischievous and not at all far from the revolutionary character she was playing! My character goes to visit Sylvia in her retirement home to ask advice from "the oldest suffragette in town". She pushes her wheelchair to the park and they discuss the controversial disposal of nuclear waste in the Yorkshire Dales and how the LFWY (the Liberation Front of West Yorkshire) should deal with the matter... to which her response was, "Wheel me to the barricades!" She tells Jill of her struggle to fight for conjugal rights of the residents in the retirement home. "It's the principle of the thing!" she says. "And a load of bollocks!" I just remember laughing with her more and more as the day went on. She was such a minx!' Beryl loved nothing more than to share naughty stories with her younger co-stars, her age and her public image as a sweet 'butter wouldn't melt' old lady providing the perfect opportunity to shock with a rude word or a near-the-knuckle anecdote.

Beryl couldn't help but demand the star treatment and word got round that if you treated Beryl well, you'd get the results you wanted whatever the situation she was required to put herself into. The marketing department at

Heinz were looking for a new face for a promotion of their tomato ketchup and Beryl agreed to do it provided she was put on a retainer in case they wanted to use her for more than one commercial. The proposal was that she should appear as an elderly duchess in the back of a car who liked the taste of the ketchup so much that she wanted to get every drop out of the bottle. Beryl was to sit in the back of a Rolls Royce and a liveried chauffeur would bump her down the stairs. She made it clear that she would give them just one morning to get their shot and that they must send a car to collect her from the cottage and to take her home again afterwards.

Will explains, 'They had a caravan for her to get ready in, and they didn't rush her. They showered her with praise, there was a huge bouquet of white flowers for her when she arrived and, when she stepped out of the car, the entire crew applauded. And she was as good as gold. She would have done anything for them. One take and it was done.' Beryl was paid £30,000 for her efforts.

In 1988, Beryl slowly became more and more reclusive, not by choice but through necessity. She would venture out to see friends in plays or pantomimes and she liked attending the odd awards 'do' or a function at the BBC. The Variety Club of Great Britain honoured her in the same year, and Beryl (resplendent in vivid green) collected her award to rapturous applause; but these were very much her peers, and the world of comedy was changing.

The alternative comedy movement had all but banished Beryl's brand of humour to the afternoon slot on BBC 2, and sitcoms such as *Are You Being Served*, once the flagship of the BBC at its best, were now cancelled with no ceremony at all. Given her age and her health, it was almost impossible to think that Beryl could make the transition to that new style of humour which was suddenly so sought after; but now an offer came from a surprising source. The comedian Alexei Sayle had written a film called 'Didn't You Kill My Brother?' for Channel 4's series *The Comic Strip Presents...*, and he was keen to include Beryl in it. She was less than impressed by the script. 'It's just awful, and I can't see where the laughs are supposed to be,' she confided to a friend. 'I've asked if I can rewrite it a little but they've said no. I have to do a television bit to be seen, but it's just not funny.' Alexei Sayle has since praised Beryl profusely and says that he enjoyed the experience of meeting her and working with her, so whatever reservations she had about this new style of comedy were clearly not conveyed. She also agreed to do one episode of *Alexei Sayle's Stuff* but, like many of her generation of performers, anarchy and bad language really didn't suit her at all – professionally at least!

When a fan wrote to Beryl asking why she hadn't been on television more recently, she replied, 'I haven't gone to meet the management just yet! Good scripts are hard to find and when I come across one, you shall be the first to know!' As Paul explains, 'She was perfectly happy to do anything if they were prepared to come to the cottage or if it could be done from bed over the telephone. She did things like Gloria Hunniford's radio show and the odd thing here and there about comedy, but it really was in the early nineties that everything suddenly started to slow and she was practically housebound.'

But her confinement to bed was not permanent, and neither was it desperately sad. Friends visited constantly, Paul and Will kept her cheerful and, on Sunday evenings during 'the God spot', Beryl would call Sue or Jan, Siân or Eileen for a good catch-up. When *Woman's Weekly* asked her to describe a typical day in her 'retirement', Beryl resented the suggestion that she had retired. 'I'm just waiting for the right thing, darling!' she protested.

In the piece, she was astonishingly frank with that typical honesty that can be so rare in other performers who want to present the best of themselves constantly. 'I don't move until Eva, my carer, comes in the morning to get me up,' she explained. 'I'm very slow getting myself together these days. I've broken my right arm twice in falls and I can't lift things any more. I've also got osteoporosis – crumbling bones. My mobility isn't very good but it's getting better so I don't allow myself to get depressed. And how could I be depressed living here right on the banks of the lovely Thames in Honeypot Cottage?' She went on, 'Once I'm up and have done my exercises on the bed and had a cup of China tea, I sit by the door and watch the Thames flowing by… I love the water and the way it changes in different lights. I used to swim across to the other bank and back but not any more. The cruisers announce my house as part of the boat trips and I always wave at them. Eva gets me a light lunch and then I might look at the scented roses etc. Or I gawk at the telly. I sometimes watch videos of my old films. It's very good to look at yourself and find out where you've gone wrong. I used to enjoy preparing dinner parties but now if I have friends over in the evening I get a girl from the village in.'

But naturally, long-standing friendships were now coming to a sudden and unexpected end. She was particularly devastated in 1989 by the death of Harry Andrews, her co-star in *Sloane*. Andrews was one of the most respected and revered actors of his generation and when he took part in Beryl's *This is Your Life*, she greeted him with an enormous bear hug, staring at him with pure love in her eyes. Harry was homosexual and for many years had lived with his partner, Basil Hoskins. Perhaps because she had met Harry when he was already involved in a committed and loving relationship, or perhaps because her experience with Hugh Paddick still stung a little, she never allowed herself to fall in love with Harry; but she always spoke of him with nothing but affection, and she relished every opportunity possible to see him. In a letter to him in 1984, she signed off 'Your devoted, dearest, darling Beryl who loves you so much'. His death came as a severe blow to her, and this was followed a year later by the death of close friend Jimmy Edwards.

Colleagues who worked with her around this time noted that she was far more introspective and, rather than try to build new friendships with the young, she spoke of nothing but those she had known in the decades gone by. There was no element of showing off to these reminiscences; she was simply comforted by the memory of friends like Harry and Jimmy who had been such an integral part of the golden age of British theatre.

This isn't to say that she became a recluse or that she didn't welcome new friendships. Even a chance meeting would result in an invitation to Honeypot, especially for those she personally admired or thought she might enjoy spending time with. Actress Rula Lenska was one of these new acquaintances from around this time: 'I worked with her very briefly on a programme which I'm ashamed to say I don't remember the title of. I was very much in awe of her; I remember her trying to impress me with little bits of Polish! I was invited to Honeypot and she was just an extraordinary, unique, wonderful actress – and a very funny lady. I would like to think we were friends; I just wish I had known her for longer.'

Offers were still pouring in for Beryl, and occasionally she felt well enough to tackle a small cameo. These brief appearances were not well paid, but it did give her the chance to leave the cottage for a day or two and to be celebrated and marvelled at by a young cast who were generally in awe of this theatre, stage, screen and radio legend in their midst. She relished the chance to offer advice and help and, when the BBC asked her to take part in a special documentary series about British comics, she was only too pleased to do so, propped up on a large wicker throne, a still-reigning Queen of Comedy. Even at the age of seventy, she was still more than willing to climb into Monica's old gymslip and do the knicker routine, pulling out a furry gobstopper and declaring with delight: 'Oh look, it's got all penicillin growing round it!' She even fired her catapult at the cameraman with glee; and, oddly, the chance to relive that character, even just for a few minutes, seemed to render her totally ageless: there were no wrinkles on her face and her twinkling, childlike grin was as delightful then as it always had been. In 1991, Beryl appeared as Lady Augusta Warlingham in a television movie, *Duel of Hearts*, an adaptation of a Dame Barbara Cartland romance starring Billie Whitelaw, Virginia McKenna and Michael York; and just a week later, she was reunited with Peter Bowles in *Perfect Scoundrels*, a kind of Arthur Daley-inspired comedy drama about a couple of con men.

Whenever she could, she liked to be taken out for a drive, and naturally the public recognised her and wanted to have a few moments with her. Paul remembers how, on a visit to an Indian restaurant, a group of workmen on some scaffolding began to shout down, 'Oi Beryl! Nice to see you, old girl!' to which Beryl replied, overcome with false modesty, 'Oh darling, it's so nice to see you too but I'm really not looking my best at all!' If this was the last shout, if this was the recognition she still needed from time to time from her adoring public, then why not? Surely she'd earned that at least?

In 1991, Beryl was stunned when she received an invitation to the British Comedy Awards and it was made clear that she really should attend: a not-so-subtle indication that they planned to honour her in some way. Clearly shocked and very moved, Beryl was given the Lifetime Achievement Award, the first woman to receive the accolade. Ronnie Barker had won the Achievement Award the year before, and he along with the other biggest names in showbusiness gave Beryl a standing ovation that seemed as though it would never end. Tearfully, she thanked all concerned; and, looking a little frail but totally overcome with emotion, she took her seat again beaming from ear to ear. But Dame Barbara Windsor noticed something wasn't quite right. 'There was a sadness there, I thought,' she says. 'She just seemed very low and frail and I thought, "Oh, bless you darling"; I just wanted to give her a hug and look after her.'

Perhaps out of boredom more than from any literary ambitions, Beryl decided that the thing to do now she was at home more often was to turn her hand to writing again, this time a children's book. *Kingfisher Jump* is typically Beryl, written in a kind of half-remembered way and centred (of course) on Honeypot Cottage and a cat, called Andy. Andy is rescued by Beryl herself and all is rosy in the garden until Andy jumps a little too enthusiastically and injures a kingfisher. Beryl nurses the bird back to health and Andy has learned his lesson. The book didn't sell terribly well, but her commitment to the local school for special-needs children was unrelenting and boxes of copies were sent there: one for each child as a gift from Miss Reid, the famous actress just down the lane. Book sales were hindered by the fact that Beryl was unable to get out onto the chat show circuit and promote it as she had done for *So Much Love* five years earlier.

In general, her diary was becoming more and more sparse with hospital appointments becoming more regular than acting work; and those parts she did take were, as Beryl said herself, 'stuff and fluff' designed to keep her hand in and her face out there but with no real bite to them. Much in the same way that Alexei Sayle had tried to include her in the so-called 'new wave of comedy', Vic Reeves and Bob Mortimer decided that she'd be perfect for a part in a pilot they were making for Channel 4's *Bunch of Five*, an anthology series along similar lines to the BBC's long-running *Comedy Playhouse*. Beryl was offered the inspiringly christened part of 'Gran' in a bizarre piece called 'The Weekenders', in which Vic and Bob play Geordie friends visiting a meat market that is suddenly besieged by aliens. It wasn't exactly *Blithe Spirit*. Out of the five pilots aired, only one ('Blue Heaven' starring Frank Skinner) was successful and commissioned for a full series; but even though Beryl hadn't actually taken part in it, the production team had been so taken with her (and keen to include a big star from yesteryear to attract older viewers) that she was offered the small part of a jewellery shop owner. Skinner played a frustrated musician with a home life dominated by his 'cowing' mother and his bovver-boy father whose favourite son is in prison, leaving Frank with only two ambitions in life: that West Bromwich Albion should win the Cup and that his pop duo, Blue Heaven, will storm the charts and become the new Kiss. Whilst many credit *The Royle Family* for being the first sitcom to dispense with a studio audience and a laughter track, *Blue Heaven* was an early pioneer of the format; but the reviews were unkind and a second series was not forthcoming.

Anyone watching *Blue Heaven* could have been mistaken for wondering what on earth had happened to Beryl. In the latter half of the 1980s, she had been in rude health and her usual buoyant self. An appearance on *Through the Keyhole* in May 1987 became memorable when she took on Chris Tarrant who dared to suggest that Honeypot Cottage was off-putting to men because it was, in his words, 'full of cats on the bed and empty gin bottles'. A clearly affronted Beryl, glittering in gold lamé, fixed Tarrant with a dangerous glint in her eye and said, 'I've had many gentlemen callers to my cottage, thank you very much, and none of them were in the least bit bothered by my cats!' When Loyd Grossman committed the cardinal sin of criticising her cooking based on the higgledy-piggledy state of the shelves and cupboards, he too got a thorough ticking-off. Beryl's last appearances on television to show her at her best came between 1986 and 1990; but, on chat shows from around that time, there is always the hint that she's slightly under the influence.

A particularly concerning example was a visit to *Wogan* in 1989. As Sir Terry explained, 'Beryl had got to the studio far too early because she said she wanted to have a good catch-up, but I was rushing around and getting myself ready for the show so I didn't really have the time to speak to her properly. She must have been waiting around for at least two hours and she was having a ball, just chatting to the hair and make-up people, just being herself. But by the time she came out on set, I knew she was really quite beyond the limit. Now, don't mistake me: she was incredibly funny, she didn't make a fool of herself, but her answers were a bit all over the place and she wasn't really in the moment as she always had been. She said to me after the show, "Was I all right, darling?" and I said she'd been great, as usual; but she just shook her head and said, "I'm too old for all this." It was quite sad to see that.'

It was a very different Beryl Reid who made that final sitcom appearance in 1994. Her hair, usually so perfectly coiffed, had been replaced with an ill-fitting wig, and she was pencil-thin. She seemed to stumble over her lines and occasionally looked directly into the camera, rather than at Frank. This time, it was not inebriation but exhaustion.

Shortly after the filming of *Blue Heaven*, Beryl agreed to give a series of exclusive interviews to close friend Dame Siân Phillips who visited Beryl at

Honeypot with a sound man and the comedienne Josie Lawrence, the aim being to make a series for BBC radio recounting the lives of female comics. Beryl received them in bed, now entirely unable to walk. In that same year, she had a knee replaced; but the doctors were realistic with Beryl. The operation would ease the pain, but it would not improve her mobility at all.

During the recording of the Radio 4 piece with Dame Siân and Josie the telephone didn't stop ringing. 'Everyone wanted to speak to her,' Siân remembers. 'I thought that was so lovely. I think she'd had a fall a few weeks before and she kept saying, "I'm so sorry, I can't get out of bed," and we tried to make her feel comfortable but she really wasn't too well at that time, she didn't seem in good spirits.' Still, lying in her bed with a bright yellow sun worked into the headboard and pretty pink curtains, she adored the opportunity; and in the series, though clearly a little weaker, Beryl proved that she could still deliver a line with perfect timing, sending Siân into fits of laughter.

The BBC had already begun work on a series for television called *Funny Women*, the first episode of which would be devoted to Beryl. It was a selection of appearances blended with interviews from co-stars and clips from Beryl's career. When a BBC producer asked her to take part, Beryl became suspicious. 'If you're making a bloody obituary, you're too early!' she cried. 'I've not dropped yet!'

Jan Linden had once been a regular visitor to the cottage, but now she noticed a change. 'Suddenly she didn't really want people to visit; she didn't want people to see that she was as ill as she was,' she says. 'Her appearance was quite important to her, she loved to be so smart, and I think the effort of getting ready was so great that she would actually put you off visiting. It was quite a trek down to Honeypot anyway, and I did offer so many times to get the train down or something; but she'd always say, "Oh no Jan, don't go to all that trouble." '

Beryl was becoming more and more wistful but one thing she refused to do was to feel sorry for herself. 'I spoke to her on the telephone every day and she was getting more tired, she was in pain and she did seem to start to push people away a little bit, but she always left you smiling and laughing,' recalls Sue.

For over sixty years, Beryl Reid had been a lynchpin of theatre, television and radio. Whether it be serious drama such as *Tinker Tailor* or farcical comedy such as *No Sex Please, We're British*, Beryl always brought a remarkable energy to her roles; and whilst she may occasionally bark at her colleagues, her bite was non-existent.

She had adored the life the theatre had given her and once said, 'I am at my happiest when the dressing room door is open and you can hear the applause of the audience ringing in your head, and then friends pour in and you give them a little drink and laugh and just delight in the company. It's the company that I adore so much.' Some of this had been transferable to small acting roles where she always received a warm welcome; but, unable to leave the cottage, Beryl did began to suffer from bouts of loneliness and depression. Company was never far away, but she was wistful for days gone by; and this, coupled with the severe pain osteoporosis wrought, meant that the brandy became a permanent and daily fixture.

When doctors suggested that her other knee might be replaced, they warned Beryl that it was quite a serious operation given her age and her general state of health. This seems to have inspired in Beryl a sudden mad dash to settle her affairs, just in case. Quite aside from the cottage, which was packed with furniture and artwork (much of it collectable), there were her cats to consider – eight of them at this time. She spoke to Sue and asked if she might take the cottage on should anything happen.

'We had a life settled up here and we had quite a few cats of her own; it's a family trait, you might say!' explains Sue. 'So when Bee asked if I'd take on the cottage and look after the cats, I knew it just wasn't practical.' When Sue declined, the offer was made to others, even to Dame Eileen Atkins. 'Beryl said, "Well, you know, the only things I care about are the cats and really I want to leave Honeypot to them," so I said, "Why don't you leave it to the RSPCA and they could put someone into the house?" but she said she didn't trust them, and then asked me if I would live in the house if she left it to me. I said no, I had my own house and couldn't take the cats on.' Beryl made a will with Barclays Bank; and one night, she said to Paul, totally dismissively as if it were an afterthought, 'Of course I've left this all to you.'

In 1995 she replied to a fan letter, the author of which had enclosed a photograph of Beryl with Brough from the *Archie* days. The picture showed her, dressed as Monica, trying to feed Archie from a jar of strawberry jam. 'I saw this again with sheer delight and you've no idea how glad I was of it!' she wrote. 'What a dear, sweet man you are to have thought of me. Sadly my health doesn't allow me to get out much these days – old moans and old bones! – but when people like you are kind and so thoughtful, it makes the sun shine.'

It is true that, in the last year of her life, Beryl had begun to drink more than was good for her. The brandy became a non-negotiable anaesthetic and, as a result, there was kidney damage which saw her in and out of Wexham Park hospital in Slough for various treatments. In June 1996, Beryl was admitted for a second knee replacement; though the surgery was a success, in the weeks that followed Beryl was in intense pain and was finding things extremely difficult to bear.

In Liverpool, Sue was also in poor health, requiring surgery on her gallbladder; and, in what was to be her last conversation with Beryl, the pair consoled each other. They shared a love of Winnie the Pooh and often quoted the stories as part of their conversations. In a particularly poignant piece, Christopher Robin realises that his friendship with Pooh will change because he's going to have to leave for school. At the very end of *The House at Pooh Corner*, Milne writes: 'So they went off together. But wherever they go and whatever happens to them on the way, in that enchanted place on the top of the Forest a little boy and his bear will always be playing.'

'We used to quote those words and burst into tears because we found it so moving, beautiful and sad,' Sue explains. For Beryl, the enchanted place was her beloved Honeypot Cottage and, by now, she had accepted that her life was drawing to its close. Beryl was saying goodbye.

Beryl telephoned Paul to explain that she was about to go into hospital again and he travelled from Bristol to see her. Sue then received a phone call to explain the full nature of Beryl's illness. She was suffering from kidney failure and was in extreme discomfort – though her hospitalisation didn't do much to quell her personality. Her physiotherapist Anne Mitchell visited Beryl in hospital only to find that she was entertaining the staff with jokes and anecdotes; nurses were often welcomed by Monica or Marlene, and she even went so far as to demand to see the chef to discuss why the hospital food was so awful. She put on a typically brave face and, when she last spoke to Anne, she said, 'I'm really feeling much better and I'm going home tomorrow to see the cats.'

But calls from concerned friends and family members were not put through, she didn't wish to speak to anyone and when Paul Strike arrived, he found Beryl very much resigned to the situation at hand. 'I'm off to the cottage now Beryl,' Paul said, and the pair said goodnight – but not goodbye.

Beryl never could say goodbye. Sue and Michael made arrangements to drive down to the hospital to see Beryl the following weekend, totally unaware of just how serious the situation was. But it was too late. Beryl went to sleep that night and never woke up. On Sunday 13th October 1996, Beryl Reid died at the age of seventy-seven.

In the midst of the immediate shock of it all, Paul telephoned Robert Luff and James Sharkey to ask what should be done. Being a Sunday, neither expected that any of the news outlets would be able to do much, but what happened next was a true testament to the love and affection that Beryl had always managed to attract. The news of her death was reported by Sky News and then by the BBC – one of the first to be given the immediate reaction of rolling news we've become so used to.

In a strange twist of events, the Variety Club of Great Britain was holding an awards ceremony that evening, and those attending were able to pause along the red carpet to give their tributes to Beryl, one after the other. During the show her death was announced, to the genuine shock and sadness of the audience; and a tribute had been put together which, when shown, resulted in a standing ovation. Beryl always felt that the praise of her peers was the mark of true success, often feeling slightly inferior owing to her lack of formal training. And yet her passing was marked with a sincere outpouring of regret from all who had worked with her – and those who had simply enjoyed her work.

The following morning, the newspapers all paid tribute to 'Sister George', 'Kath', 'Monica' and 'Marlene', united in their adoration of the woman who brought those characters to life so memorably. Columnists lined up to celebrate her long career in whichever way they could. Ronnie Wolfe wrote a special obituary for *The Stage* in which he praised Beryl's professionalism and unique talent. 'I'll never forget Beryl, spectacles on the end of her nose, looking up at me with brandy in hand and a twinkle in her eye, asking, "Yes, it's funny darling but... could we make it funnier?" ' Over fifty years in showbusiness, Beryl Reid always did so.

*

Beryl's funeral was held on a crisp but sunny October afternoon ten days after her death. Since she had no formal religious faith (and an aversion to funerals), nobody was really sure what form the service should take; and, with Sue still recovering in Liverpool, it was to Paul that the decisions fell. The choice was made to hold a Service of Thanksgiving at St Andrews, the picturesque Anglican church a short distance from Honeypot in Wraysbury. The congregation included Dame Eileen Atkins, Bernard Cribbins, Sir Harry Secombe, Susannah York and the ever devoted Robert Luff as well as Beryl's closest friends and family members.

The press gathered, of course, and many of the guests spoke to them happily, sharing their favourite memories. One told the press how, when they unexpectedly popped along to Honeypot to see how Beryl was getting on with things, she answered the door in a fluster and said, 'Excuse me for not asking you in, darling, but I'm in bed with somebody I don't know very well!'

This was not a time for hushed tones; this was very much a celebration of everything Beryl was. The service included the rousing hymns 'All People That on Earth Do Dwell', 'Immortal Invisible God Only Wise' and 'Praise My Soul the King of Heaven'. 'She was adorable,' Dame Eileen told the congregation. 'She was my very dear friend for over thirty years and I adored her. And what's more, nobody can ever replace Beryl Reid.'

A reading from St John's Gospel seemed more another invitation to Honeypot than a call to faith: 'If I go and prepare a place for you, I will come back and take you to be with me that you also may be where I am. You know the way to the place where I am going.' There was another reference to Honeypot during the service, naturally coming from Beryl's favourite writer, A. A. Milne:

'I have a house where I go
When there's too many people.
I have a house where I go
Where no one can be...
Where nobody ever says "no"
Where no one says anything – so
There is no one but me.'

And whilst it had been a life lived so ferociously independently, the villagers of Wraysbury were not willing to let her go without saying their own goodbye. As the coffin was taken from the cottage to the church, friends and neighbours lined the route and treated her to one final round of applause. Opposite the church was a small café. Instead of the 'Dish of the Day', written on the blackboard outside were two simple words that summed up the high esteem the Wraysbury locals had for their most famous and most celebrated resident: 'Goodbye Beryl'.

After the service, her nearest and dearest gathered at Honeypot; and, enjoying a few glasses of something sparkly with the River Thames rushing by and the cats weaving their way among the guests, they shared their memories of Beryl. It was a day of laughter, just as Beryl would have wished it to be. She was cremated and her ashes scattered in the gardens of the cottage.

For a month or two, the newspapers kept printing nothing but positive news stories about Beryl. Victor Lewis Smith, writing in the London *Evening Standard*, even waged a one-man crusade to give the BBC a thorough ticking-off. They had broadcast a tribute to Beryl a day after she died, but in Smith's view: 'For the BBC to "celebrate" Miss Reid's career with such a hastily and lovelessly constructed half hour (followed by an equally ill-considered assembly of clips from her 1968 series) was an insult to one of Britain's greatest and much-loved performers. She was a woman who could oxygenate the screen (unlike the human bell jars who infest the medium nowadays) and her myriad talents deserved a far cooler and more intelligent appraisal than this.' He had a point. So quick were the BBC to throw together a tribute programme that they even got their own logo wrong. BB Cone (rather than BBC One) had apparently put the thing together and the only person to be included who actually knew Beryl well was Sir Terry Wogan, who had clearly been told some years prior to speak in general terms about Beryl – just in case. Still, many channels made the effort to re-run *Sister George* or *Mr Sloane* and Radio 4 even broadcast an episode of *Educating Archie*, the only time it would be repeated until the creation of BBC 7 which specialised in the broadcast of vintage radio comedies.

Less than six months after she died, Beryl was once again in the news, but this time not for reasons she would have approved of. In 1985, Beryl had been asked to comment on why she had chosen to make a life at Honeypot for a feature in *Good Housekeeping* magazine. 'It's a house full of my hopes, my dreams and ideals,' she said. 'A house full of love and laughter. I don't know who I'll leave it to but I hope that whoever follows me here will feel exactly the same as I do. My roots here are so well planted that I will be hard to dig up, even when I'm not here in person any more.' By the time of her death, Beryl had chosen to leave the cottage to Paul

Strike; and, as well as the cottage itself and Beryl's furniture, books, clothes, personal archive and showcase of awards, he'd also inherited seven cats. Seven. Not thirty. When Beryl was alive, she was ever frustrated by interviews talking about her tumbledown house by the river, full of flood water and empty gin bottles, cats and a lack of male company. What the press wanted was to cast her in the role of a 'crazy cat lady', an eccentric spinster with lesbian leanings who had something of the Miss Havisham about her. Nothing could have been further from the truth but with Beryl no longer around to correct them, the press had a field day.

It began with a piece in the *Sunday Express* which claimed that Beryl had left Honeypot Cottage to Paul on the condition that he care for the cats. No such condition existed legally, though naturally Paul understood how important Beryl's cats were to her. When Beryl died, she had seven cats: Boon, Coco, Eileen, Hamish, Tufnell, Paris and Snowball. Boon had been a recent addition and named for Michael Elphick's character in the series of the same name in which Beryl had made a brief cameo a few years before her death. He was elderly and clearly unwell and so the decision was taken, with the full agreement of Muriel Carey, to have him put to sleep.

Whilst Paul was willing to do all he could, he had suddenly found himself in sole charge of a cottage miles away from his own home in Bristol; and it was felt best by all concerned that, whilst he would keep Coco, Beryl's remaining brood would be rehomed with close friends, most of whom lived in Wraysbury and were well known to Beryl's neighbours.

'The Killing of Sister Beryl!' screamed the *Daily Mail*. 'Beryl Reid left this man everything she owned,' it insisted, 'and what did he do to repay her? He killed her cats.' Suddenly Paul was public enemy number one and treated to a thorough pasting in the dailies. It was deeply unfair and Beryl would have been distraught at the way Paul was being treated.

At the same time, the Beryl Reid myth was fast gathering ground. 'Britain lost one of its most iconic lesbian actresses last month,' cried the *Pink Paper*, whilst the *Express* claimed that Beryl had been hiding a secret battle with alcoholism that had caused her death, citing claims that all she'd done in her remaining years was sit in front of the television, totally alone, watching her old performances and weeping into a bottle of Courvoisier.

The unpleasantness surrounding the cottage and the newly invented version of Beryl Reid's latter years now permeated, and it wasn't until 2000 that Beryl was brought back to the fore when she was featured in the series

The Unforgettable…. But the broadcast didn't go as planned. Owing to a few choice words, ITV decided to show the episode at 11.35 p.m. on New Year's Eve – when most people are blind drunk and getting ready for the countdown. It was never shown again and the episode seems to have been lost entirely. Beryl, who had always been so concerned at the thought of being forgotten, seemed to be in danger of just that.

Epilogue

'I never want them to be sick of me. I never want them to think, "Oh, there's that silly Beryl Reid again." I want them to want me. Always.'

WITH HER WIDE, BROWN SPARKLING EYES and infectious giggle, Beryl Reid was a familiar face to British audiences for decades, and with each new generation there was a reason to fall in love with her. For children growing up in the 1950s, there was Monica. For liberated adults looking for cinema to break taboos, there was Sister George. For those thrill seekers who love political intrigue and drama, there was Connie Sachs. And for children growing up in the 1980s, the thought of Beryl humming along with Stephen and Mooncat remains a special memory from their formative years. But so insistent was Beryl that she didn't wish to get caught up in a long-running series, and so keen was she to avoid being typecast, that her performances are rarely seen today.

'I think she slightly lost out because she wasn't a part of something like the *Carry On* series,' explains Dame Siân Phillips. 'She wasn't really a part of the public consciousness in the same way as Hattie Jacques or Joan Sims; they have been kept alive because the *Carry Ons* are always being shown, but Beryl didn't have that.'

And her legacy? 'It's impossible to talk in terms of legacy, though clearly Beryl's is that she was incredibly funny,' she says. 'But there'll be actors training today who haven't heard of Peggy Ashcroft; that happens, it's a natural thing and one mustn't be too sad about it.'

Sue agrees that Beryl's career, though incredibly varied and full of brilliant performances, does not lend itself to a constant presence. 'The films she did were quite adult and they're usually shown quite late or on a bit of an obscure channel,' she says. 'Nobody really repeats Archie and it's all sort of fallen away a little bit, which is sad, but people do still remember her and they want to see more of her work.'

Shortly after her death, the *Daily Mail* wrote: 'One could imagine Beryl at 110, still treading the boards, playing crusty dowagers with a naughty twinkle in her eye'; and as Nicky Henson says, 'If she were alive today, I've no doubt she'd be a huge television star. She'd be in absolutely everything and she'd be wonderful at it all of course.' And though she took great pains not to be typecast, there are very definitive 'Beryl Reid' roles. Would it be Dame Beryl Reid as the Dowager Countess, reigning over Downton Abbey with waspish wit and impeccable timing? Would she have been a resident of the Best Marigold Hotel, or would she have settled into the bar of the Rovers Return, a familiar face to a whole new audience?

It appears Beryl was offered the chance on more than one occasion to join long-running serials; there was even interest from *Crossroads*, but Beryl declined – she didn't want to end up a real-life June Buckridge, dreading the day when her character caught the 'flu. Her legacy therefore is left to the body of work she created, specifically designed to be diverse and to showcase her enormous variety of skills.

Beryl was sometimes extremely modest (not something you'd associate with a lady who had her own perfume created especially for her, christened 'Easy Virtue'!) and she was always keen to try and reduce her approach down to the familiar 'shoes' line. But there was so much more to it. The late Susannah York, in her tribute to Beryl, explained, 'She took me to one side and said, "Now here's what I'm going to do, do you think you can keep up?" and then there was this little display of fireworks as she transformed into George. A critic has said that I was far too wide-eyed in the film and I would agree but I was wide-eyed because I was staggered by her presence as an actress. You couldn't try and compete, you had to complement; but when the spotlight had to shift, she was more than happy to complement you. That's a very rare skill and she had it in spades – because, basically, she was a nice person who wanted everyone to do well.'

Much of Beryl's work was confined to a time and a place. The thought of a ventriloquist on the radio would have us questioning the BBC's sanity today; in an era when we've not only seen lesbian relationships hinted at on screen but explicitly played out with full frontal nudity, Beryl's performances remain very much a part of television history but they remain timeless. Nobody can watch Beryl's performance as Connie Sachs and fail to be impressed, touched by the magic she brings to the screen in just six minutes. Thanks to an ever present yearning for nostalgia, many of Beryl's performances are finding themselves a new home on DVD; and, though Beryl didn't have much luck in the world of sitcom, generally making turkeys of her own but appearing in the very best of everyone else's, series such as *Alcock and Gander* are now finding a brand-new audience who want to see more Beryl Reid.

So when actress Elaine Pantling was asked by a producer if there was anyone she admired and whose story she might want to retell, there was no question that it had to be Beryl. 'I didn't really have to think about it, she just popped into my head. For me, she was brave and fearless, extremely funny, naughty but beautifully fragile. She was the first lady of comedy and a brilliant actress who just wanted to be loved. I felt that her story must not only be heard but must be seen. I didn't want her to be forgotten.' Elaine put together the stage show *Roll Out the Beryl*, which not only brings to the fore the story of the lady herself but also revives Monica and Marlene to the delight of the audience.

'Marlene was warm and funny, but also an ordinary working-class girl and I think people recognised themselves in her,' says Elaine. 'Marlene helped people to laugh at life and find the funny in the everyday. Monica was so mischievous and naughty and we all want some of that naughtiness in our lives, childish antics and adventures. I sometimes take "Monica" into school assemblies and the kids just love her!' Through Elaine, Beryl is winning yet another generation of devoted fans.

'It isn't that there aren't funny women around today,' observed Sir Terry Wogan. 'It's that there aren't funny women around like her. She was unique and I think that her style of comedy will always be regarded as a textbook example of what it means to entertain.'

And so perhaps that is Beryl's true legacy. Wood and Walters, French and Saunders, Catherine Tate, Tracey Ullman – these are comediennes very much cast in the Beryl mould. 'I always thought she was slightly too early,' said Sir Harry Secombe, speaking of Beryl to the *Radio Times* a year after her death. 'If I speak about her today, people always tell me that they've just seen a script that would be perfect for her and then they smile. Now that's a lovely memory to leave, isn't it?' Certainly Nicky Henson agrees: 'She had a comic timing that is so rare, it's unique and there is no doubt in my mind that today, she would be a huge television star, stealing every single scene and being adored by the public for it.'

'The Beryl Reid Myth' continues to be the abiding memory the public have of her. On the whole, people remember her extremely fondly and, as Paul Strike says, 'They remember her as their favourite auntie or their granny, and it's affectionate but they don't know much else – they only know the Beryl they saw on screen, and there was so much more to her than that.' Instead of being remembered as a Tony award-winner or a stalwart of the Old Vic, Beryl is regarded as the eccentric old lady who lived with thirty cats in a cottage by the river, who drank herself to death and who was probably 'a collar and tie job'. There is no malice behind the myth: it hasn't been created because people wished to denigrate Beryl or to see her name slandered. It has grown from rumour and gossip, reprinted as fact over the years until it has taken root. Beryl had a very set account of her life: there was an official version which focused on the comical and the cheerful – she always wanted a happy ending. But just as she gave so many layers to her many characters, she too was multi-faceted and, like any human being, she had her flaws and her foibles.

'Every day when I walked from Brixton to Shaftesbury Avenue with no money for the bus and slopping about in the pouring rain, not knowing if they wanted me or if I'd ever be a success, I'd tell myself one thing over and over again,' she said with dogged determination. 'Beryl: you will be a success. You will make it. You must make it.' The awards and the acclaim paled into insignificance in her later years. She was content enough to know that she *had* made it, just as she always said she would.

*

In writing this book, I have not set out to prove Beryl's account of her life in *So Much Love* wrong. Neither have I tried to expose anything controversial or tear down the walls of Honeypot Cottage to find the monster within. It is my hope that this book will not be taken simply as a tribute to a great actress or much-loved comedienne, but as an objective look into the life of someone so unique and so unconventional that, from the moment she stepped onto the stage at the age of four in her little pink tutu, the course was set. The world was always going to know Beryl Reid and it has been my huge pleasure and enormous privilege to make sure that they still do. It is my sincere hope that having read this book, you'll now go off and rediscover Monica, Marlene, George and Connie all over again. Beryl didn't want to be forgotten. Let's make sure she gets her wish and always remember her fondly, with so much love.

Appendix: Honeypot Catalogy by Miss B. Reid

BERYL CALLED HER FELINE FAMILY 'The House of Reid' and in her 1987 book *The Cat's Whiskers* she painstakingly created a family tree of every cat she'd owned at Honeypot. Those who had not yet arrived at the cottage at the date of publication have been added by the author.

Ella (Beryl's first cat), discovered at Wraysbury in 1953.

Fred (1953–1970), son of Ella.

Footy (1953–1971), son of Ella.

Furry Wee (1962–1964), adopted in Weston-Super-Mare at an advanced age.

Andy (1965–1974), born at Honeypot.

Georgie Girl (1968–1984), born in Chelsea and spirited away to the banks of the Thames!

Patrick (1970–1983), Georgie Girl's son, named for Patrick Cargill.

Emma (1970–1984), Georgie Girl's daughter.

Kath (1969–1971), adopted whilst filming *Entertaining Mr Sloane* in Camberwell.

Lulu (1979–1984), adopted from the Reading Cat Protection League.

Ronnie (came to Honeypot in 1973), adopted in Windsor, named for Ronnie Corbett.

Elsie (came to Honeypot in 1979), adopted in Bristol during the run of *Born in the Gardens*.

Penny (came to Honeypot in 1980), given as a gift from her
  housekeeper.

Sir Harry (came to Honeypot in 1982), adopted from the RSPCA and
  named after Sir Harry Secombe.

Muriel (came to Honeypot in 1981), adopted from the RSPCA and
  named for friend Muriel Carey.

Dimley (came to Honeypot in 1982), adopted from the RSPCA.

Billy and Jenny (came to Honeypot in 1984 as a pair), adopted from
  the RSPCA.

Paris and Tufnell (came to Honeypot in 1985 as a pair), adopted from
  the RSPCA.

Clive (came to Honeypot in 1986), adopted from the RSPCA.

Eileen (came to Honeypot in 1986), adopted from the RSPCA, named
  for Dame Eileen Atkins.

Boon (came to Honeypot in 1990), adopted from the RSPCA, named
  for Michael Elphick.

Coco (came to Honeypot in 1992), adopted from the RSPCA.

Snowball (came to Honeypot in 1992), adopted from the RSPCA.

Hamish (came to Honeypot in 1992), adopted from the RSPCA.

Many of these feline friends now share Beryl's final resting place in the
grounds of Honeypot Cottage. In life, they were joined by a plethora of
visiting moggies (including Nikki and Mountbatten), a pair of Greek tor-
toises called Jean and Arthur, two ducks called Jeremy and Jemima and
many unnamed foxes, water rats, mice, voles, seagulls, assorted birds and
squirrels – some of whom outstayed their welcome in the thatch of the roof
and were dispatched… often during dinner parties…

Appendix: Beryl's Recipe for Pissy Pork Pie

THIS RECIPE FIRST APPEARED in Beryl's 1987 book *Food and Friends* and she was so delighted with it, she sent a copy to friend Sheila Cooke. Here is Beryl's original letter to Sheila and the accompanying recipe.

Darling Sheila,

I need your help. I'm doing another book, this time a cookery one, and I want to include this very special recipe by Hannah Glasse. But it's 17th century and I just can't make it out! Are the ffs supposed to be ssess I wonder?

Do advise, your loving, Beryl xxx

Take a loin of pork, fkin it, cut it into fteaks, feafon it with falt, nutmeg and pepper, make a good cruft, lay a layer of pork, then a large layer of pippinf, pared and cored, a little fugar, enough to fweeten the pie, then another layer of pork: put in half a pint of white wine (half a bottle to you and me), lay fome butter on the top and clofe your pie.

If your pie be large, it will take a pint of white wine (a whole bottle, no less) – in which case, you'll end up with a very piffy pork pie!

(If you don't find this funny, tell me to piff off!) – B x